Joseph Conrad's Fiction

Joseph Conrad's Fiction

A Study in Existential Humanism

SUMAN BALA

INTELLECTUAL PUBLISHING HOUSE
NEW DELHI

Sole Distributors
Intellectual Book Corner
23, Daryaganj, Ansari Road
New Delhi 110002
Ph. 275860

ISBN: 81-7076-029-1

First Edition: 1990

Price [illegible]
US $40

Published by
D.R. Chopra
Intellectual Publishing House
New Delhi 110002

Phototypesetting by
data culture
Ph. 6431070

Jacket Design by
Three-A Corporation
New Delhi 110002

Printed by
Chaman Offset Printers
1626, Suiwalan, New Delhi 110002

Contents

Preface

My interest in Joseph Conrad began in the early seventies while teaching *Heart of Darkness* which I found remarkable for its psychological subtlety and philosophical depth. Subsequently, I read other novels of Conrad and came to conclude that in Conrad's fictional world the existential perception of the void is at the centre of things. Indeed it goes to the credit of Conrad who, as early as the first decade of the twentieth century, became conscious of human condition and explored man's freedom and responsibility in an absurd world. But, Conrad has no room for despair. As an existential humanist, he holds his faith in man's courage and his ability to face a hostile universe. This aspect of Conrad, I came to realize, has not been sufficiently explored hitherto. The present book seeks to examine Conrad's major novels in the light of existential philosophy and to show that Conrad anticipates the modern humanistic school of existentialism.

In the year 1984, I had the privilege of visiting the United States and conducting the present research study at some of its universities especially the Ohio State University and the New York State University. Over there, I had many opportunities to discuss ideas embodied in this work. My special thanks go to the Conradian scholar Dr. William Carigan of the University of Utah to whom I owe suggestions that have been of inestimable value to me.

I must place on record my deep sense of gratitude to several British and Scottish scholars who, during my stay in Great Britain, not only provided me with the books but also offered suggestions which have contributed to the enrichment of my book. In this connection, I will like to mention Mr. Peter Messent (Nottingham University), Mr. Steve Watts

(Cambridge University) and Mr. Angus Calder (Open University of Scotland).

In the end, I must acknowledge my debt to the staff of the British Museum library, the Leicester University library, the Edinburgh University library and the Polish Centre, London which generously made available to me critical books and periodicals on Conrad. It gave me an opportunity to go through some rare manuscripts and articles which have great relevance to this study. Also, I benefitted a great deal from the Delhi University library and the British Council library, New Delhi.

Existential Humanism and Joseph Conrad

Joseph Conrad's work is complex owing to its highly introspective nature; that is why he is still regarded as an enigma or a challenge by the critics. The scholars have conveniently dubbed him either as a thorough pessimist or as a robust optimist, either as a nihilist or as an idealist. Such a labelling of the novelist is too sweeping, for it fails to encompass the totality of Conrad's views on man's role in the universe and the meaning of his existence.

A close study of Conrad's fiction reveals that Conrad shares the chief tenets of existential humanism, advocated so vigorously by Albert Camus and Jean-Paul Sartre in the mid-twentieth century. Conrad's obsession with the concept of random, responsible choice, his study of the extremes of human experience, its agonies and monstrosities, his view that death is one experience which gives shape to life, his faith in human values are classically existential attitudes. In all of his work, fiction as well as non-fiction, Conrad expresses a conception of the world which synchronizes with the one held by the philosophers of the existentialist school.

A number of critics have pointed out similarities between Conrad and the modern existentialist writers of Europe, especially Camus and Sartre. One of the most striking similarities between these writers is their emphasis on isolation of their major characters and the anguish resulting from this isolation. In Conrad's novels man is alone before a hostile universe and from the crisis resulting from the loneliness he must forge a moral ethic by which to live. M.D. Zabel was one of the early critics who pointed out Conrad's affinities with the existentialist writers. Conrad dramatizes, says Zabel,

> the plight of the man or woman on whom life closes down. By divesting him or her of the familiar supports and illusory protection of friendship, social privileges, or love; by throwing the individual violently out of an accepted relationship with family or society, this

> crisis suddenly makes him aware of a hostile or unknown world which must be learned anew, conquered or mastered, before survival is possible. . . . It is this drama of alienation and spiritual recognition which appears . . . in the novels of the French existentialists, who have given tragedy a new dimension in the irrationality or absurdity of the universe.[1]

In his article entitled "Conrad, Camus, and Sisyphus,"[2] Stavrou shows how the thought of Joseph Conrad and Albert Camus is similar in many ways. Adam Gillon in his article entitled "Conrad and Sartre" notes that Conrad, like Sartre, was aware of the absurdity and the inscrutability of nature and the human condition. Gillon feels that this "justifies an examination of his work in the light of existential thinking."[3] John A. Palmer notes the significance of these comparisons and feels that Conrad's response to the void at the heart of the human condition is a broadly existentialist response: "Themes of isolation, alienation and guilt, a willed commitment to human solidarity in the face of a metaphysical void, and the like, exist in all these writers (Conrad, Camus, Sartre), in some broad form."[4] Discussing *Heart of Darkness*, Ted Billy points out that "*nothing* lies at the heart of Conrad's conception of the self and the meaning of life."[5] And Iris Murdoch, in her brilliant book entitled *Sartre: Romantic Rationalist*, considers both Conrad and Sartre as phenomenologists.[6]

A number of critics have thus exhibited affinities between Conrad and the existentialist writers. Also, some attempts have been made to examine specific novels within an existential framework.[7] However, there has as yet been no detailed study of Conrad's novels in terms of existentialist philosophy and no attempt has been made to place Conrad in a definite school of existentialism. The avowed purpose of this study is to examine Conrad's major fiction in the light of existential philosophy and to prove that Conrad belongs to its humanistic school, the one that upholds the values of Existential Humanism.

It is noteworthy that existentialism is only a recent phenomenon; it has caught the imagination of the literate only during the last four decades of the century although its roots lie far back in the nineteenth century. Soren Kierkegaard, the Danish philosopher, is commonly regarded as the father of modern existentialism, and is the first European philosopher who bears the existentialist title. Existentialism receives its philosophical support from Martin Heidegger and Karl Jaspers in Germany, and Gabriel Marcel, Jean-Paul Sartre and Albert Camus in France.

Modern existentialism permeates literature as well as philosophy. It was Sartre who gave the school of existentialism its present name though the term eludes an exact definition. "Existentialism," says John Macquarrie, "is a style of philosophizing rather than a body of philosophical doctrines."[8] It is not a rigid system and in an anthology of existentialist writers, one finds such literary names as Dostoevsky, Nietzsche, Rilke and Kafka alongside the more technical professional philosophers. It is however commonly agreed that existentialism aims at describing and evaluating the situation in which every man finds himself, and from which he looks upon society, nature and God. It is a philosophy which states that man is everything; its concern for the individual is unique. It is concerned primarily with an analysis of human existence.

Though there are important differences between the existential thinkers, as a group they adhere to a common philosophic claim. All of them put a great stress on subjectivity and individuality of human existence. Kierkegaard goes so far as to choose the words "That Individual" as the inscription for his tombstone.[9]

Existentialism maintains the priority of existence to essence, of action to thought, of the particular to the universal. It rejects the objective idealistic tradition in philosophy that dominated Western thought in the nineteenth century. All the existentialists agree that man's essence is what he freely creates himself. In *Existentialism and Humanism*, Sartre defines it thus: "What do we mean by saying that existence precedes essence? We mean that man first of all exists, encounters himself, surges up in the world—and defines himself afterwards. . . . Man is nothing else but that which he makes of himself."[10] Sartre's statement establishes the supremacy of individual freedom; man exists first and then defines himself. At every moment in his life, he wills his future by choosing freely. The existentialists exhort man to make authentic choice in a crisis by using his absolute freedom. The world is not preordained and man has to define himself repeatedly in the course of his life. Sartre makes it clear when he says:

> If, however, it is true that existence is prior to essence, man is responsible for what he is. Thus, the first effect of existentialism is that it puts every man in possession of himself as he is, and places the entire responsibility for his existence squarely upon his own shoulders. And, when we say that man is responsible for himself, we do not mean that he is responsible only for his own individuality, but that he is responsible for all men.[11]

The existentialists believe that man has to assert his choice or be destroyed. Kierkegaard comprehends human existence in the sense of its perennial freedom. To him, the existentialists owe the Either-Or contingence and the concept of *angst*. Kierkegaard had a stern religious upbringing and his philosophy arises in an ethical religious context, as he was preoccupied with the religious problems and with how to become a true Christian. He experienced the existential feeling that something is wrong with the world and life as it is lived. Interested in man's inner life, he insists on the need for commitment and resolute decision. Man is responsible not only for himself but for the whole mankind. This responsibility is simply crushing: it makes us dizzy.[12]

The fundamental rule of truth in Kierkegaard is uncertainty. Nothing that is absolutely certain and without any possibility of being erroneous can be attributed to the reality of the existent: "When the question of truth is raised in an objective manner, reflection is directed objectively to the truth, as an object to which the knower is related. Reflection is not focused upon the relationship, however, but upon the question of whether it is the truth to which the knower is related."[13]

According to the existentialist thesis, truth signifies constant revelation of creation whose nature is not confined to anything encountered as readymade and completed. The dynamism of passionate living which characterizes the transformation of the existing individual itself constitutes the uncertainty of truth. The gravest problem is that the conditions of practical life arouse in man a sense of frustration. It is a disorderly universe in which we live, and it gives us only an experience of futility and worthlessness. Kierkegaard believes that we can discover ourselves and can come to understand the human situation only if we commit ourselves. The ultimate for the Danish philosopher is surrender to God: the core of his thinking is Christian.

Friedrich Nietzsche may be regarded as important as Kierkegaard in the genesis of modern existentialism. He did not hesitate to proclaim that for all intents and purposes God is dead. In a most provocative manner, he declared: "God is dead! God remains dead! And we have killed him!"[14] This truth, he urged, should be accepted with courage and upon it should be built a new conception of human existence. Both Heidegger and Jaspers have written at length about Nietzsche and regard him as a key figure in the rise of existentialism.

All religious existentialists hold the conviction that man's anguish is due to the Original sin of Man's fall from Grace. Marcel, however, does not believe in an all-seeing, all-powerful, benevolent God. Nothing is preordained; what is indubitable is the existence of the universe and the human being who plays his part in this universe. Marcel feels that true existence can be revealed directly through participation in being. Man is free to choose, to decide. But economic, social, moral and religious pressures restrain his freedom. This means that to Marcel a sphere exists in which man may live and discover the absurdity of life. This will lead to the ultimate realization of the hopelessness of the situation. Man, according to Marcel, is never at the goal but always on the way to self-realization.

Jaspers found that rapid development of science and technology was resulting in intellectual and moral instability. Man can get out of these problems through true philosophy. It is through reason, Jaspers asserts, that existence becomes lucid and clear. Thus reason and existence, says he, "are not two opposed powers which struggle with one another for victory. Each exists only through the other. They mutually develop one another and find through one another clarity and reality."[15] Jaspers believes in free decision. At any crucial moment of decision, man sees the self before nothingness or the divinity. It is concentration upon such crises which has led the existentialists to centre their ethics in choice, indeed to insist that man is a product of his choices and creates himself bit by bit as he chooses. The self that makes decisions, the authentic self for Jaspers, is something over and above the unauthentic self. Man recognizes the shallowness of the unauthentic self when the ultimate situations arise. The authentic self's interpretation of the world is a free decision: "Man can seek the path of his truth in unfanatical absoluteness, in a decisiveness which remains open."[16]

Heidegger is a systematic metaphysician. His main thesis is that the "Being" of the human being consists in his movement through the world. He finds man forlorn and abandoned. Man is thrown into the world; it is not a place chosen by him to live in. The circumstances of human life have not been so arranged that man can discover what he is, what is expected of him, what he can hope for. He cannot discover these things because they are not preordained. Heidegger considers the experience of death to be of vital importance because it individualizes man.

Albert Camus, one of the chief exponents of modern existentialism, is concerned with man's spiritual character, his place in the world, and his relations to other human beings. Camus's ideas can be summarized by two terms: absurdity and revolt. He sees man as a lonely exile struggling for happiness and meaningfulness beneath the immense and senseless burden of existence. If the world is cold and unfriendly, perhaps existence is not worth the struggle.

In his *The Myth of Sisyphus*, Camus raises the question: how can a life that has no meaning best be lived? Why should a man continue to suffer if he cannot find any logic behind the chaos of this world? Camus considers the possibility of suicide as "one truly serious philosophical problem"[17] for the fully conscious individual. The logic of absurdity concludes to the necessity for suicide. Suicide seems to be a logical answer to the irrational universe but it does not accord with experience. Camus rejects suicide; it cannot be ethically justified. To take one's life would be, in the final analysis, an act of cowardice; suicide is the consummation of the defeated conscience. Moreover, killing oneself destroys the absurd for the individual only; it continues for other men. Suicide then merely escapes the problem; it does not solve it.

Camus finds self-destruction to be an unsatisfactory answer to the absurd. The true answer is rebellion. Man must rise up in protest against the irrational universe that challenges human existence and its significance. Rebellion is courageous; it is a rising of conscience. We must live if we wish to maintain what we believe to be true: "Living is keeping the absurd alive. Keeping it alive is above all contemplating it. Unlike Eurydice, the absurd dies only when we turn away from it. One of the only coherent philosophical positions is thus revolt."[18] Revolt is a creative effort that makes absurdity meaningful. By protesting against the absurdity of human condition, man transcends it.

In *The Rebel*, Camus states that man defines himself by what he opposes for it is only then, in the act of resisting exterior pressures, which would make him a naturalistic object, that he establishes the primacy of his individual consciousness. Man's cry of revolt is the result of some inherent value in man: "I proclaim that I believe in nothing and that everything is absurd, but I cannot doubt the validity of my own proclamation and I am compelled to believe, at least, in my own protest. The first, and only, datum that is furnished me, within absurdist experience, is rebellion."[19]

The absurd depends upon a world which is without reason. If man can postulate a reason, if he can attribute purpose and design to the world, then the absurd would be destroyed. The main problem is not how to resolve the absurd, but how to live authentically in it. Rebellion is the ethical key to authenticity: "In order to exist, man must rebel."[20] The rebel realizes that existence is absurd for every rational individual and hence the human tragedy is not a solitary struggle. Thus the maxim, "In order to exist, man must rebel," becomes, "I *rebel*, therefore we *exist*."[21]

Revolt is the conscious or unconscious affirmation by man of his own humanity in the face of a destiny which will ultimately crush him.

The best exposition of existential philosophy is Camus's description of Sisyphus's task. Sisyphus is condemned by the gods to roll a rock to the top of a mountain, only to have it fall back down again. What interests Camus is that, like Sisyphus, man is an "absurd hero."[22] Man must always roll that proverbial stone in toil and efforts to the top—and inevitably it rolls down. So he trudges down again to begin the inevitable process once more. Camus observes that Sisyphus "knows the whole extent of his wretched condition"[23] and yet continues to act. It is then, as in life, that Sisyphus has moments of clarity: he comprehends his destiny. It is during the pause at the top of the mountain and during the return to his endeavour that Sisyphus is superior to his fate, is stronger than his rock. He realizes his fate: despite his slavish work, he becomes his master:

> His fate belongs to him. His rock is his thing. Likewise, the absurd man, when he contemplates his torment, silences all the idols. . . . There is no sun without shadow, and it is essential to know the night. . . for the rest, he knows himself to be the master of his days. At that subtle moment when man glances backward over his life, Sisyphus returning towards his rock, in that slight pivoting, he contemplates that series of unrelated actions which becomes his fate, created by him, combined under his memory's eye and soon sealed by his death.[24]

Camus concludes the essay with the remark: "One must imagine Sisyphus happy."[25] Out of absurdity and human tragedy, Camus develops faith. He comes to the conclusion that life is meaningless but precious, all existence is absurd but worthwhile.

All Camus's works are concerned primarily with the crisis of the individual, with man as a lonely exile struggling for happiness and meaningfulness beneath the immense and senseless burden of existence. Meursault, the hero of *The Outsider,* is a stranger to his own life because he cannot give his existence a meaning. He realizes the complete pointlessness of life; family affection, love and friendship have no meaning for him. And he becomes a stranger to the society because of his mother's death.

The novel opens with the words, "Mother died today. Or, maybe, yesterday; I can't be sure."[26] Mother's death constitutes Meursault's first encounter with the absurd. For him, only the present counts. He is indifferent to everything except the immediate physical sensations. When he receives the news of his mother's death, his only worry is that he will have to ask for two days's leave from his employer.

Meursault shocks the society when he refuses to act according to its set conventions. At his mother's funeral, he shows no sadness or regret. He feels only the physical inconveniences of watching over the body and following the hearse to the cemetry under the burning sun. He declines to see his mother's body, smokes cigarettes and sleeps and drinks coffee during his vigil at night beside the dead body. The following day, he strikes up an intimate friendship with Marie Cardona, a stenographer formerly employed in the office where he works. He meets her by chance at one of the bathing beaches in the harbour, takes her to a movie and even goes to bed with her. His statement at the end of all this shocks the reader: "It occurred to me that somehow I'd got through another Sunday, that Mother was now buried, and tomorrow I'd be going to work as usual. Really, nothing in my life had changed."[27]

Meursault is one of those persons whose existence consists in nothing worth-noting. His drifting way of living—his not caring whether he accepts the offer of a job in Paris or not, whether he marries Marie or not—carries him into an absurd situation. In a chance-encounter, he kills an Arab and is put on trial for the murder.

The debate in the courtroom as to whether or not Meursault loved his mother is absurd. The lawyer strikes at the root of the problem when he asks: "Is my client on trial for having buried his mother, or for killing a man?"[28] Meursault's actions during and after his mother's funeral seem wrong to the conventional lawyers, press and jury; the police find these a proof of his callousness. The courtroom crowd condemns him for not conforming to the society's conventions. His insensitivity at his mother's funeral weighs overwhelmingly against him and he is sentenced to death.

Meursault ends his life in revolt against the absurdity of the world. He does not believe in absolute moral standards. For him, morality lies in the private domain. He feels that a court of law cannot decide the matter of innocence and guilt. That is why he remains indifferent to everything until the very last page of the novel. He never thinks of self-defence. Nor does he have any remorse or feeling of guilt about his victim.

While awaiting execution, Meursault rejects the chaplain's offer of the consolation of religion. The priest tries to salvage him for the divine city but Meursault realizes that nothing matters: "Nothing, nothing had the least importance."[29] When Meursault can contain himself no longer, he revolts and unleashes a storm of abuse. The global effect of his retort to the priest is a rejection of pseudo-values and the affirmation of existential values. Meursault affirms the meaning of physical existence in his realization that all men are outcasts and condemned to death: "All alike would be condemned to die one day."[30]

The novel ends on a promising note. Meursault has his revelation on the last page of the novel. He realizes that though faced with death he is free to maintain his own integrity. He feels himself liberated at last from the meanings society has tried to force upon him. He becomes aware for the first time that he has been happy in his life and that he would like to re-live it all over again. He hopes that there will be many people at his execution and that they will greet him with cries of hatred:"all that remained was to hope that on the day of my execution there should be a huge crowd of spectators and that they should greet me with howls of execration."[31]

The Plague again has the sentence of death as its theme. The action takes place in the Algerian coastal city of Oran which has fallen prey to the epidemic of the plague. Living in a city shut in upon a universe of exile and separation, people are physically isolated from the rest of the world and from each other. The outbreak of plague separates Dr. Bernard Rieux from his wife who has gone to a sanatorium for getting treatment for her tuberculosis. Rambert, the journalist, who has come to the city of Oran to write a story for one of the big Paris newspapers on living conditions among the Arabs, feels doubly exiled when the state of plague is declared: he is separated both from his mistress and from his country.

The plague links people as they face the epidemic. They feel that meaning may be given to human life by fighting collectively a natural calamity. They want to continue earthly life in revolt against death. Faced with the threat of death, Dr. Rieux, Tarrou, Rambert, Grand and Father Paneloux organize medical resistance against the epidemic and show man's determination to make the cause of man triumph. Through their efforts, hospital units are set up, isolation camps are created, and the burial of the dead is organized. Rambert decides to stay on in the plague-ridden city and work with Dr. Rieux until he can find "some way of getting out of the town."[32] He realizes that he is no longer a stranger to the city: "I know that I belong here whether I want it or not. This business is everybody's business."[33] M. Othon, after his child's death, joins Dr. Rieux's plague-fighting organization. The plague is an indisputable scourge and everyone joins in to combat it. Through their collective struggle against the common enemy, the people of Oran find meaning in their lives.

Dr. Rieux dedicates himself to the task of fighting the plague which represents the absurd world, the finality of death and its ever-present threat to life. He lets his wife go away and neglects his personal happiness to defend the happiness of others. He does not believe in an all-powerful God because if he did, he would cease curing the sick and leave the entire matter to God: "But no one in the world believed in a God of that sort; . . . And this was proved by the fact that no one ever threw himself on Providence completely."[34]

Dr. Rieux believes that it is his personal responsibility to fight the plague. For him, fighting the plague is not a matter of heroism. It is simply a matter of common decency which for him consists in doing his job well. He feels that the battle is worth fighting unto death. The plague is an interminable defeat and he defends mankind against death without losing sight of the fact that all victory is temporary and that sooner or later death will conquer. But the fact that his victories will not be lasting, Rieux feels, is "no reason for giving up the struggle."[35] He refuses to despair and faces his destiny heroically. It is through the exercise of his private responsibility that Dr. Rieux enters the community of men.

Perhaps no other thinker in the twentieth century has wielded as much influence on philosophy and literature as Jean-Paul Sartre. Every individual, says Sartre, is born free. For an individual to be free is to choose himself. He is not born with any given human nature; his acts constitute his whole existence. His chief distinction thus is involvement: "he is what he wills."[36] Placed in a world of probables, man has to act, to decide, to involve himself. He comes to exist through such involvements. Whatever meaning and value man can find in his life is the outcome of his own choices. Each of man's acts is free in the sense that it is wholly disconnected from what has previously happened. The past does not determine the course of action. Man cannot avoid involvement; even passivity or neutrality involves decision. Whatever a man may be, he is free to be something else if he chooses; but he is not free to choose to give up his freedom. Every man stands perennially and inescapably on the brink of new, still-to-be-posited action.

In the domain of existence, one feels unusually free but despaired and forlorn. Sartre is tormented by the feeling that we are forced to take decisions at every moment in our lives: "Man is condemned to be free. Condemned, because he did not create himself, yet is nevertheless at liberty, and from the moment he is thrown into this world he is responsible for everything he does."[37] Man did not ask for any freedom but he finds himself possessed of freedom. Freedom is man's triumph as well as tragedy. The picture of the world that Sartre presents is a terrifying one. The sense of futile but inescapable responsibility results in anguish. Man experiences forlornness from his knowledge that he lives in a purposeless world in which all things perish. Since man must rely upon himself, his normal condition is despair. He realizes that all events are contingent, that nothing is certain. All human experience is founded on nothingness. The impermanence, the restlessness, innate in life, is deeply felt by Sartre.

Since there is no universal human nature, Sartre feels that the individual has no real intimacy with other individuals. Man is alone, completely and irredeemably alone. His freedom thus becomes an inseparable burden, a source of perpetual anguish. He cannot shirk decisions for which he alone is responsible; that is his existence. His existence commits others yet he can never hope to be one with them. Nor can he measure the value of his decisions. All human pursuits culminate in frustration.

One of Sartre's most important ideas, and which is on the borderline between philosophy and psychology, is that of bad faith, the intellectual and emotional sleight-of-hand whereby we try to hide our freedom from ourselves. Bad faith is the self-deception derived from routinizing one's exterior world into pre-established patterns, from accepting pre-given roles in which to present oneself to others.

Sartre puts stress on personal freedom in all decisions which goes along with personal responsibility, a responsibility which is not limited to one's private affairs but extends to all that happens in the world in which one is placed. The limitless freedom of choice in which man's existence consists is thus at the same time a boundless responsibility for what he makes of himself. This feeling is most strongly expressed by Sartre in the chapter "Freedom and Responsibility":

> Thus, totally free, undistinguishable from the period for which I have chosen to be the meaning, as profoundly responsible for the war as if I had myself declared it, unable to live without integrating it in my situation, engaging myself in it wholly and stamping it with my seal, I must be without remorse or regrets as I am without excuse; for from the instant of my upsurge into being, I carry the weight of the world by myself alone without anything or any person being able to lighten it. [38]

Sartre does not discuss whether or not God exists; he assumes at the outset that He does not. That being the case, human beings are neither created nor pervaded by anyone. Sartre believes that man's fate is not determined by a prior super-imposed essence. Since there is no God to give man any guaranteed security or any set of objective standards, man must give them to himself. He has to create his own values. Man is thus the source of all meaning in his life. He has freedom to shape his destiny: "What man needs is to find himself again and to understand that nothing can save him from himself, not even a valid proof of the existence of God."[39]

It is significant to note that existentialism as advocated by Camus and Sartre is humanistic in approach; it is not a philosophy of disaster, of pessimistic irrationalism. It is to meet the commonplace-charge of pessimism that Sartre came out with a strong defence of existentialism in his famous lecture *Existentialism is a Humanism.* It makes the most explicit exposition of existentialism as an optimistic doctrine. This is Sartre's best known work and has been translated into English by Philip Mairet and published under the title *Existentialism and Humanism.*

At the very outset, Sartre makes his intention clear: "My purpose here is to offer a defence of existentialism against several reproaches that have been laid against it."[40] He notes that existentialism has been decried as having made "an invitation to people to dwell in quietism of despair" and "for having underlined all that is ignominious in the human situation."[41] He strongly refutes these allegations and declares that existentialism is essentially a humanism. He regards existentialism life-affirming and defines it as "a doctrine that does render human life possible; a doctrine, also, which affirms that every truth and every action imply both an environment and a human subjectivity."[42]

Sartre seeks to find out the truly real and significant in experience. He sees man as a struggling and hopeful being and defines his glory by affirming his freedom. He feels that anguish, forlornness and despair are spurs to heroic action. Sartre says that existentialism "cannot be regarded as a philosophy of quietism since it defines man by his action; nor as a pessimistic description of man, for no doctrine is more optimistic, the destiny of man is placed within himself."[43] He goes on to suggest that existentialism is nothing but "a form of humanism."[44]

An existentialist does not take man as the end, since man is still to be determined. There is no other universe except the human universe, the universe of human subjectivity. This is what Sartre calls "existential humanism"[45] and goes on to add: "This is humanism, because we remind man that there is no legislator but himself; that he himself, thus abandoned, must decide for himself."[46] Man therefore has to create his own values in order to comprehend the true meaning of his existence."The conclusion of Sartre's philosophy," in Stumpf's words, "is . . . that if man expresses his genuine humanity in all his behaviour, he will never deceive himself; and honesty will then become not his ideal but rather his very being."[47]

Existentialism stands for the recovery and restoration of the dignity of the individual and his personality. It presents a philosophy of life with hope and exultation among grim facts of life. Man gives his life meaning through action, through choice, or through revolt. Sartre concludes his *Existentialism and Humanism* thus: "existentialism is optimistic, it is a doctrine of action, and it is only by self-deception, by confusing their own despair with ours that Christians can describe us as without hope."[48]

Nausea, published in 1938, is Sartre's most deeply philosophical novel and the most explicit analysis of the phenomena of nausea. Existence is of central concern in the novel and there are echoes of Kierkegaardian and Heideggerian thought. The novel is presented in the form of the diary of Antoine Roquentin which he started writing after his first experience of nausea. A desire to show life in its most gloomy colours forms the basis of the novel. It is from the basic reality of his own vision of life as formless and superfluous that Roquentin judges the rest of humanity to be either hopelessly deceived or deliberately blind. He sees his own life as tasteless and obscene, and the very thought of it gives him an insidious desire to be sick.

The novel gives expression to a warning as to what happens when a man cuts himself off from action and from the society of his fellows. A disillusioned French intellectual, Roquentin settles down in Bouville at the age of thirty-five after having led an adventurous life. He lives there all alone. He has no family, no friends, and no work except the self-imposed task of writing the scholarly biography of an eighteenth-century rake and intriguer, Marquis de Rollebon. Before coming to Bouville, Roquentin has had hectic experiences including his extensive travelling abroad for six years: "I can see the rigorous succession of circumstances. I have crossed the seas, I have left cities behind me. . . . I have had women, I have fought with men."[49] After coming back from his travels, Roquentin could just as well have settled in Paris or in Marseille but since most of the documents pertaining to Rollebon are available in the Municipal library of Bouville, he decides to stay in this town.

Roquentin is highly reflective and analytical. One day as he stands on the sea-shore, he undergoes a disturbing sensation. He bends down to pick up a pebble which he wants to throw into the sea. And he suddenly finds that he cannot do that: "How unpleasant it was? And it came from the pebble, I'm sure of that, it passed from the pebble into my hands. Yes, that's it, that's exactly it: a sort of nausea in the hands."[50] Overcome by a curious sickly horror, he drops the pebble and goes away. Later on, one morning when he is going to library to pursue his research on Rollebon, he bends down to pick up a piece of paper. Once again, he finds that it is physically impossible for him to do so. He senses that he is wasting his time, that life must be something more than this. Similar other experiences assail him and he begins to fear various objects but cannot decide whether a change has occurred in him or in these things.

Roquentin experiences a sense of emptiness and meaninglessness which the existentialists call *ennui*. He discovers the contingency of the world and realizes that his being is superfluous and therefore absurd. He becomes aware that human consciousness is not the centre of the universe. Nothing in the universe has any specific function to fulfil. No established scheme or pattern can protect man from essential inhumanity of nature. The world of dead objects confronts him with silent hostility and the thought of an unnecessary and inescapable existence makes him feel sick. Around Roquentin, there is no one except a shadow of himself and he feels the sordidness and wretchedness of being alone.

Most men on earth attribute a definite meaning to their existence, without ever experiencing any nausea. Such naive, unpremeditated belief and confidence are the very things that provoke Sartre's ridicule. These people pretend to justify their existence through their prejudices, their patterns of behaviour, and their superficial conventions. Sartre calls such people *salauds*. They lead quiet, confident lives and believe themselves justified and, unlike Roquentin, pose no questions of justification. They readily believe that their lives are coherent; they never feel that their existences are stale and unjustified. They live surrounded by institutions of state and family, and borne up by a consciousness of their own claims and virtues. Sartre denounces in vehement terms the false sense of security of these men who try to become important enough to believe in themselves—in their superficial lives—and thereby to elude the fundamental problems of existence.

The uneasy sense of boredom, weariness and dissatisfaction leads Roquentin to abandon his book on Rollebon. As a consequence, he decides to leave Bouville. He sits in the cafe and listens for the last time to his favourite gramophone record, "Some of these days" sung by a negress. As he listens to the melody, Roquentin is "like a man who is completely frozen after a journey through the snow and who suddenly comes into a warm room."[51] Almost miraculously his nausea disappears. He suddenly perceives a possibility of salvation. He realizes that he should create something, a novel perhaps which, like the jazz tune, shall be "beautiful and hard as steel."[52] He feels that the completion of such a work of art would enable him to enjoy an instant of happiness and henceforth he will be able to recall his past without disgust. By resolving his doubt, he finds a deliverance from the curse of absurdity. His resolution is to live meaningfully in a world without meaning.

Like the existentialist thinkers, Conrad views the universe as meaningless—one which has no apparent concern with people's lives, where consciousness is really a curse and Nature permanently alien to man. Man's existence in this universe is of a kind which he can neither comprehend nor control. There are many aspects of this universe which appear unreasonable and inexplicable to his mind. He tries to find a rational scheme or order in the universe but discovers none.

In each of Conrad's novels, the accent is placed upon the absurdity of the world and of the human condition, on the eternal denial of justice to man. Man's position in this world is thus precarious; he confronts need, necessity and death. In relation to the universe, man is irredeemably little. Thus Jim appears as a little speck in Marlow's last vision of him. Again, in *Lord Jim* only, Stein seems to be voicing Conrad's concern with man's place in the universe when he says:

> Man is amazing but he is not a masterpiece.... Sometimes it seems to me that man is come where he is not wanted, where there is no place for him; for if not, why should he want all the place? Why should he run about here and there making a great noise about himself, talking about the stars, disturbing the blades of grass?[53]

It is indeed very disturbing for man to feel that he has come into a world where he is not wanted. Conrad, like the existentialists, sees the world without order or value. He feels convinced that there is ultimately no life-style which can be recommended as a means of redeeming the human condition, for they all eventually prove to be inadequate. Like Nietzsche, Conrad believes that there is no absolute truth. All knowledge is fragmentary and truth as a whole can never be known.

Conrad shares the atheistic existential view that God is dead. He however refuses to despair at the absence of God and, like Camus and Sartre, creates for himself a faith without dogma and an ideal of fidelity and responsibility. He holds the belief that man has the capacity to transcend himself and find a meaning in his life. Man, frustrated by his experiences in the world, turns to his inner self to comprehend life's significance. The problems besetting man's precarious life necessitate the establishing of customs, principles and standards of behaviour. These help man in his attempt to grapple with the enigmas and insecurities of existence.

The individual, Conrad believes, must establish his own code of behaviour and assert positive values in order to combat the hostile world. Conrad's novels constantly reiterate that in a universe devoid of meaning, man has to create his own values. In a letter to Edward Noble, Conrad gives expression to this view: "Everyone must walk in the light of his own heart's gospel. No man's light is good to any of his fellows. That's my creed from beginning to end. That's my view of life,—a view that rejects all formulas, dogmas and principles of other people's making. These are only a web of illusions. We are too varied. Another man's truth is only a dismal lie to me."[54]

Almost all Conrad's heroes—Willems, Marlow in *Youth* and *Heart of Darkness*, Jim, Nostromo, the young captain in *The Secret Sharer*, Razumov, Heyst—cherish a dream of ideal self which is not in keeping with certain hard facts of existence. The protagonist in each novel is in search of a justification for his existence. As a solitary being, he has to live with his own self and his own conscience. Guilt arises when he is not able to accept his own deeds and sits in judgment on his own self; it arises when he is aware that he has violated some personal or public norm. His guilt is an existential one, for it has arisen out of his knowledge that human dignity has been violated.

The existences of central characters in Conrad's novels are significantly marked by frustrations and failures. They make us aware that the paths of our lives are not preordained but depend solely on us. There are no rules to govern our conduct and no systems to bring us stability and steadfastness. Conrad himself experienced a sense of uncertainty and incompleteness. In a letter to Edward Garnett, he suggests: "If we are 'ever becoming—never being' then I would be a fool if I tried to become this thing rather than that: for I know well that I will never be anything."[55]

Conrad thus shares the existentialist belief that man is always *becoming*, never *is*. The protagonists in his novels are capable of sudden growth and change. Although they first appear at a moment of apparent certainty, the direction of their lives alters radically. Almayer, Willems, Jim, Nostromo, the captain in *The Secret Sharer*, Razumov, Heyst—all of them are startlingly alike in their conviction at the outset of their tales that they are what they will always be. However, the events take a sudden turn to reveal how incomplete the man is when confronted by a crisis. The apparently paradoxical incompleteness of these protagonists is existentialist in essence.

Like Camus and Sartre, Conrad places great premium upon a responsible decision. He shares the existential belief in revolt against the absurdity of existence. Conrad demonstrates that man must create values out of despair of his life and the absurd world in which he lives. Conrad's belief that man must struggle against a hostile universe leads in a positive way to his belief that this struggle results in energy and the creation of man's individual morality. Conrad's quest for significant action and faith in human soul is best expressed in the "Author's Note" to *Chance:* "The history of men on this earth since the beginning of ages may be resumed in one phrase of infinite poignancy: They were born, they suffered, they died . . . Yet it is a great tale!"[56]

In order to demonstrate existential humanism in Conrad's fiction, it is necessary to examine Conrad's own life and his views on man and universe. The life and work of Conrad bear a close relationship. Human experience is the basis on which Conrad builds his fictional world. In the essay entitled "Books," Conrad discusses the novelist's craft and warns the artist not to restrict himself to the experience of his own imagination in violation of the actuality of human experience: "In truth every novelist must begin by creating for himself a world, great or little, in which he can honestly believe. This world cannot be made otherwise than in his own image: it is fated to remain individual and a little mysterious, and yet it must resemble something already familiar to the experience, the thoughts and the sensations of his readers."[57] It is a firm conviction of Conrad that the duty of the artist is to give a consistent form to the shapeless facts of human experience

The present study attempts to explore Conrad's existential humanism in his early work and trace its development into his significant work in a chronological order, concluding with *Victory*, the last of his novels still indicative of a major talent. Such a study makes the subsequent readings of Conrad's novels more rewarding and brings out the full scope of Conrad's art and meaning not sufficiently apprehended hitherto.

NOTES

1. M.D. Zabel, "Joseph Conrad: Chance and Recognition," *The Art of Joseph Conrad: A Critical Symposium,* ed. Robert W. Stallman (East Lansing: Michigan State University Press, 1960), p. 28.
2. C.N. Stavrou, "Conrad, Camus, and Sisyphus," *Audience,* VII (1960), pp. 80-96.
3. Adam Gillon, "Conrad and Sartre," *Dalhousie Review,* XL (1960), p. 61.
4. John A. Palmer, *Joseph Conrad's Fiction: A Study in Literary Growth* (New York: Cornell University Press, 1968), p. 196.
5. Ted Billy, "Dead in the Centre—Conrad's Confrontation with Nothingness," *Studies in the Humanities,* V (1976), p. 39.
6. Iris Murdoch, *Sartre: Romantic Rationalist* (London: Collins, 1967), p. 9.
7. For example, Tony Tanner, "Nightmare and Complacency: Razumov and the Western Eye," *Critical Quarterly,* IV (1962), pp. 123-40; Ira Sadoff, "Sartre and Conrad: Lord Jim as Existential Hero," *Dalhousie Review,* XLIX (1969), pp. 518-25; P.L. Brown, "*The Secret Sharer* and the Existentialist Hero," *Conradiana,* III (1971), pp. 22-30.
8. John Macquarrie, *Existentialism* (London: Hutchinson, 1972), p. 3.
9. Soren Kierkegaard, "That Individual," *Existentialism from Dostoevsky to Sartre,* ed. Walter Kaufmann (New York: New American Library, 1975), p. 100.
10. Jean-Paul Sartre, *Existentialism and Humanism,* trans. Philip Mairet (London: Methuen, 1948; rep. 1970), p. 28.
11. *Ibid.*, p. 29.
12. "Dread and Freedom," *Existentialism from Dostoevsky to Sartre,* p. 105.
13. "Concluding Unscientific Postscript." *Existentialism from Dostoevsky to Sartre,* p. 114.
14. *The Joyful Wisdom* (New York: Frederick, Ungar, 1960), p. 125.
15. "Reason and Existenz," *Existentialism from Dostoevsky to Sartre,* p. 225.
16. *Ibid.*, p. 232.
17. *The Myth of Sisyphus and Other Essays*, trans. Justin O'Brien (London: Hamish Hamilton, 1960), p. 11.

18. *Ibid.*, p. 47.
19. *The Rebel*, trans. Anthony Bower (London: Penguin, 1973), p. 16.
20. *Ibid.*, p. 27.
21. *Ibid.*, p. 28.
22. *The Myth of Sisyphus and Other Essays*, p. 97.
23. *Loc. cit.*
24. *Ibid.*, p. 99.
25. *Loc. cit.*
26. *The Outsider, The Collected Fiction of Albert Camus* (London: Hamish Hamilton, 1960), p. 3.
27. *Ibid.*, p. 15.
28. *Ibid.*, p. 54.
29. *Ibid.*, p. 67.
30. *Ibid.*, p. 68.
31. *Loc. cit.*
32. *The Plague, The Collected Fiction of Albert Camus*, p. 166.
33. *Ibid.*, p. 191.
34. *Ibid.*, p. 144.
35. *Ibid.*, p. 145.
36. Jean-Paul Sartre, *Existentialism and Humanism*, p. 28.
37. *Ibid.*, p. 34.
38. *Being and Nothingness*, trans. Hazel E. Barnes (London: Methuen, 1977), p. 577.
39. *Existentialism and Humanism*, p. 56.
40. *Ibid.*, p. 23.
41. *Loc. cit.*
42. *Ibid.*, p. 24.
43. *Ibid.*, p. 44.
44. *Ibid.*, p. 54.
45. *Ibid.*, p. 55.
46. *Ibid.*, pp. 55-56.
47. Samuel Enoch Stumpf, *Socrates to Sartre* (New York: McGraw Hill, 1966), p. 470.
48. *Existentialism and Humanism*, p. 56.
49. *Nausea*, trans. Robert Baldick (Penguin, 1965), p. 39.
50. *Ibid.*, p. 22.
51. *Ibid.*, p. 251.
52. *Ibid.*, p. 252.
53. *Lord Jim* (Garden City, New York: Doubleday, Page, 1925), p. 208.

54. Jean-Aubry, *Joseph Conrad: Life and Letters* (Garden City, New York: Doubleday, Page, 1927), I, p. 184.

55. Edward Garnett, ed., *Letters from Joseph Conrad: 1895-1924* (Indianapolis: Bobbs-Merrill, Charter Books, 1928), p. 46.

56. *Chance* (Garden City, New York: Doubleday, Page, 1925), p. viii. Ellipses Conrad's.

57. *Notes on Life and Letters* (Garden City, New York: Doubleday, Page, 1925), p. 6.

Formative Influences

Anyone who investigates into Conrad's childhood and adolescence cannot avoid feeling that the recurrence in his novels of characters obsessed with some guilt and faced with extreme situations is an evidence of obsessional motifs in a single pattern established in his early years. It is because much of the experience communicated in his novels flows from Conrad's memories and is based on his early life spent in Poland. His unhappy childhood has had a seminal influence on all his fiction. It is possible to gather evidence from his writings of the miserable days of his early life and the impact it had on his mind. The irrational and hostile universe portrayed in Conrad's novels can be traced to his appalling experiences in the Poland of his childhood which tends to undermine any vision of a stable society.

Indeed, one need not go beyond Conrad's own life to find reasons for his lifelong preoccupation with exile, loneliness, isolation and issues pertaining to man's existence in the world. Conrad's art is closely related to its author's life. In order to explore the background of Conrad as a philosophic-novelist, we must look farther into the past than the period 1894-1924 during which he produced his fiction. This biographical inquiry involves, besides other things, a study of psychological factors which determined the meaning and significance of his creations.

A number of biographers-have discussed the outer story of Conrad's life: his readings, schooling, life as a sailor, family life. It is now necessary to trace the development of the inner man, the formative intellectual influences which finally produced the philosophical novelist that Conrad is. This has a great significance when one considers the unusual if not bizarre nature of Conrad's early life. Before settling down as a novelist, Conrad had acquired a vast and variegated experience of life. During his infancy years there were events which made indelible impressions on his susceptible mind. Often without his conscious knowledge, there worked in his mind the effects of his Polish nationality, his years in Russia, his interrupted and uneven education, his long years as a seaman, and his naturalization as an Englishman. Perhaps there is no other writer in English who has had such an unorthodox preparation for his craft. As Conrad himself points out: "That which in their grown-up years may appear to the world about them as the most enigmatic side of their natures, and perhaps must remain forever obscure even to themselves, will be their unconscious response to the still voice of that inexorable past from which their works of fiction and their personalities are remotely derived."[1]

Polish life contributed little direct material for Conrad's plots but it considerably moulded the bent of his mind. Man's writing is conditioned essentially by what resides in his unconscious, his memories, his experiences, the various impacts that life has made. In his mind are stored all sorts of latent responses which are called forth at a point in time, often to his great surprise, by a certain stimulus. In the consideration of any work of art, and fiction writing in particular, it is therefore most profitable to make use of the biographical material as it helps a great deal in throwing light on the artist's choice of the subject and his attitude towards it.

Although a Pole by birth, Conrad was a Russian national—Poland in those days being under the oppressive rule of Russia. His early life was darkened by the savage repressions which Tzarist Russia inflicted on the Poles after the failure of the rebellion of 1863. His father, Apollo Korzeniowski, was one of the rebel leaders who vehemently opposed the Russian imperialism. In October 1861, he was arrested by the Russian authorities and imprisoned in the citadel.

When Conrad was only four years old, Apollo was exiled from Warsaw to Vologda, a cold marshy Russian province. Conrad's mother, Evelina, voluntarily joined her husband in exile and took the young boy with her. On way, Conrad had an attack of pneumonia and suffered serious illness. The murderous climate of Vologda adversely affected the health of Evelina and Conrad. The condition of Evelina, a tuberculosis patient, deteriorated and she died two years later, on 18th April 1865, at the age of thirty-two. Conrad was then seven years old, and he spent the next four years of his life mainly with his father who had to move from one place to another. The failure of the 1863 insurrection and the premature death of his beloved wife crushed Apollo's spirit; he was given to occasional fits of depression. Left with the full responsibility of bringing up his little son, he was broken, grieved and totally disillusioned. As for Conrad, there was hardly any chance to have the full experience of youth; he had no companions, no friends to play with. He was a lonely boy, defenseless against the outside world. He passed his weary days all alone, his first consciousness being that of solitude. It is obvious that school could by no means exercise the same lasting influence on him as his father did. Through manifold bitter experiences Apollo had become pessimistic. In a letter to his cousin Jan Zagorski, Apollo gave vent to such feelings:

> I have passed through heavy and even terrible days of brooding on God's blessings. . . . I know I have not suffered and never could suffer like our Saviour, but then I am only a human being. . . . It is sad indeed for a man to see the two doors through which alone he can approach the presence of God shut against him, but such is the will of Providence.[2]

Apollo's pessimism made a deep impression on Conrad's tender mind. And when Apollo died in 1869, Conrad was completely shaken: "I had an awful sensation of the inevitable. I had also moments of revolt which stripped off me some of my simple trust in the government of the universe."[3] A streak of fatalism accompanied by a strong distrust in God is evident in his utterance.

Orphaned at the age of eleven, Conrad was placed in the charge of his uncle, Thaddeus Bobrowski. It was a period of sadness and loneliness, the sorrow of his bereavement being in unison with his environment—the environment of Cracow, that sombre city.

It is interesting to note the similarities between Conrad's life and the lives of Camus and Sartre. Both the French writers lost their fathers when they were very young. Camus was only a year old when his father was killed in the First World War; Sartre was still a young boy when his father died. Both Camus and Conrad were exiles from their native lands.

The early years of Conrad's life were marked by exile, solitude and death. Miseries and privations that his parents suffered made a deep impression on the child's mind. No wonder, one can easily trace these feelings in his writings. Conrad was speaking largely of his own life and torment when he spoke of man's lifelong solitariness. His protagonists are heroes—lonely, doomed, overcome, yet unyielding. His view of life is founded on the inherent paradox that the individual is completely isolated in a universe in which he is somehow inextricably involved.

When speaking of these unconscious influences one must not forget Conrad's love for reading books which he inherited from his father. His father, a renowned literary scholar, had translated Shakespeare, Victor Hugo and Alfred de Vigny into Polish.[4] During his last illness, he got his son to read aloud to him the proofs of some of his works. And during his long, lonely and unoccupied hours, Conrad turned to his father's library. Apart from many foreign writers, the leading Polish romanticists Mickiewicz and Slowacki had a deep influence on Conrad. These two writers are the strong advocates of the idea of moral and national responsibility.[1] "Ethical principles," observes Najder, "were based on the idea that an individual, however exceptional he might be, is always a member of a group, responsible for its welfare."[5] Even a superficial reader will detect what importance Conrad attributes to responsibility in his fiction.

At the age of fifteen, Conrad divulged his desire to go to sea. In making up his mind, he was torn with a conflict whether going to sea would tantamount to deserting his country. Finally, he decided he should go. The remonstrances of his tutor, the advice of his uncle, the entreaties of his grandmother, and the astonished indignation of his relations failed to stop him. In 1874, at the age of seventeen, he left Poland, the land for which his ancestors—indeed his own father and mother—had suffered and died. It was not till sixteen years later that he set foot again upon his native soil.

Conrad's profound concern with problems of moral failure, of desertion, of betrayal, in a large part sprang from guilt feelings about his own abandonment of Poland. In his essay, "Poland Revisited," Conrad admits that his departure from Poland had for him the character of a betrayal. In *A Personal Record*, hc alludes to this decision as "the only case of a boy of my nationality and antecedents taking a . . . standing jump out of his racial surroundings and associations." (121) *Lord Jim* is a dramatization of Conrad's sense of having deserted Poland in her crisis. Jim's fatal jump from the *Patna* parallels Conrad's departure from Poland.

As a writer, Conrad was obsessed with the thought of suicide. In 1878, in a fit of depression, he made an attempt to commit suicide by shooting himself in the chest. Luckily, the bullet missed the heart. To his uncle, he described it as despair over financial ruin. Some of Conrad's biographers attribute it to an unsuccessful love-affair with Dona Rita. The facts of the case seem likely to remain a mystery. Conrad, however, remained susceptible to morbid depression for most of his life. Throughout his work, he constantly returned to the contemplation of death. The thought of suicide repeatedly appears in his novels in which no fewer than nine major characters take this way out. Some others sacrifice themselves in what may be called a form of suicide. Growing frustrations, bitterness, disappointments bring the characters to the brink of self-destruction. The suicides remind us of the bitterness of life that creates the need to consider ending it all.

The event that made the deepest impact on Conrad's mind was his trip to Stanley Falls on the Congo in 1890. Jean-Aubry tells us of Conrad's remark to Garnett: "Before the Congo I was just a mere animal."[6] Before he reached the Congo, Conrad knew that the prospects of life in the Congo were far from rosy. While still on board the *Ville de Maceio,* he wrote to his cousin Charles Zagorski: "What makes me rather uneasy is the information that 60 percent of our Company's employees return to Europe before they have completed even six months' service. Fever and dysentery! There are others who are sent home in a hurry at the end of a year, so that they shouldn't die in the Congo."[7]

Conrad's health was also ruined by the adverse climate of the Congo. The complete breakdown of his health through fever and dysentery caused him to resign his post and return to Europe. The malarial gout which troubled him for the rest of his life became special source of vexation by affecting the wrist of his right hand. His Congo experience was terrible; he felt totally disgusted with existence. Dissatisfied with the seeming emptiness of his existence, Conrad was in a state of mind which is often a prelude to creative activity. From Stanley Falls, he brought back a copybook which contained the first seven chapters of *Almayer's Folly.* Conrad had been guided by a random pursuit of adventure for its own sake but the Congo experience forced him to examine the many kinds of adventure; it gave birth to Conrad's moral imagination. Jean-Aubry confirms this when he declares: "It may be said that Africa killed Conrad the sailor and strengthened Conrad the novelist."[8]

We find the literary transposition of Conrad's Congo journey in *Heart of Darkness.* The novel, with its tone of outraged humanism and its consciousness of evil, shows how deeply Conrad was affected by the sight of human baseness and degradation. The story is an introspective journey into the self—the very heart of darkness. The enigma of existence that Conrad confronted in the Congo persisted in his mind and the subsequent fiction that he wrote invariably centred around this.

The great bulk of Conrad's fiction indeed stems from his adventurous life as a seaman. A skimming of Aubry's biography will show that almost every one of Conrad's stories has some autobiographical basis. Such an approach, it must be said, concerns itself with the literal view only and fails to discover any profundity in the work. In *Heart of Darkness*, as also in other novels, Conrad was not merely fictionalizing real experience and his work is not a simple rehash of his life. Conrad expressed his full aversion to this approach. He frankly admits the autobiographical origin of most of his work,[9] but always insists that every work of art has an independent existence. While Richard Curle explored the sources of the work in real events, Conrad observed: "It is a strange fate that everything that I have, of set artistic purpose, laboured to leave indefinite, suggestive ... should have that light turned on to it. ... Didn't it ever occur to you, my dear Curle, that I knew what I was doing in leaving the facts of my life and even of my tales in the background? Explicitness, my dear fellow, is fatal to the glamour of all artistic work, robbing it of all suggestiveness, destroying all illusion."[10]

Writing in an alien language was another factor that accentuated Conrad's sense of frustration and solitude. One of the most important matters for Conrad as a writer was the problem of communication. Interestingly, he could not speak the language of England until he was twenty years old. For Conrad, English was his third language. He encountered the difficulty of learning to write in his adopted tongue. In a letter to Arthur Symons, Conrad expresses himself thus: "I had to work like a coal-miner in his pit quarrying all my English sentences out of a black night."[11]

Conrad felt more at home while conversing in French and discussed with Ford important theoretical issues and problems of literary craft in this language only. And when he met Cunninghame Graham for the first time, Conrad wrote to Sanderson, they talked in two languages—in English and in French.[12] We have the testimony of Ford who writes: "Conrad's dislike for the English language, then, was, during all the years of our association, extreme, his contempt for his medium unrivalled."[13] To say, as does Ford, that Conrad had contempt for English would be highly unfair. Conrad, in a span of few years only, had mastered the nuances of the English language and made it a fit tool of artistic expression. However, there is no doubt that throughout his life Conrad spoke English with a marked foreign accent and even mispronounced certain words. He was well aware of his linguistic shortcomings. In a letter to Graham, Conrad writes: "But you know I am shy of my bad English."[14]

Conrad always remained in a state of anxiety about his financial position. He wrote his novels under the pressure of earning a livelihood. He would normally receive advances from J.B. Pinker, his literary agent, and spend them before he could write the books for which he received them. In a letter to Pinker, Conrad makes it clear that he cannot be trusted to adhere to any set schedule of work: "I generally sell a work before it is begun, get paid when it is half done and don't do the other half till the spirit moves me. I must say that I have no control over the spirit neither has the man who has paid the money."[15] His ill-health and the pressing domestic problems distressed Conrad and he found it difficult to concentrate upon his work. In the early years of his writing life, the terrible feeling of loneliness gripped him. He confides to Sanderson in a letter: "I fear I have not the capacity and the power to go on—to satisfy the first expectations of those who are dependent on my exertions. I fear! I fear! And sometimes I hope. But it is the fear that abides."[16] In his novels, Conrad continually stresses the loneliness and the hazard of life and the implacable responsibility of each soul to itself.

It is not certain how far Conrad was influenced by Nietzsche, but he was quite familiar with the nihilistic philosophy advocated by the German philosopher. In a letter to Garnett, dated 26th October 1899, Conrad speaks of having received a copy of Garnett's essay on Nietzsche: "I had letters about your Nietzsche from all sorts of people. You have stirred some brains!"[17] It may be stated without reluctance that like Nietzsche, Conrad admires and subscribes to Schopenhauer's attitude towards life.

Undoubtedly, Conrad's early life contributed significantly to his scepticism. He came to hold, like Schopenhauer and Nietzsche, a pessimistic view of life. For this, he was constantly reprimanded by his uncle, Thaddeus Bobrowski, under whose tutelage he came after the death of his father. Uncle Thaddeus was a parental figure and his guidance and admonitions made a deep impact on young Conrad. In 1891, when Conrad felt highly frustrated owing to his physical disabilities, his uncle reproached him in strong terms: "The tone of your letter of September 26th gave me very little comfort. To say that it is better to die young, a man must be either very discouraged or really ill. Such a philosophy could not proceed from a young man of thirty-four who was in good health."[18] Another of his uncle's letters throws light on the stress and despair which Conrad experienced after the Congo journey, in effect, throughout his life. Starting the letter with "MY DEAR BOY," Thaddeus writes to Conrad: "I begin as I always do but I ought to address you as 'my dear pessimist': for judging from your letters that description would fit you best. . . . I am sure that with your melancholy temperament you ought to avoid all meditations which lead to pessimistic conclusions. I advise you to lead a more active life than ever and to cultivate some cheerful habits."[19]

Yet another factor that contributed to Conrad's frustration in life was the realization that he as a writer had been misunderstood by his contemporaries. Conrad's stories, rooted as they are in his rich experiences at sea, earned for him "such headings as 'spinner of sea-yarns—master-mariner—seaman writer'."[20] Some of his comtemporaries failed to go beneath the romantic surface of the stories and found nothing intrinsically human in them. They often associated his name with writers like Marryat, Cooper and Kipling. In a letter to Sidney Colvin, Conrad laments this lack of understanding on the part of his contemporaries: "Perhaps you won't find it presumption if, after 22 years of work, I may say that I have not been very well understood. I have been called a writer of the sea, of the tropics, a descriptive writer, a romantic writer—and also a realist."[21] To Richard Curle, he expresses his wish "to get freed from that infernal tail of ships" and points out that "in the body of my work barely one-tenth is what may be called sea stuff, and even of that, the bulk, that is *Nigger* and *Mirror*, has a very special purpose."[22] Conrad was specially distressed by the American press which projected him as a writer of sea stories: "I do wish that all those ships of mine were given a rest, but I am afraid that when the Americans get hold of them they will never, never, never get a rest."[23] One may unhesitatingly assert that Conrad does not restrict his writing to the world of ships. It is the fundamental existential questions that concern him, and his writings are an expression of his quest into life.

NOTES

1. *A Personal Record* (Garden City, New York: Doubleday, Page, 1925), p. xxi.
2. Jean-Aubry, *Joseph Conrad: Life and Letters*, I, p. 16.
3. Quoted in Edward Harold Visiak, *The Mirror of Conrad* (New York: Humanities Press, 1968), p. 32.
4. *A Personal Record*, p. ix.
5. Z. Najder, ed., *Conrad's Polish Background: Letters to and from Polish Friends* (London: Oxford University Press, 1964), p. 16.
6. Jean-Aubry, *Joseph Conrad: Life and Letters*, I, p. 141.
7. *Ibid.*, p. 126.
8. *Ibid.*, p. 142.
9. "Every novel," says Conrad, "contains an element of autobiography—and this can hardly be denied, since the creator can only express himself in his creation." *A Personal Record*, pp. xv-xvi.

10. Richard Curle, ed., *Conrad to a Friend* (Garden City, New York: Doubleday, Doran, 1928), p. 142.
11. Jean-Aubry, *Joseph Conrad: Life and Letters,* II, p. 84.
12. *Ibid.,* I, p. 219.
13. Ford Madox Ford, "Conrad on the Theory of Fiction," *Conrad: A Collection of Critical Essays* (New Jersey: Prentice-Hall, 1966), p. 175.
14. Jean-Aubry, *Joseph Conrad: Life and Letters,* I, p. 121.
15. *Ibid.,* p. 278.
16. *Ibid.,* p. 282.
17. Edward Garnett, ed., *Letters from Joseph Conrad:1895-1924,* p. 157.
18. Jean-Aubry, *Joseph Conrad: Life and Letters,* I, p. 147.
19. *Ibid.,* pp. 147-48.
20. Richard Curle, ed., *Conrad to a Friend,* p. 189.
21. Jean-Aubry, *Joseph Conrad: Life and Letters,* II, p. 85.
22. Richard Curle, ed., *Conrad to a Friend,* pp. 188 and 189.
23. *Ibid.,* p. 189.

Conrad's Views on Man and Universe as Revealed in his Non-Fictional Writings

Conrad's work is so rich and complex that it is open to infinite interpretations. Its inscrutability is also owing to the fact that Conrad did not talk much about his works. "The intention of temperamental writing is infinitely complex," Conrad wrote in response to a publisher's request for blurb material, "and to talk about my work is repugnant to me beyond anything."[1] To unravel Conrad's mind, one must turn to his non-fictional writings. His essays, prefaces, and letters yield a consistent account of his art and present an exhaustive statement of his philosophic vision. These writings amply reveal Conrad's views on human nature and on man's place in the universe.

Three volumes of autobiographical nature must be noted in particular as depositories of Conrad's ideas on art and life. The first, *The Mirror of the Sea*, is partly autobiographical; it is descriptive of various aspects of life at sea. In Conrad's own words, "it is the best tribute my piety can offer to the ultimate shapers of my character, convictions, and, in a sense, destiny—to the imperishable sea, to the ships that are no more, and to the simple men who have had their day." (viii) The second, *A Personal Record*, was written to depict "the man behind the books" and "to give the record of personal memories by presenting faithfully the feelings and sensations connected with the writing of my first book and with my first contact with the sea." (xxi) The third, *Notes on Life and Letters*, is a collection of essays written between 1898 and 1920. Conrad describes these essays as "a thin array . . . of really innocent attitudes: Conrad literary, Conrad political, Conrad reminiscent, Conrad controversial." (v-vi)

Conrad was a prolific writer of letters and these constitute a large body of his literary output. His letters bear many resemblances to his essays and were a safety-valve which enabled him to air his views on various topics. A thorough combing of the numerous letters that he wrote to his friends over a period of thirty years reveals Conrad the man and his views on human life. Most of his letters are informal, done on the spur of the moment, and quite frank and sincere. They thus make the most valuable contribution to the understanding of Conrad's mind.

Conrad corresponded in three languages—Polish, French and English. Though Conrad wrote numerous letters in Polish, in many cases the originals have been lost. The French letters are addressed to Marguerite Poradowska, Andre Gide and Jean-Aubry. Letters to Mme. Poradowska are extremely important as these throw a great light on Conrad's early career; those to Andre Gide are helpful in understanding his middle career when the French writer supervised the translation of Conrad's work into French. The number of letters in English runs beyond 3000. These are written to J.B. Pinker, H.G. Wells, John Galsworthy, Ford Madox Ford, Stephen Crane, Edward Garnett, R.B. Cunninghame Graham, Arnold Bennett and others.

Conrad had a close literary association with Edward Garnett who encouraged and sponsored his writings. In his letters to Garnett, Conrad could afford to put aside all reserve and express his true feelings. Between 1897 and 1899, Conrad wrote a series of letters to his friend Cunninghame Graham. These letters are significant for they contain some forthright and eloquent statements on man's condition and his place in the universe. It may be borne in mind that Conrad held Graham in high esteem and often claimed that he trusted Graham's critical judgment and sympathy. "I've always felt," he wrote to Graham, "that there are certain things which I can say to you because the range of your feelings is wider and your mind more independent than that of any man I know."[2] Again in 1921, Conrad wrote: "I never wrote a book since (1897, when they met) without mental references to you of whom I alone almost among my readers always thought that HE will understand."[3] No wonder, sometimes serious epistolary debate ensued between the two friends and they expressed in their letters matters of deepest concerns.

It may be emphasized that Conrad's pronouncements in his letters and other non-fictional writings are not a methodical exposition of a philosophy. These are marked by the novelist's protean moods and vacillations. Over and again, Conrad modified his opinions on various matters. But, despite some variations, his basic ideas remained the same throughout his life. For example, in 1898, Conrad wrote: "If this miserable planet had perception, a soul, a heart, it would burst with indignation or fly to pieces from sheer pity."[4] Twenty years later, in 1918, he seems afflicted with the same helplessness: "bitterness is the very condition of human existence."[5]

Conrad's primary aim as man and artist is his existential search for truth. In the famous Preface to *The Nigger of the "Narcissus,"* Conrad expresses himself emphatically thus: "A work that aspires, however humbly, to the condition of art should carry its justification in every line. And art itself may be defined as a single-minded attempt to render the highest kind of justice to the visible universe, by bringing to light the truth, manifold and one, underlying its every aspect."[6] Conrad is concerned with the inner truth of experience. Art, he writes, is an attempt "to find in its forms, in its colours, in its light, in its shadows, in the aspects of matter and in the facts of life what of each is fundamental, what is enduring and essential . . . the very truth of their existence."[7]

The search for truth is no mean task: "One must explore deep and believe the incredible to find the few particles of truth floating in an ocean of insignificance."[8] The expression "ocean of insignificance" has a large ring of existential awareness. Throughout his writings, Conrad investigates the facts, enigmas and hidden motives of life. This search for the sense of life and its meaning is truly existential.

Conrad could never grasp the entirety of any situation at once. Temperamentally, he was a sceptic. To Galsworthy, he recommended scepticism as the only attitude in a writer: "Scepticism, the tonic of minds, the tonic of life, the agent of truth,—the way of art and salvation."[9] Throughout his life, Conrad was gripped with the problems of human existence.

Whereas Conrad was preoccupied with the search for truth in his writings, he was also conscious that truth is the most evasive of all illusions: "And suppose Truth is just around the corner, like the elusive and useless loafer it is? I can't tell. No one can tell. It is impossible to know. It is impossible to know anything."[10] To Garnett, he wrote: "All is illusion—the words written, the mind at which they are aimed, the truth they are intended to express, the hands that will hold paper, the eyes that will glance at the lines. Every image floats vaguely in a sea of doubt—and the doubt itself is lost in an unexplored universe of incertitudes."[11]

Like that of Camus and Sartre, Conrad's attitude towards faith, God, and religion is basically one of doubt. His scepticism finds its best expression in his letter addressed to Garnett: "I wish I could believe in an intelligent, benevolent Supreme Being to whom I could leave the task of paying my debts—such debts as the one I owe you for instance. And perhaps there is one. I don't know but it is clear that unless there be a God to repay you in some heavenly coin I shall die in your debt."[12] Much later, in another letter to Garnett, Conrad states that the God under whom he was educated is no longer his God: "I always suspected him (the Jewish God) of being a Futile Person."[13] He refers to the gods as "blind, deaf-mute gods'' whereas we, the human beings, are "so clear-eyed; eloquent and sharp of hearing.''[14]

Conrad expressed in unequivocal terms his distaste for Christianity. In a letter to Edward Garnett, he writes: "Moreover, the base from which he (Tolstoy) starts—Christianity—is distasteful to me. I am not blind to its services but the absurd oriental fable from which it starts irritates me. Great, improving, softening, compassionate it may be but it has lent itself with amazing facility to cruel distortion and is the only religion which, with its impossible standards, has brought an infinity of anguish to innumerable souls—on this earth.''[15] Conrad, as a matter of fact, is reluctant to accept the ethical view of the universe. "I have come to suspect,'' he writes in *A Personal Record*, "that the aim of creation cannot be ethical at all. I would fondly believe that its object is purely spectacular.'' (92) Much like Nietzsche, Conrad finds the world to be devoid of anything except spectacular value.

Even the scientific approach to the world does not provide grounds for ascribing meaning to reality. Conrad speaks of values as mere illusion: "Theory is a cold and lying tombstone of departed truth.''[16] One of his favourite analogues for the universe in which we live is a self-perpetuating knitting machine. Appalled with the notion of the indifferent universe, Conrad cannot find any coherent principle according to which the creation took place. In a letter to Cunninghame Graham, he describes universe as a mere tragic accident, a vast inhuman machine:

> There is a,—let us say,—a machine. It evolved itself (I am severely scientific) out of a chaos of scraps of iron and behold!—it knits. I am horrified at the horrible work and stand appalled. I feel it ought to embroider,—but it goes on knitting. You come and say: "This is all right: it's only a question of the right kind of oil. Let us use this,—for instance,—celestial oil and the machine will embroider a most beautiful design in purple and gold.'' Will it? Alas, no! You cannot by any special lubrication make embroidery with a knitting machine. And the most withering thought is that the infamous thing has made itself: made itself without thought, without conscience, without foresight, without eyes, without heart. It is tragic accident,—and it has happened. You can't interfere with it. The last drop of bitterness is in the suspicion that you can't even smash it. In virtue of that truth one and immortal which lurks in the force that

> made it spring into existence it is what it is,—and it is indestructible!
>
> It knits us in and it knits us out. It has knitted time, space, pain, death, corruption, despair and all the illusions,—and nothing matters.[17]

It may be noticed that there is a striking resemblance between Conrad's presentation of universe as a knitting machine and Nietzsche's observation on world in *The Will to Power:*

> This world: monster of energy, without beginning, without end; a firm, iron magnitude of force that does not grow bigger or smaller, that does not expend itself but only transforms itself; as a whole of unalterable size, a household without expenses or losses, but likewise without increase or income; enclosed by 'nothingness' as by a boundary.[18]

In this respect, both Conrad and Nietzsche anticipate Camus who portrays man and the universe as odd-shaped pieces in some gigantic, meaningless puzzle. Devoid of any cosmological design, the universe is irrational. Man is condemned to a barren and aimless existence, without any hope of escape.

Man is aware of his existence in a world which does not fulfil his aspirations and necessities. In a letter to Graham, Conrad comments on the meaninglessness of life and questions the validity of any positive commitment to the world:

> "Put the tongue out,'' "why not?" One ought to really. And the machine will run on all the same. The question is whether the fatigue of the muscular exertion is worth the transient pleasure of indulgent scorn. On the other hand one may ask whether scorn, love, or hate are justified in the face of such shadowy illusions.
>
> The machine is thinner than air and as evanescent as a flash of lightning. The attitude of cold unconcern is the only reasonable one. Of course reason is hateful,—but why? Because it demonstrates (to those who have the courage) that we, living, are out of life,—utterly out of it.[19]

Even Nature offers no solace; it reminds man of his personal problems and the enigmas of existence. The stormy sea suggests the restlessness of the human beings. The vastness of the sky makes man conscious of his insignificance in the world. In *The Mirror of the Sea*, Conrad reflects: "It is the malicious pleasure of the East Wind to augment the power of your eyesight, in order, perhaps, that you should see better the perfect humiliation, the hopeless character of your captivity." (97) Nature is totally indifferent to human life. There is a chasm between nature and man:

> The mysteries of a universe made up of drops of fire and clods of mud do not concern us in the least. The fate of a humanity condemned ultimately to perish from cold is not worth troubling about. If you take it to heart it becomes an unendurable tragedy. . . .
>
> Life knows us not and we do not know life,—we don't know even our own thoughts. Half the words we use have no meaning whatever and of the other half each man understands each word after the fashion of his own folly and conceit. Faith is a myth and beliefs shift like mists on the shore: thoughts vanish: words, once pronounced, die: and the memory of yesterday is as shadowy as the hope of to-morrow,—only the string of my platitude seems to have no end. As our peasants say: "Pray, brother, forgive me for the love of God." And we don't know what forgiveness is, nor what is love, nor where God is. *Assez!* [20]

Again, in a letter to Garnett, Conrad writes: "I must let out a howl upon things in general—which are things that interest me in particular."[21]

Like the existentialists, Conrad believes that human nature remains essentially the same. He views character as innate and conduct as its manifestation. In the "Author's Note" to *Under Western Eyes*, Conrad writes: "The world is brought face to face with the truth of the saying that the tiger cannot change his stripes nor the leopard his spots."[22] Discussing Graham's schemes of radical social reform, Conrad feels that Graham has been misguided by the desire of the Impossible: "Alas! what you want to reform are not institutions,—it is human nature. Your faith will never move that mountain. Not that I think mankind intrinsically bad. It is only silly and cowardly."[23] Conrad is aware of the destructive potential in human nature. He sees this destructive potential as a threat not only to the individual, but also to the very fabric of society.

The knowledge of his own insignificance and life's absurdity may drive a man to despair. In a letter to Mme. Poradowska, Conrad remarks that it is necessary to drag the ball and chain of one's selfhood to the end, as it is the price one pays for the devilish and divine privilege of thought.[24] Thought is an incongruity, and the tragedy of man's condition lies in consciousness. Suffering is contingent upon man's being in this world; he cannot escape from it. And consciousness of suffering afflicts man terribly. Writing to Graham, Conrad points out that without the illusions generated by ego, the sense of our insignificance in the universe would crush us:

> Egoism is good, and altruism is good, and fidelity to nature would be the best of all, and systems could be built and rules could be made,—if we could only get rid of consciousness. What makes mankind tragic is not that they are the victims of nature, it is that they are conscious of it. To be part of the animal kingdom under the conditions of this earth is very well,—but as soon as you know of your slavery, the pain, the anger, the strife,—the tragedy begins. We can't return to nature, since we can't change our place in it. Our refuge is in stupidity, in drunkenness of all kinds, in lies, in beliefs, in murder, thieving, reforming, in negation, in contempt,—each man according to the promptings of his particular devil. There is no morality, no knowledge and no hope: there is only the consciousness of ourselves which drives us about a world that, whether seen in a convex or a concave mirror, is always but a vain and floating appearance.[25]

Each person, Conrad feels, is confined to the solitariness of self. Man is aware of his solitariness in this universe. In his essay "Well Done," Conrad reflects on man's awareness of the fact that the secrets of his heart cannot be read by his fellows.[26] Man realizes that he is different from all the others in this world. One significant reason of man's solitariness is that his life is quite uneventful. Discussing the content of *The Nigger of the "Narcissus,"* Conrad writes: "As to the lack of incident well—it's life. The incomplete joy, the incomplete sorrow, the incomplete rascality or heroism—the incomplete suffering. Events crowd and push and nothing happens. You know what I mean. The opportunities do not last long enough. Unless in a boy's book of adventures. Mine were never finished. They fizzled out before I had a chance to do more than another man would."[27]

Conrad feels that there can be no set method for man to solve his problems in life. Man faces the problems and tries to find solutions. But the basic problem is that one individual's solution is not useful to another.

Man is aware of his limitations and shortcomings. In his essay on Anatole France, Conrad comments on man's aspirations: "He knows that our best hopes are irrealizable; that it is the almost incredible misfortune of mankind, but also its highest privilege, to aspire towards the impossible; that men have never failed to defeat their highest aims by the very strength of their humanity which can conceive the most gigantic tasks but leaves them disarmed before their irremediable littleness."[28] Conrad realizes that nothing lasts in this world. There are few remedies and there is no universal panacea: "Political institutions, whether contrived by the wisdom of the few or the ignorance of the many, are incapable of securing the happiness of mankind."[29]

Several such pronouncements throw ample light on Conrad's profound disenchantment with life and hostility to God and religion. It will however be misleading to suggest, as some critics do, that Conrad has no faith in human existence and the values it manifests. Reacting to the criticism that he was a pessimist and one who enjoyed portraying scenes of cruelty and brutality, Conrad writes:

> One thing I am certain of is that I have approached the object of my task, things human, in a spirit of piety. The earth is a temple where there is going on a mystery play, childish and poignant, ridiculous and awful enough, in all conscience. Once in I've tried to behave decently. I have not degraded any quasi-religious sentiment by tears and groans; and if I have been amused or indignant, I've neither grinned nor gnashed my teeth. In other words, I've tried to write with dignity, not out of regard for myself, but for the sake of the spectacle, the play with an obscure beginning and an unfathomable denouement.
>
> I don't think that this has been noticed. It is your penitent beating the floor with his forehead and the ecstatic worshipper at the rails that are obvious to the public eye. The man standing quietly in the shadow of the pillar, if noticed at all, runs the risk of being suspected of sinister designs. Thus I've been called a heartless wretch, a man without ideals and a poseur of brutality. But I will confess to you under seal of secrecy that *I don't believe* I am such as I appear to mediocre minds.[30]

Conrad has glimpsed at the darkness but he also knows the values of human community. "It must not be supposed," he writes, "that I claim for the artist in fiction the freedom of moral Nihilism. I would require from him many acts of faith of which the first would be the cherishing of an undying hope.''[31] He rejects nihilism as an acceptable absolute:

> What one feels so hopelessly barren in declared pessimism is just its arrogance. It seems as if the discovery made by many men at various times that there is much evil in the world were a source of proud and unholy joy unto some of the modern writers. That frame of mind is not the proper one in which to approach seriously the art of fiction. It gives an author—goodness only knows why—an elated sense of his own superiority. And there is nothing more dangerous than such an elation to that absolute loyalty towards his feelings and sensations an author should keep hold of in his most exalted moments of creation.
>
> To be hopeful in an artistic sense it is not necessary to think that the world is good. It is enough to believe that there is no impossibility of its being made so.[32]

Conrad seems to believe that it is difficult to achieve ideals in life, though he does not dissuade man to attempt these. The present age, permeated by considerations of profit and utility, is immune to noble ideals. To the question whether one could have a set of rules to follow in life, Conrad replies in a letter to Graham:

> You and your ideals of sincerity and courage and truth are strangely out of place in this epoch of material preoccupations. What does it bring? What's the profit? What do we get by it? These questions are the root of every moral, intellectual or political movement. Into the noblest cause, men manage to put something of their baseness: and sometimes when I think of you here, quietly, you seem to me tragic with your courage, with your beliefs and your hopes. Every cause is tainted: and you reject this one, espouse that other one as if one were evil and the other good, while the same evil you hate is in both, but disguised in different words.[33]

But soon after making this gloomy observation, Conrad goes on to add: "I am more in sympathy with you than words can express."[34] Men and not ideals are the subject of his scepticism.

Although Conrad appears totally estranged from the natural world, from other people, and from the self, he leaves a sense of a much wider commitment to the main ethical, social and literary attitudes. He entertains, in his non-fictional writings, certain convictions about the value of work, fidelity, and solidarity in the face of a universe that is without meaning. He feels that in a hostile and uncomprehending universe, work—an unconscious devotion to the task at hand—offers the chance of sanity and survival. It is a fit alternative to despair and cynicism. Work, for Conrad, is something which stands between man and the vast indifference of things: "For the great mass of mankind the only saving grace that it needed is steady fidelity to what is nearest to hand and heart in the short moment of each human effort."[35]

Throughout his writings, Conrad is preoccupied with the moral question of responsibility and with work as a method of survival. "A man," declares Conrad in his essay "Well Done," "is a worker. If he is not that he is nothing. Just nothing—like a mere adventurer."[36] In his essay on "Confidence," Conrad praises those men who are fashioned by hard work and tradition. In "Tradition," he stresses on man's necessity to work, the solidarity and morality of seamen and the fascination of the sea. Conrad begins his appreciation of the merchant seamen with a quotation from Leonardo da Vinci: "Work is law. Like iron that lying idle degenerates into a mass of useless rust, like water that in an unruffled pool sickens into a stagnant and corrupt state, so without action the spirit of men turns to a dead thing, loses its force, ceases prompting us to leave some trace of ourselves on earth."[37] Again, in "Some Reflections on the Loss of the *Titanic*," Conrad describes the nature of authority and responsibility on board a ship. He is all praise for those who understand responsibility to their jobs.

Conrad is conscious of the benefits of work. Man requires contact with the everyday realities and the ordering quality of work as a counterbalance to the chaotic world outside. In "Tradition," he points out the positive results of work: "From the hard work of men are born the sympathetic consciousness of a common destiny, the fidelity to right practice which makes great craftsmen, the sense of right conduct which we may call honour, the devotion of our calling and the idealism which is not a misty, winged angel without eyes, but a divine figure of terrestrial aspect with a clear glance and with its feet resting firmly on the earth on which it was born."[38]

In some of his letters, Conrad gives his reaction to the First World War that broke out in Europe in 1914. The war had global repercussions, and the event affected Conrad's inner life decisively. In a letter to Wedgewood, Conrad expresses the horror of war:"the thoughts of war sit on one's chest like a nightmare. I am painfully aware of being crippled, of being idle, of being useless with a sort of absurd anxiety."[39] Though immensely shocked by the war, Conrad cherishes a hope nonetheless: "but the door of Mercy is not closed: neither can it kill the hope of better things."[40]

In a letter to Edward Noble, Conrad praises him for his distinct individuality and exhorts him to have faith in future: "Hope is the best and the worst of life. Half of it comes from God and half from the devil, but it behoves men to take gifts and curses with a steady hand and an equable mind,—because of such is made up Fate,—the blind, the invincible."[41] In a more optimistic moment, he writes to H.G. Wells: "The future is of our own making—and (for me) the most striking characteristic of the century is just that development, that maturing of our consciousness which should open our eyes to that truth—or that illusion."[42]

Conrad's non-fictional writings thus manifest his preoccupation with questions of the nature and meaning of universe and man's significance, his hopes and his destiny. Within this area, Conrad has established a positive humanism.

NOTES

1. Jean-Aubry, *Joseph Conrad: Life and Letters*, II, p. 34.
2. C.T. Watts, ed., *Joseph Conrad's Letters to R.B. Cunninghame Graham* (Cambridge: Cambridge University Press, 1969), p. 180.
3. *Ibid.*, p. 191.
4. Jean-Aubry, *Joseph Conrad: Life and Letters*, I, p. 246.
5. Edward Garnett, ed., *Letters from Joseph Conrad: 1895-1924*, p. 258.
6. *The Nigger of the "Narcissus"* (Garden City, New York: Doubleday, Page, 1925), p. xi.
7. *Loc. cit.*
8. Jean-Aubry, *Joseph Conrad: Life and Letters*, I, p. 301.
9. *Loc. cit.*
10. *Ibid.*, II, p. 204.
11. *Ibid.*, I, p. 208.
12. Edward Garnett, ed., *Letters from Joseph Conrad: 1895-1924*, p. 215.
13. *Ibid.*, p. 282.
14. *Ibid.*, p. 164.

15. *Ibid.*, p. 245.
16. Jean-Aubry, *Joseph Conrad: Life and Letters*, I, p. 216.
17. *Loc. cit.*
18. Friedrich Nietzsche, *The Will to Power*, trans, Walter Kaufmann and R.J. Hollingdale (New York: Vintage Books, 1967), p. 550.
19. Jean-Aubry, *Joseph Conrad: Life and Letters*, I, p. 222.
20. *Ibid.*, pp. 222-23.
21. Edward Garnett, ed., *Letters from Joseph Conrad: 1895-1924*, p. 60.
22. *Under Western Eyes* (Garden City, New York: Doubleday, Page, 1925), p.x.
23. Jean-Aubry, *Joseph Conrad: Life and Letters*, I, p. 229.
24. John A. Gee and Paul J. Sturm, trans. and ed., *Letters of Joseph Conrad to Marguerite Poradowska* (New Haven: Yale University Press, 1940), p. 72.
25. Jean-Aubry, *Joseph Conrad: Life and Letters*, I, p. 226.
26. *Notes on Life and Letters*, p. 179.
27. Edward Garnett, ed., *Letters from Joseph Conrad: 1895-1924*, p. 80.
28. *Notes on Life and Letters*, p. 33.
29. *Loc. cit.*
30. Jean-Aubry, *Joseph Conrad: Life and Letters*, II, pp. 83-84.
31. *Notes on Life and Letters*, p. 8.
32. *Ibid.*, pp. 8-9.
33. Jean-Aubry, *Joseph Conrad: Life and Letters*, I, p. 229.
34. *Loc. cit.*
35. *Notes on Life and Letters*, pp. 190-91.
36. *Ibid.*, p. 190.
37. *Ibid.*, p. 194.
38. *Loc. cit.*
39. Jean-Aubry, *Joseph Conrad: Life and Letters*, II, p. 162.
40. *Ibid.*, p. 163.
41. *Ibid.*, I, p. 176.
42. *Ibid.*, p. 323.

The Early Phase: First Statements

Conrad's novels show a remarkable continuity of theme and concern with existential problems. Conrad's view of life seems to have been formed very early in his writing career. *Almayer's Folly*, *An Outcast of the Islands*, *The Nigger of the "Narcissus"* and *Youth* are the first statements of Conrad's existential humanism and reveal preoccupations with the problems that he was to examine in his later works.

Conrad was still a seaman while working for about six years on *Almayer's Folly* until its publication in 1895. *An Outcast of the Islands* was published in the year 1896 which incidentally was the year of Conrad's marriage also. *The Nigger of the "Narcissus"* was originally planned by Conrad to be only a story but during the course of writing, it lengthened to become a novel. It was serialized in *New Review* from August to December 1897 and was published in book form in 1898. *Youth* was originally published in *Blackwood's Magazine* in September 1898 and was later included in the volume *Youth: A Narrative and Two Other Stories* published in 1902. These four works form the early phase of Conrad's writing career.

The works during the early phase represent not only Conrad's literary apprenticeship but are also indicative of concerns which were to remain basic throughout his career. These foreshadow the existential themes with which Conrad was to deal extensively in his later works. Jean-Aubry notes Conrad's awareness, in Kaspar Almayer, of "a vivid example of that discord between the imagination in man and his power to perform, which was to be one dominant theme, at once magnificent and pathetic, of his work as an artist."[1] Almayer and Willems—like Jim, Nostromo, the captain in *The Secret Sharer* and Heyst in later novels—are devoted to ideals beyond themselves. They find no intelligible pattern in the universe or in their own lives and feel that there can be no permanent escape from the condition of existence. Significantly, Conrad himself was faced with this dilemma of existence. In a letter to Edward Garnett written as early as August 1898, Conrad expresses his predicament as a writer: "I am appalled at the absurdity of my situation—at the folly of my hopes, at the blindness that had kept me up in my gropings. Most appalled to feel that all the doors behind me are shut and that I must remain where I have come blundering in the dark."[2]

One of the main themes of Conrad's early fiction and the one that unites all his major work is the theme of the essential isolation and loneliness of the individual. In *Almayer's Folly* and *An Outcast of the Islands*, Conrad touches upon this universal theme which was to occupy him ceaselessly. A sense of solitude and loneliness hovers over Almayer, Nina, Willems and Aissa and at times overwhelms them. An important factor that adds to the sense of isolation in Almayer and Willems is that they are representatives of European civilization in an alien land.

The emphasis Conrad lays upon isolation is evident from the letter that he wrote to Henry S. Canby. Talking about the problem the crewmen face in *The Nigger of the "Narcissus,"* Conrad says that theirs is not a problem of the sea, "it is merely a problem that has arisen on board a ship where the conditions of complete isolation from all land entanglements make it stand out with a particular force and colouring."[3] It is, therefore, not the setting but the isolation which gives significance to Conrad's novels.

It is interesting to note that *The Nigger of the "Narcissus"* is an important precursor of Camus's novel *The Plague*. Conrad in his novel portrays the collective struggle of the crew against the threat of death at sea and in this lies the meaning they have "wrung out" from their "sinful lives." (173)[4] The people of the plague-ridden Oran in Camus's novel confront death in the form of epidemic and find a new meaning in their lives through their collective struggle against the common enemy.

Youth anticipates the dark vision of *Heart of Darkness*. Immersed in a meaningless world and driven to the point of exhaustion by irrational needs to keep moving, Marlow in *Youth* finds meaning in life when he defines himself in his action and gains authenticity. The works of the early phase thus are the first statements of Conrad's existential themes which he was to deal more fully in his subsequent novels.

II

Almayer's Folly, Conrad's first novel, contains in embryonic form many ideas which existentialists focus upon and which are developed and reiterated in almost all Conrad's fiction. It is a record of the dreary existence of a solitary Dutchman named Kaspar Almayer. Displaced from his origins, he represents European culture in an altogether different society. Away from his native place, he struggles hard to retain a sense of moral firmness and certainty in the face of alien, apparently slothful, codes. One of Conrad's favourite themes, the consciousness of "the opportunity missed," finds its first expression in this novel. Almayer is devoted to an ideal beyond himself. This is a trait which he shares with other protagonists of Conrad. He is imprisoned in the fundamental isolation of his being and tries desperately to give his life meaning. He sees the failure of the projected life which his imagination had dreamed of. *Almayer's Folly* tells a sad tale but it is not depressing.

The subject of *Almayer's Folly* is man and his place in the universe. In the "Author's Note" to the novel, Conrad makes his intention obvious. His concern, he writes, is with humanity at large, with the feelings and emotions of human beings whether they live in Europe or Malaya: "And there is a bond between us and that humanity so far away. . . . I am content to sympathize with common mortals, no matter where they live; in houses or in tents, in the streets under a fog, or in the forests behind the dark line of dismal mangroves that fringe the vast solitude of the sea."[5]

The novel provides an intense description of racial discrimination in society and its effects upon an especially strong bond between a white father and his half-caste daughter. Almayer is an emissary of European civilization—a white man with a Westernized outlook and dominated by the ideologies of the West. The world he builds for himself in Malaya is a microcosm of the world from which he has come. In spite of the ties of family and friends, in spite of man's religious and social ideals that all men are equal and should love each other, racial conflicts continue to flare up in this absurd, meaningless world. A sense of unresolved tension, the confrontation of one culture with another, governs the novel.

The character of Almayer, like that of an existentialist hero, is not static but tentative and groping. In his response to other characters, he perceives himself and defines his identity. In the beginning, we find him to be a singularly unheroic protagonist who has allowed Lingard, a wealthy old trader, to make important decisions for him. His only reason for being in Sambir is that Lingard has put him there. In existential terms, he lives in an unauthentic way and commits the initial mistake of letting others direct the course of his life. He is essentially a selfish man who has gone in for a loveless marriage with a Malay girl, the adopted daughter of Lingard, in the hope of a share in the trader's wealth and a position in his firm.

When the offer for marriage is made by Lingard, Almayer envisions only the possible wealth that might be his as the result of this alliance. He dreams of "great piles of shining guilders, and . . . an opulent existence." (10) He is a man whose life is couched in illusion. He is not bothered about the girl he is going to marry and fondly wishes that "she may mercifully die. . . . He had a vague idea of shutting her up somewhere, anywhere, out of his gorgeous future." (10) The dream of immense wealth to be gained through trade with the natives has lured him to the decaying jungles of Sambir. And all his later woes spring from this initial mistake.

As the novel opens, Almayer is shown musing on his glorious future in Europe, rich with the gold for which he has despatched Dain Maroola, a native Malay chief. His dream of wealth is worked into the scene when we are told that he likes to look at the river at the time of sunset "perhaps because at that time the sinking sun would spread a glowing gold tinge on the waters of the Pantai." (3) His thoughts turn to "gold; gold he had failed to secure; gold the others had secured." (3) The river is pivotal to the novel and controls Almayer's internal and external qualities—his aims, ambitions, downfall and death.

Almayer feels imprisoned in Sambir and wants to get away from it. He peers wistfully at the river as it swirls turgidly past, and identifies himself with the tree being carried by the stream. He envies the happy lot of the tree when its course becomes "free down to the sea." (4) He would also like to be as free as the tree but, in total contrast, is confined to the Malay jungle with the sea totally inaccessible to him. Much later in the novel, he expresses his desire for freedom—his wish to get away from the shackles of Malay jungle:

> I have been trying to get out of this infernal place for twenty years, and I can't. You hear, man! I can't and never shall! Never! (142)

Almayer is a typical Conradian protagonist who exists far from his original home. An insignificant man separated from his own kind and his surroundings, he is left to cope with the debilitating climate and native intrigues. Though surrounded by half-savage Arabs and Malays, he is an isolated man. He is an individual, placed in opposition to the tribe. The jungle becomes a symbol of the isolation which strips man of all his refinements and leaves him entirely to his own resources and inner strength.

Ill-at-ease and lonely in the river settlement of Sambir, Almayer has almost no insight into his own character or life and correspondingly less into that of the Malays and Arabs who share the river banks. When the novel opens, he is already a defeated man, though he refuses to accept his defeat. Dreaming of recovering Lingard's buried treasure, he fails to face the reality of his sordid existence and plans to forget twenty-five years of heart-breaking struggle on the coast. Buoyed up by the hope of returning some day to his far-off home in Holland with wealth sufficient to secure his ease and comfort, Almayer goes through all the bitter experience of a life-long exile among an inferior race.

Not only Almayer, but his daughter Nina also is isolated. The presence of the jungle is so overwhelming that the people in contrast seem mere pawns in the grasp of uncontrollable forces. The vast jungle drives home the severe isolation of Nina. Before meeting Dain, she is dreamy, silent, calm and impassive. She seldom speaks to the natives of Sambir and moves among them "calm and white-robed, a being from another world and incomprehensible to them." (38)

There exists a mutual and deep-rooted distrust among the Malays and the Europeans. Almayer fails to understand the nature of Mrs. Almayer and Nina. He does not understand what his women see in Dain and belittles the man by regarding him a petty trader: "I believe all you women are crazy. . . . The man wants to collect trepang and birds' nests on the islands. He told me so, that Rajah of yours." (57) Dain's tale of trepang-hunting deceives no one in Sambir except Almayer. The others wait for the revelation of his real purposes, and eventually their persistence is rewarded.

Because of his inherent blindness to native differences, Almayer fails to perceive the danger Dain's presence represents for him. In remaining unaware of what Dain really is, he projects his own needs upon Dain. He depends on the active Dain for the fulfilment of his plan of obtaining gold in order to get away from the coast. But despite his reliance upon Dain, Almayer fails to distinguish Dain's humanity or identity.

Almayer confronts his daughter when his plans to obtain gold have gone awry. Mistaking a mangled corpse for the body of Dain, he feels highly dejected. Staring at the body of the dead Malay at the edge of the river, he has a horrified realization of failure. Identifying himself with the dead Malay, he feels inclined to weep "over the fate of a white man he knew; a man that fell over a deep precipice and did not die." (99) He upbraids Nina for not grieving for Dain. Her calm posture evokes an outburst of violent indignation: "You have no heart, and you have no mind, or you would have understood that it was for you, for your happiness I was working. I wanted to be rich; I wanted to get away from here. I wanted to see white men bowing low before the power of your beauty and your wealth." (101) He had planned so much for her. Now that Dain is dead, all is lost. He feels relieved to think that he has "laid clear before his daughter the inner meaning of his life." (102)

Aware of the secret of Dain's hidden existence after his presumed death in the river, Nina says nothing to comfort her father. She refuses to give Almayer the pity and sympathy he asks of her because she fears betraying Dain's life. Since Almayer cannot understand her fears, Nina's silence exasperates him: "Are you content to live in this misery and die in this wretched hole? Say something, Nina; have you no sympathy? Have you no word of comfort for me? I that loved you so." (102) However, his heart is filled with a great tenderness and love for his daughter: "The sense of his absolute loneliness came home to his heart with a force that made him shudder." (102)

Unaware of his daughter's love for Dain, and of her part in the substitution of the boatman's body with Dain's, Almayer comprehends the death of Dain through visions of his own annihilation. Viewing the body later, Almayer bursts out: "First one hope, then another, and this is my last. Nothing is left now." (144)

It is ironical that the search for gold with which Almayer hopes to provide Nina with a new life is instrumental in driving his half-caste daughter forever from European civilization. Almayer lives in the hope of finding gold up the Pantai river with the help of Dain, his ally in the gold scheme. But Dain involves himself and Almayer in an abortive revolution which ruins the trading post. All Almayer's dreams about a luxurious future are shattered. Nina, the only person besides himself for whom he really cares, feels contempt for her father as also for all Europeans. She revolts against the restraints of civilization and relapses to a barbaric life.

Ambivalence towards white culture is expressed through Nina. She represents in her person the complicated fusion of white and Malay cultures. She is torn between a sincere affection for her father and a fascination for the savage ravings of her mother. Her dual nature is the result of the unhappy mating of the civilized and the primitive which characterizes her parents's marriage. The European father and the native mother are the forces of two opposite cultures which try to pull her to their side. This tension between the European and the Malayan continues throughout the novel.

Almayer hopes to give Nina wealth and prestige in Europe, as well as a European marriage. It is rumoured that Lingard has a mountain of gold and a treasure of diamonds. Almayer thinks of himself as the legitimate heir to Lingard's wealth, and dreams of the day when he and his half-caste daughter can leave Sambir and live in Europe, where they "would be rich and respected " where "nobody would think of her mixed blood in the presence of her great beauty and of his immense wealth." (3) In his desire for gold, Almayer thinks of establishing his daughter as a white woman, buying respectability for her with the wealth he dreams about. Devotion to Nina and regard for money are indeed the ruling passions of his life. Nina's mother on the other hand wants to prevent Nina's marriage to a white man. She encourages her to choose Dain and the jungle he represents rather than a white man and Europe.

Nina is almost as savage as her mother. Her life, like her mother's, is sharply divided between Malayan and European surroundings. Mrs. Almayer had suffered silently when she was kidnapped from a pirate ship full of dead and dying Malays and placed in the Christian atmosphere: "She bore it all—the restraint and the teaching and the new faith—with calm submission, concealing her hate and contempt for all that new life." (22) She has spent four years in a convent, but the native savagery is inherent in her.

Like her mother, Nina is uprooted from the native surroundings by Lingard who takes her to Mrs. Vinck in Singapore to get educated. He puts her into overly refined Christian surroundings but the Vinck episode makes it clear to Nina how the whites think of the half-castes. Her upbringing among Europeans comes to an abrupt end, "in a scene of humiliation, in an outburst of contempt from white people for her mixed blood." (42) Later she recalls her stay in Singapore as "her days of restraint, of sorrow, and of anger." (72)

In a sense, Nina relives her mother's experience. In the long and garbled recitals of her mother, she recognizes her own pain and humiliation, and also the glory of Malayan pride and savagery. Only she reverses the order of experiences which her mother had. She makes the conscious choice which her mother did not have the opportunity to make.

Nina faces a difficult situation and eventually makes the choice her mother advocates. Her choice constitutes another victory for the jungle. She prefers to live in Sambir with her Malay kinsmen because she knows the hypocrisy, pretences, and prejudices of the white society in which she was educated. Love for Dain awakens her from passivity to intense aliveness. Trying to account for her love for Dain, Nina tells Almayer: "When he came, all doubt disappeared, and I saw only the light of the blue and cloudless heaven." (191) To Nina, Dain means life, fulfilment and freedom: "With the coming of Dain she found the road to freedom." (152) As John Hicks suggests, Nina recognizes in Dain "a means by which to realize her own individuality . . . to give her impoverished life significance."[6]

For both Dain and Nina, it is a case of love at first sight. Nina's first impression of Dain is of "an erect lithe figure of medium height with a breadth of shoulder suggesting great power." (55) And as for Dain, he falls in love at first sight when Nina bursts in upon the trading discussion he is having with her father. Dain is "dazzled by the unexpected vision, forgot . . . all things else, in his overpowering desire to prolong the contemplation of so much loveliness met so suddenly in such an unlikely place." (55)

Love gives Dain and Nina a new awareness of life. They find fulfilment in their intense and all-absorbing love which detaches them from the outside world. The love and union of Dain and Nina flowers on the Pantai river. As they go in a small boat on the river, they forget the existence of the great forests surrounding them: "To those two nothing existed then outside the gunwales of the narrow and fragile craft." (69) The external world is totally excluded from their private world.

Dain's involvement with Nina has its positive as well as negative aspects. Dain realizes the debilitating effects of his love for Nina: "He had not the courage to stir a limb. He had lost faith in himself, and there was nothing else in him of what makes a man." (168) Love also causes many anxious moments to the lovers. In his long wait for Nina while preparing his escape, Dain experiences the anguish of time passing: "He could not sleep, but he felt a great numbness in all his limbs. His restlessness was gone, and he was content to lie still, measuring the time by watching the stars." (169)

Nina's choice is between two kinds of society, between a world characterized by isolation and a world in which people are able to establish a real communion. These are represented by the civilized Almayer and the Malay Dain who are dramatized as cultural opposites. Both vye for the love of Nina—their struggle for her affection forming the axis through which the ideological conflicts of the novel are developed. Dain, the active searching man, is much distinct from the decaying and hesitant Almayer. In fact, he is very nearly the opposite of Almayer. His world is one of action and he is able to participate more fully in life as his love for Nina attests. He offers to Nina an alternative to her isolated existence with Almayer and she gladly opts for it.

Almayer has invested his entire life in Nina but she does not understand his ambitions and his feelings. She breaks Almayer's heart and feels no remorse at leaving. For Almayer, Nina's going away is the end of all his hopes. Abandoned by Nina, he experiences a chaotic disorder of his thoughts and an acute sense of physical pain. His face mirrors his futile existence; it becomes "a blank, without a sign of emotion, feeling reason . . . like the blank wall of a prison enclosing sin, regrets, and pain, and wasted life." (190)

The final torture when Nina begs him not to forget her, is too much for Almayer. Just after she sails, he falls on his knees and vigorously wipes out her footsteps from the sand. He tries to erase from his mind every memory of the daughter he has loved so much. But he is not able to forget her till the end. Conrad sums up the absurdity of Almayer's attitude both as a father and as a man: "Only one idea remained clear and definite—not to forgive her; only one vivid desire—to forget her. . . . That was his idea of his duty to himself—to his race—to his respectable connections; to the whole universe unsettled and shaken by this frightful catastrophe of his life." (192)

Almayer has a choice of action as Nina plans to go away from him. For a moment, he thinks of following Nina to her new existence: "Great things could be done! What if he should suddenly take her to his heart, forget his shame, and pain, and anger, and—follow her!" (192) But soon his hesitation disappears and he reasserts himself as a white man: "I will never forgive you, Nina!" (192) Probably he loves his dream more than his daughter.

The concluding section of the novel reveals the rapid deterioration of Almayer. Forsaken by all, he is destroyed by the weight of his failure and remorse. Somehow, he has become entangled in a web of circumstances from which he cannot free himself. Consumed by his own wishes and influenced by the bigotry of European society, he rejects the union of Nina and Dain by withdrawing to his deserted decaying house named "Almayer's Folly," which symbolizes the failure of his materialistic hopes. He falls further into personal and social isolation; his life becomes monotonous and sordid. Henceforth, it is a death-in-life existence for him.

Captain Ford, a monthly visitor to Sambir, expresses the continuing despair of Almayer. He tells us that Almayer, once a boisterous speaker, has become the silent type "as if he was forgetting how to speak." (203) On learning that Nina has got a son, he begins to smoke opium and dies in the house that was once a symbol of his ambitions. One day, the natives find him "dead, and his soul delivered from the trammels of his earthly folly." (208) Death bestows upon him "that serene look which follows the sudden relief from anguish and pain." (208) The novel ends with Abdullah whispering the name of "Allah! The Merciful! The compassionate!" (208)

The existentialists believe that the key to identity lies not in self-assertion but in an act of sacrifice. By returning to the primitive source of life, Almayer tries to discover a more authentic world but fails. The success of the natives shows the folly of the ego-centred existence of Almayer whose life has revealed that existence without love and compassion is not worthwhile. Nina's life and the birth of her son, on the other hand, show that Nina has attained personal and social fulfilment.[7]

III

An Outcast of the Islands again has the Malayan setting. Some of the characters are also used again, though the events take place before those in *Almayer's Folly*. Thus the second novel goes back to the past lives of the characters of the first novel. It repeats the themes of betrayal, the dangers of imagining a splendid future, the tensions between black and white, and the perils of isolation. However, it marks an advance over the earlier novel in that it presents a much more complex central character in a convincing manner. Peter Willems, the protagonist of the novel, reminds us of Kaspar Almayer, especially in his relation to Lingard. His character also looks forward to the complex character of Lord Jim. And the love-affair between Willems, a white man, and Aissa, a native Sambir girl, becomes central to the import of the tale.

The epigraph of *An Outcast of the Islands* strikes an existentialist note and applies to the whole novel. Taken from Calderon's La Vida Es Sueno, it may be translated as "Man's greatest crime is having been born." The fundamental belief of the existentialist philosophy is that man runs a hopeless course from birth to death. The journey of Willems's life too is an existential one. He is a man in process. The novel proceeds with Willems at the peak of his power to his decline into futility, frustration, and finally death.

The existentialists believe that man is always *becoming*, never *is*. The events in life take a sudden turn to reveal how incomplete the man is when confronted by a crisis. The event which precipitates a crisis of character in Willems's life is a violation of a code of conduct: he embezzles his employer Hudig's money. The novel opens with a description of Willems, having strayed from the path of rectitude, making "an inward assertion of unflinching resolve to fall back again into the monotonous but safe stride of virtue as soon as his little excursion into the wayside quagmires had produced the desired effect." (3)[8] His theft is without any moral justification but he is "unable to conceive that the moral significance of any act of his could interfere with the very nature of things." (3) Engrossed in "weaving the splendid web of his future," (11) he feels no remorse for his crime. He defines his guilt as a mere "idiotic indiscretion" (22) and remains unaware that the outward form of his life was a facade hiding deeper forces that would rise up to destroy him.

Willems, like Jim later, suffers his fall from a position of trust and responsibility. The opening section presents the civilized ethos of Willems; it shows him at the peak of his influence and power. The De Souza family's admiration makes him have a feeling of unquestionable superiority: "He loved to breathe the coarse incense they offered before the shrine of the successful white man; the man that had done them the honour to marry their daughter, sister, cousin; the rising man sure to climb very high." (4) Willems is an excessively proud man and enjoys belittling his wife and relatives; their financial dependence gives him a sense of power and authority. He thinks of himself as "their providence; he kept them singing his praises. . . . It is a fine thing to be a providence, and to be told so on every day of one's life." (4) This early portrait of Willems reveals his power and munificence and is, what Sartre terms, "subjectivism"[9] of existential humanism.

The discovery of the theft leads to the rapid fall of Willems. He realizes that his life has changed totally. Standing in front of his pretty little house where he had always reigned with thoughtless security, he suddenly experiences a tremendous dislocation of self: "Willems the successful, the smart; . . . And what was Willems now? Willems the . . . He strangled the half-born thought and cleared his throat to stifle a groan." (24) From the beginning he had equated power with existence. So the withdrawal of power leaves him shaken. His wife accuses him of being arrogant and scolds him for the disgrace he brings them: "Oh! you great man! . . . And you think that I am going to starve with you." (27) The shocking revelation that only the trappings mattered to his wife and her innumerable relatives sends Willems back to his point of origin—back to the edge of the water where Lingard had first found him.

In existentialist terms, Willems's refusal to accept personal responsibility for his actions is an act of bad faith. Hudig holds him responsible for embezzling money, but Willems deceives himself into thinking that he is merely borrowing money from his employer. Again, recalling the last few hours of his life, he begins to see himself as another man and shirks responsibility: "He had assaulted brutally his brother-in-law, . . . He did. Well, no! It was some other man." (30) In this way he detaches himself from his unseemly behaviour which he is not willing to accept. This is the real beginning of the story when Willems faces the condition of powerlessness.

Willems is the paradigm of the Conradian protagonist, a man poised to jump, suspended between one life and another, free to choose, having made a wrong choice a moment ago: "For the first time in his life he felt afraid of the future, because he had lost his faith, the faith in his own success. And he had destroyed it foolishly with his own hands!" (31) He faces social disgrace and punishment and realizes that he must "leave this house, leave this island, go far away where he was unknown." (26) He abandons his wife and child, what he calls "those encumbrances of his life." (25)

Once again Lingard takes Willems under his protection and provides him with an opportunity to rehabilitate himself in Sambir, an up-river settlement where he enjoys a flourishing monopoly. The conflict of feelings and attitudes which Willems experiences involves an attempt to resolve suffering and inner tension. Through suffering he knows that he exists, reflects upon himself and life, and tries to know the conditions of his existence. He suffers shame and humiliation as an outcast but pride, arrogance, and anger prevail upon him. He tries to find comfort through passion—his love for Aissa, the daughter of a blind Arab chieftain Omar, dominates the action henceforth.

In his new life at Sambir, Willems experiences loneliness and isolation. He finds himself separated from his natural surroundings and from his kind in space, and feels "a sense of bitter loneliness . . . as if he was the outcast of all mankind." (30) His moral and geographic isolation leads to the dissolution of his consciousness under the insidious influence of Aissa. He feels that he alone was "left outside the scheme of creation in a hopeless immobility" and this feeling fills him "with tormenting anger and with ever-stinging regret." (65)

Willems's loneliness, like that of Almayer, is self-imposed. He is an egotist who is alone chiefly because he has thoughts for no one else but himself. He fails to establish a rapport with Almayer, another white man living in Sambir. The two hate each other and scarcely permit conversation without perpetual overtones and intimations of sibling rivalry. In their exchanges they snarl at each other: "Those two specimens of the superior race glanced at each other savagely for a minute, then turned away their heads at the same moment as if by previous arrangement, and both got up." (63) Willems is jealous and mistrustful of Almayer and a sense of hostility exists betwen the two: "From cold civility in their relations, the two men drifted into silent hostility, then into outspoken enmity." (64)

Willems lives in physical isolation and even love proves ineffective in dispelling his solitude. From the first moment, the timeless world of Willems and Aissa is simply an illusion covering their real isolation from each other. When Aissa appears in her native dress, Willems sees her as no more than "an animated package of cheap cotton goods." (128) He feels that the veil seals off real contact between them, leaving him doomed as a human being, cut off from civilization and civilized feeling. Such a feeling leads him to reflect that "they had nothing in common—not a thought, not a feeling; he could not make clear to her the simplest motive of any act of his." (128)

Soon after falling in love with Aissa, Willems becomes conscious of their underlying isolation from each other. And this realization makes him feel miserable. He feels indignant as Aissa refuses to give up veiling herself. To feel and to suffer without knowing why one must suffer is perhaps the most exasperating and seemingly irrational aspect of life. Precisely because man suffers, he finds himself absurd: "He (Willems) was not, of course, able to discern clearly the causes of his misery; but there are none so ignorant as not to know suffering, none so simple as not to feel and suffer from the shock of warring impulses. The ignorant must feel and suffer from their complexity as well as the wisest; but to them the pain of struggle and defeat appears strange, mysterious, remediable and unjust." (129)

The savage beauty of Aissa enraptures Willems and blinds him to the demands of civilization. Aissa evokes the latent savagery in his nature and performs a function similar to Nina's by representing for Willems, as Nina did for Dain, the paradox of life involvement: the need for submission to it, and the degradation it entails. Soon after falling in love, Willems experiences "the fear of something unknown that had taken possession of his heart, of something inarticulate and masterful which could not speak and would be obeyed." (72) The glimpse of Aissa awakens unknown and hitherto dormant feelings in him. Through his growing attachment to Aissa, he experiences a revolution of perspective that brings to fore the transient, the momentary, the instantaneous. He seems to lose all conscious control and feels as if "his very individuality was snatched from within himself by the hand of a woman." (77) He surrenders his will to the unknown, to the unidentifiable forces, working within and without, which sap life and reduce resistance.

When the network of associations that binds Willems to the civlized world is dissolved, unconscious forces usurp rationality. The savage overcomes the civilized. A concomitant effect is the loss of civilized value systems. His growing relationship with Aissa results in the loss of all identity for Willems. The passionate sensuality of his love accelerates his downfall. After he has yielded to her, Willems sits up suddenly "with the movement and look of a man awakened by the crash of his own falling house." (77) Later, he listens to "the voice of his fate . . . a sound inarticulate but full of meaning." (80) His relation with her terrifies him. When she looks into his eyes, it seems to him that she is drawing his very soul from within him. And her look of surrender leads to the complete subjugation of his will. When she clasps him passionately, he recoils "in repulsion, in horror." (285)

Isolation surrounds Willems on Lingard's departure and he experiences the enforced severance from a community, "the cruel solitude of one abandoned by men." (327) A sense of solitude and loneliness overtakes all the three—Willems, Aissa and the serving-woman—as they sit by the side of the river:

> Those three human beings abandoned by all were like shipwrecked people left on an insecure and slippery ledge by the retiring tide of an angry sea—listening to its distant roar, living anguished between the menace of its return and the hopeless horror of their solitude—in the midst of a tempest of passion, of regret, of disgust, of despair. (328)

In fact, Willems and Aissa suffer an ultimate isolation from each other: "Those two, surrounded each by the impenetrable wall of their aspirations, were hopelessly alone, out of sight, out of earshot of each other; each the centre of dissimilar and distant horizons; standing each on a different earth, under a different sky." (333-34) They are imprisoned in their isolated worlds and cannot reach each other through love.

As she looks longingly at her lover, Aissa has the expression of unfulfilment in her eyes, "the wonder and desolation of an animal that knows only suffering, of the incomplete soul that knows pain but knows no hope." (334) And Willems, in extreme need of consolation, feels "afraid of his solitude, of the solitude of his body, of the loneliness of his soul." (337) His driving need to be someone, to create an identity haunts Willems. In his relationship with Aissa he discovers that he is "robbed of his passion, of his liberty, of forgetfulness, of consolation." (339) He realizes the need for identity and its loss: "he murmured with conviction—speaking half-aloud to himself in the shock of the penetrating thought: 'I am a lost man.'" (340)

In a letter to Edward Garnett, Conrad explains the situation Willems and Aissa are in: "Nothing lasts! So with Aissa. Her passion is burnt out too. There is in her that desire to be something for him—to be in his mind, in his heart."[10] Like existentialists, Conrad emphasizes the fact that in life, each person is confined to the solitariness of his self. Aissa has a single-minded desire to make Willems wholly intelligible to her but she fails. After the failure of her appeal to Lingard, she realizes "the tremendous fact of our isolation, of the loneliness impenetrable and transparent, elusive and everlasting; of the indestructible loneliness that surrounds, envelopes, clothes every human soul from the cradle to the grave, and, perhaps, beyond." (250) No one in this world is immune to this feeling of isolation.

Isolated from the trading and financial white world in which he had formed himself, Willems often responds to Aissa by becoming almost literally paralysed, suspended in a trancelike state and incapable of waking himself to real activity. With his limited understanding of the complexity of self, he turns his back on the real world. As he lays dreamily with his head in Aissa's lap, Willems is

> perfectly happy but for the annoyance of an indistinct vision of a well-known figure; a man going away from him and diminishing in a long perspective of fantastic trees . . . but never getting out of sight for all his steady progress. He felt a desire to see him vanish. There was something familiar about that figure. Why! Himself! (145)

Willems desperately tries to cling to his identity as a white man but his falling rapidly into a trancelike state denotes his powerlessness before Aissa's savagery. In fact, he lives in terror of the native influence upon his nature and his vision of loss of self takes the image of a fall into the abyss:

> Now and then he would grasp the edge of the table and set his teeth hard in a sudden wave of acute despair, like one who, falling down

> a smooth and rapid declivity that ends in a precipice, digs his finger nails into the yielding surface and feels himself slipping helplessly to inevitable destruction. (78)

In existential terms, the imagery of walking away from a sleeping self or falling over an abyss may be interpreted as a subconscious prompting to resolve his life and return to his family. All this seems absurd to Willems who is quite aware of "the absurdity of his own emotions." (145)

In the course of the novel, Conrad makes a number of comments describing man's moments of bitterness or frustration with life and the human condition. Willems experiences a horrible fear "which destroys hope and despair alike." (148) He suffers both physically and mentally. He bites himself to forget the pain in his heart and strikes himself so hard with his fist that he reels under his own blow. (91) The horror of absolute isolation and inevitable death puts him in a state of non-existence. It is a "horror of bewildered life where he could understand nothing and nobody round him; where he could guide, control, comprehend nothing and no one—not even himself." (149)

In her moments of anxiety, Aissa asks Lingard if he knows "the fear without voice—the fear of silence—the fear that comes when there is no one near—when there is no battle, no cries, no angry faces or armed hands anywhere? . . . The fear from which there is no escape!" (252, ellipses Conrad's) Herself, she heaves a sigh which is "full of pain and fear, like the sigh of those who are about to face the unknown: to face it in loneliness, in doubt, and without hope." (286)

As a consequence of a choice of action or inaction, Willems confronts the conditions of his existence. He betrays the trust that Lingard had put in him and the proclaimed ideals of his race. Enthralled by Aissa, Willems gets crazy when the local politicians separate him from his beloved for a few days. Their plan is to use Willems to undermine the power of Lingard. And they succeed when Willems pilots Abdulla's brig up the river through the secret entrance which Lingard had revealed to him. Willems soon discovers that he will profit nothing by his crime. The Malay chiefs have no further use of him and refuse to accept him into their society. This turns Willems's passion for Aissa into loathing.

Significantly, Willems founders when isolated from the sustaining hand of Lingard. The latter is inexplicably detained far from his river settlement and in desperation Willems guides Abdulla into the river. He thus opens the gates of Sambir to Lingard's trade rivals and enemies—the Arabs. When Lingard returns, he realizes that he has lost his navigational secret and commercial monopoly. The secret channel is the key to the country which Almayer had hoped to exploit. But once the Arabs have come, the white men have no further prospect of riches; what is valuable will be taken away by the intruders. Lingard holds Willems accountable for the betrayal and this leads to the shattering of the personality of Willems, a determined and self-confident man. Consequent to his cold-blooded treachery, the forces of disorder enter Lingard's world and destroy his rule. The office of Lingard remains neglected and deteriorates gradually. Finally, there is a "hopeless disorder—the senseless and vain decay of all these emblems of civlized commerce." (301)

Betraying the confidence of Lingard is an example of ultimate degradation. But once again, Willems fails to understand the implications of his mistakes and misdeeds. As he had done earlier when he betrayed Hudig, Willems envisions himself as having strayed from the path of honour to which he would return very soon. He has a faint consciousness of having gone wrong somewhere but fails to pursue the thought to its logical conclusion.

In his last meeting with Lingard, Willems perceives his kinship with the white man. He attempts to free himself of Aissa and to resume his relation to Lingard who represents the white race and whose society he desperately craves. Willems tells Lingard that he could have easily hurt and destroyed him—he could have shot him. But Lingard reacts with assurance: "You would have missed, . . . There is, under heaven, such a thing as justice." (265)

In an attempt to execute justice upon Willems, Lingard administers unsatisfactory beating to him. But this beating is nothing more than an expression of human frustration, blind anger, and wounded pride: "the anger of his outraged pride, the anger of his outraged heart, had gone out in the blow; and there remained nothing but the sense of some immense infamy. . . . Was there, under heaven, such a thing as justice?" (265) His query is charged with the disillusionment of an atheistic existentialist who is disgusted with the life he is leading.

In the beginning, Lingard is bitterly scornful of Willems. Gradually he is won to the sense of his own responsibility in Willems's plight. He brings Willems's wife and son to Sambir, for he thinks he has created problems for Willems by bringing him there. He makes a pertinent comment on the situation: "life is foul." (191) He also reflects upon the "cold unconcern the high dignity of lifeless matter that surrounds, incurious and unmoved, the restless mysteries of the ever-changing, of the never-ending life." (242)

The novel shows Conrad's insistence upon the destructive and devouring nature of a woman's love. Willems wants to be saved from Aissa whose possessiveness has become oppressive for him. Overcome with remorse, he pleads to Lingard for forgiveness, begging to be taken away so that he can make yet another start somewhere else. In his complete frustration, he tries hopelessly to summon some human dignity: "I will live. I shall repent. I may escape. . . . Take that woman away—she is sin." (278, ellipses Conrad's) Lingard however is furious in righteous indignation and remains adamant. Earlier when Aissa had attempted to plead for the life of Willems, Lingard had commanded her to get out of his path. Now he orders Willems the outcast to stay where he is—in Lakamba's deserted settlement. He condemns Willems to the solitude and bitterness of his existence with the woman he loved so passionately, and whom he detests now, to perpetual exile in the jungle outskirts of the community.

Willems is caught in a trap of frustration and exhaustion. He is conscious of the destructive death lying at the centre of life: "he saw death looking at him from everywhere; from the bushes; from the clouds—he heard her speaking to him in the murmur of the river, filling the space, touching his heart, his brain with a cold hand. He could see and think of nothing else. He saw it—the sure death—everywhere." (330-31) The vision of death unsettles Willems. He sees the world full of life—the mad turmoil of tropical life going around him noiselessly. But for himself, he visualizes the time when "he would lie stiff, passive, rotting slowly; while . . . the endless and minute throngs of insects . . . would swarm countless, persistent, ferocious and greedy—till there would remain nothing but the white gleam of belching bones in the long grass." (332) He realizes that his disappearance will change nothing in the world and that soon he will be completely forgotton: "nobody would miss him; no one would remember him." (332) His feelings here are like that of an existentialist hero—a trapped man, constantly trying to escape.

Standing out strongly in his isolation against the background of tropical forest, Willems has a presentiment of his end. The huge trees tower over him and bring into focus his loneliness. He senses in the forest around him a "merciless and mysterious purpose, perpetuating strife and death through the march of ages." (337) For the second time in his life, he feels the need to send a cry for help in the wilderness,and realizes the hopelessness of its unconcern. Nature is deathless in its omnipotence and man in his struggles becomes frailer and more ephemeral. Willems imagines himself "peering into a sombre hollow, into a deep black hole full of decay and of whitened bones; into an immense and inevitable grave full of corruption where sooner or later he must unavoidably fall." (339) However he refuses to accept personal responsibility for his acts by assuming that his situation in Sambir is the accumulation of one indignity after another "added to an intolerable load of humiliations." (341)

Eventually, however, at the novel's close, the fully-disillusioned Willems regains the husk of his former self. His abandoned wife Joanna reaches his sanctuary with her small child and confronts him at the height of his affair with Aissa. From a distance, she appears to him as an unrecognizable apparition, and he remains seated in stunned silence as she approaches him and asks for forgiveness. Willems finds himself embroiled in still further conflict and seems "to struggle in the toils of complicated dreams where everything was impossible, yet a matter of course, where the past took the aspects of the future and the present lay heavy on his heart—seemed to take him by the throat like the hand of an enemy." (347)

Willems sees the river as a means of escape but it turns out to be the source of frustration, and finally of death. He tries to leave the island in a boat, leaving behind his mistress, his wife and child. But Aissa, instrumental earlier in destroying his mind, now ends his life with a bullet. Seeing him with his wife and child—the family of which she had been unaware—Aissa realizes that he has deceived her. She resents Willems's commitment to the white woman. To her, Willems's deception and betrayal of trust become the cruel manifestation of the evil and hypocrisy of white society. Conrad considers her feelings as she prepares to aim the gun at Willems: "Hate filled the world, filled the space between them—the hate of race, the hate of hopeless diversity, the hate of blood; the hate against the man born in the land of lies and of evil from which nothing but misfortune comes to those who are not white." (359)

The final comment on the world comes in the drunken, deserted cry of Almayer: "The world's a swindle! A swindle! Why should I suffer? What have I done to be treated so?" (367) Assuming a rebellious attitude towards the scheme of the universe, he questions Providence for having treated him shabbily and for having favoured Willems. The novel ends on a sardonic use of the word "hope" when Almayer says: "Where are you, Willems? Hey? . . . Hey? . . . Where there is no mercy for you—I hope!" (368, ellipses Conrad's)

In order to remain sane and whole, Willems strives desperately to rejoin the white civilization. He seems to hear a loud voice shouting in the heavens that soon "he would step into another existence; that all this, the woman, the madness, the sin, the regrets, all would go, rush into the past, disappear, become as dust, as smoke, as drifting clouds—as nothing." (356) In the rapid vision of his hopeful future, he finds himself to be much above the others: "Nothing mattered. He cared for nothing. He had forgotten Aissa, his wife, Lingard, Hudig—everybody." (356) His eventual return and a genuine horror of what he has become puts Willems on a higher plane and is existentialist in spirit. Like the existentialist hero, he discovers the mystery of human freedom: the more liberty you have, the less you can use. The fact that he wants to and does make an attempt to return to the white world raises Willems above the common run of humanity.

IV

The Nigger of the "Narcissus" concerns itself with the problem of existence. It deals with the conduct of the crewmen and their consequent anguish in the face of death. The sea-voyage represents man's passage through life and tests the manhood of all on board the *Narcissus*, from Captain Allistoun to mutinous Donkin. The presence of James Wait on board the ship poses a serious threat to the crew's strength. Wait has an uncanny ability to evoke the deepest longings and weaknesses of the crew. The absurdity of death stems from the fact that death comes to everybody and it may treacherously come at any time. Its unavoidability and unpredictability create a terror in the minds of men. Death—the most impenetrable mystery—makes the crew indecisive. They do not know whether Wait is really dying or just pretending. To prove their worth, the crewmen have to overcome this dread of death.

In the beginning, Mr. Baker, the chief mate of the ship, asks Knowles to send the men aft for mustering. This is followed by a description of the members of the crew, preparing themselves for the voyage ahead. What emerges as significant in these pages is the figure of Singleton—the experienced, reliable sailor—who is presented as the best example of the professional code of seamen. He is the oldest able seaman in the ship and resembles a learned and savage patriarch, the incarnation of barbarian wisdom serene in the blasphemous toil of the world. Engrossed in reading Bulwer Lytton's *Pelham*, he is not disturbed by all the noise made by the crowd on the *Narcissus*. Throughout the voyage, he remains unperturbed by the dread of death which inflicts the whole crew. He unquestioningly accepts the maritime code and embodies the rational order prevailing on board the ship.

Going into the reason of Singleton's reading *Pelham*, the narrator reflects in the form of a question: "Are those beings who exist beyond the pale of life stirred by his tales as by an enigmatical disclosure of a resplendent world that exists within the frontier of infamy and filth; within that border of dirt and hunger, of misery and dissipation, that comes down on all sides to the water's edge of the incorruptible ocean, and is the only thing they know of life, the only thing they see of surrounding land—those life-long prisoners of the sea?" (6-7) In a letter to Cunninghame Graham, Conrad writes that Singleton possessed "the knowledge of how to live" and was "in perfect accord with his life."[11]

The call to muster brings all hands from the lighted forecastle to the dark deck. This action of the crewmen is quite significant. Till the call, they were listening to Donkin, offering him their old clothes, but when the call for duty comes, none of the crowd notices him. They assemble on the dark deck and Mr. Baker musters them with a white paper in his hand. As he reads out a name, one of the men answers and, detaching himself from the shadowy mob, steps barefooted into the circle of light, and in two noiseless strides passes into the shadows on the port side. The momentary stay in the light points to the brevity of life.

Mr. Baker involuntarily ejaculates "O Lord" when the incredibly dilapidated figure of Donkin appears in the light. With a malevolent grin, Donkin asks: "Is there anythink wrong with me, Mister Mate?" (16) His insolent query brings out praises from the other men on board who slap him on the back and flatter him in whispers.

Mrs. Baker's inability to make out the last name on his list which is "all a smudge" is symbolic. Till the end, the crewmen will not be able to read the true nature of this inscrutable figure. As the group of sailors begins to move forward, a deep, ringing voice breaks the stillness: "Wait!" Mr. Baker, who has turned away yawning, turns back. Furious at the insolent cry, he blurts out: "What's this? Who said 'Wait'? What?" (17) In the light of the lamp, the whites of the newcomer's eyes and his teeth can be seen distinctly but the face is indistinguishable. His black face makes it clear that he is a nigger. Because of his blackness, Wait remains a lonely and isolated figure in an all-white crew. As Conrad remarks in the "Author's Note" to the first American edition: "a Negro in a British forecastle is a lonely being. He has no chums." (ix)

Wait explains to Mr. Baker that his name is Wait—James Wait. To Baker's inquiry as to who he is and why he is there, he remains calm, cool, towering and superb. From his height of six foot three, he announces confidently: "I belong to the ship." (18) Ordered to take his place on the deck, the nigger coughs twice—a cough metallic, hollow and tremendously loud. Throughout the journey, he uses these fits of cough as a weapon against the crew members. He begins to cast his influence upon them from the very beginning: when he asks the people to help him in bringing the luggage, the refusal seems impossible.

The idea of death is introduced even before Wait begins to influence the crew's feelings and thoughts about death. Podmore, the cook, is startled when Wait greets him. Later on, he would often say of this encounter: "The poor fellow had scared me. I thought, I had seen the devil." (19) We are told that the religious-minded cook would daily sleep with his lamp turned full, and an open Bible in his hand. With a benign serenity, he would say: "I am ready for my Maker's call . . . wish you all were," (20) which would make Belfast, the sentimental guy, say: "I don't want you to die. . . . What's the hurry? . . . Think of Us . . . of Us . . . of Us." (20)

As the men settle for the night, Singleton keeps the watch. Alone in the dim emptiness of the sleeping forecastle, he appears bigger, colossal, very old; old as Father Time himself. He is one of those men who know how to exist beyond the pale of life and within sight of eternity.

The *Narcissus* sets sail the next morning and moves on smoothly. Away from the gloom of the land, she moves on lonely and swift like a small planet. Life on board the compact and orderly ship represents a microcosm of human society. Dissociated from the land, the crewmen resume their daily routine. Healthy and contented, they begin their voyage in a world governed by a benevolent providence. The narrator comments: "The true peace of God begins at any spot a thousand miles from the nearest land; and when He sends these the messengers of His might it is not in terrible wrath against crime, presumption, and folly, but paternally, to chasten simple hearts—ignorant hearts that know nothing of life, and beat undisturbed by envy or greed." (31) It is a calm atmosphere where the soft breeze stirs the tumbled hair of the crew "with a touch passing and light like an indulgent caress." (32)

In the evening, the crewmen relax and talk, forgetting their toil. However, their peaceful life is disrupted by Wait's coughing, who appears on the deck and condemns them for being noisy in their leisure near his cabin. He unceasingly flaunts the idea of death before them: "Leave me alone. It won't be for long. I'll soon die. . . . It's coming right enough!" (35) Presented as the incarnate symbol of the dread of death, he exploits to the full the awe and pity that his declaration of death arouses:

> He seemed to take a pride in that death which, so far, had attended only upon the ease of his life; he was overbearing about it, as if no one else in the world had ever been intimate with such a companion; he paraded it unceasingly before us with an affectionate persistence that made its presence indubitable, and at the same time incredible. (36)

With his knowledge of death, Wait exerts a terrifying moral blackmail on the crew. The presence of death, a hostile annihilating force at the centre of existence, brings in the crewmen a sense of their vulnerability to it.

The narrator finds it difficult to analyse the effect Wait exercises over the crew. Wait is a mysterious figure who at first seems unaccountable. The crewmen are not sure whether he is shamming or really dying. They are uncertain as to how best to conceive of Wait. They hesitate between pity and mistrust; Wait's presence on the ship evokes ambiguous emotions in them. Though confused by his behaviour, they proceed to yield to his insidious influence and become his willing victims. They comply with his demands while resenting them. They serve him in his bed with rage and humility, as though they had been "the base courtiers of a hated prince; and he rewarded us by his unconciliating criticism." (37) Wait seizes every chance to remind the crew of the spectre of death and makes himself master of every moment of their existence. The narrator makes implicit the men's adoption of Wait when he refers to him as "our nigger." (34)

Wait's presence demoralizes the small world of the ship and it threatens to founder both physically and morally. Wait appeals to the crew in an underhand and irresistible manner. The crewmen are ready to go to any length for his sake. Belfast steals a pie to appease the nigger and this contaminates the whole atmosphere. Baker no longer heaps jocular abuses upon his favourites and grunts suspiciously at everyone. The *Narcissus* is still a peaceful ship, but the mutual confidence is shaken. Donkin does not conceal his delight at the situation. He refuses to believe that Wait is seriously ill and accuses him of malingering.

None of these tensions seems to affect Singleton who lives untouched by human emotions. As the crewmen vacillate in their attitude to Wait, Singleton seems immune to his capricious tyranny. One day, at dinner, he asks Wait directly if he is dying. The question startles all, including Wait who answers shakily: "Why? Can't you see I am?" (42) Singleton faces this affirmative answer with calm contempt which confounds all: "Well, get on with your dying . . . don't raise a blamed fuss with us over that job. We can't help you." (42)

Later, however, even Singleton proves weak in countering Wait's complex appeal. When the crewmen seek his advice on the issue of Wait's death, he says calmly: "Why, of course he will die." (42) The assurance from the oracle gives relief to everybody: at last, they know that their compassion is not misplaced. But Donkin's statement that death is a common fate destroys the effect of Singleton's assurance. The crewmen perceive that Singleton's answer means nothing. They are totally under Wait's control and, in existential terms, feel unauthentic:

> All our certitudes were going; we were on doubtful terms with our officers: the cook had given us up for lost; we had overheard the boatswain's opinion that "we were a crowd of softies." We suspected Jimmy, one another, and even our very selves. We did not know what to do. At every insignificant turn of our humble life we met Jimmy overbearing and blocking the way, arm-in-arm with his awful and veiled familiar. It was a weird servitude. (43)

Wait uses the pretence of illness to escape his duties aboard the ship. From the very beginning, he does not do his share of work. He shrewdly exploits the unfair advantages of his sickness and soon becomes "the tormentor of all our moments . . . worse than a nightmare." (44) Gullible to his subtle influence, the crew members are confused once again. They can perceive that though Wait coughs often, mostly it is when it suits his purpose. One day he appears hale and hearty on the deck, and next time he has to be carried to his cabin. Eventually, he is removed from the uncomfortable quarters of the forecastle and is installed in a private cabin from where he continues to dominate the lives of the crew: "He fascinated us. He would never let doubt die. He overshadowed the ship. Invulnerable in his promise of speedy corruption he trampled on our self-respect; he demonstrated to us daily our want of moral courage; he tainted our lives." (46-47) Wait holds not only the crew but also the reader in suspense because he remains uncertain whether the illness from which Wait appears to be suffering throughout the ship's stormy passage is genuine or sham.

There is a kind of unpredictable malice in Nature. The crew of the *Narcissus* is tested by the direct assault of the sea. As the ship approaches the Cape of Good Hope, she is struck by a gale. The crewmen valiantly serve the storm-tossed ship, which bears the "anguished remnant of sinful mankind, through the distress, tumult and pain of an avenging terror." (54) Captain Allistoun remains constantly on deck and none of the men sleeps that night. Nature reminds man of his personal problems and the enigmas of existence. The restlessness of human beings is suggested by the stormy sea. Man becomes aware of his insignificance when he looks at the vastness of the sky. In *The Mirror of the Sea*, Conrad reflects: "It is the malicious pleasure of the East Wind to augment the power of your eyesight, in order, perhaps, that you should see better the perfect humiliation, the hopeless character of your captivity." (97)

The threat of death at this moment comes from a nature that is presented as blind. Seeing a large roller topple the ship onto her side, Singleton shouts a warning. The masts are inclining nearly to the horizon and the crewmen call for them to be cut to prevent the vessel from turning over altogether. They consider the cutting of masts to be their only chance to save themselves. But the captain refuses to permit such a move and the men comply obediently. They resign themselves to the captain's order; not even a murmur of remonstrance comes out from them. Holding on where they can, the men wait in cold and misery. The high seas wash away their belongings. For about sixty hours, the seamen cling to the vertically sloping deck.

The instinctive devotion to duty saves the crew from complete disintegration. The storm threatens their life and makes existence frightening. It does its worst to the men but they remain almost unshakable. They work together to save themselves and the ship. They uphold the honour of the service—sink or swim—and maintain its composure.

In his alertness and control, Captain Allistoun exemplifies the concept of self-discovery through work. The long, sleepless vigil that he keeps during the storm shows his exceptional powers of endurance. His behaviour during the storm is unimpeachable.[12] At the end of the storm, he feels neither dismayed nor discouraged. The captain and the crew defeat the weather that assailed them; they subdue the alien and hostile nature.

The storm, with its immense demands upon the bodies and spirits of the crew, makes them forget Wait. The nigger vanishes from their minds. They concentrate on saving the ship but suddenly someone cries, "Where's Jimmy?" and the reminder terrifies all. Wait's shelter is nearly submerged and the door itself under water. At great risk to themselves and with immense efforts, a group of five men rescues Wait trapped in his little cabin. To reach him, his shipmates have to cross through the carpenter's shop. When they bring him back, the crewmen have a strange feeling: "on the very brink of eternity we tottered all together with concealing and absurd gestures, like a lot of drunken men embarrassed with a stolen corpse." (71) Completely exhausted, they lie upon the deck. In rescuing Wait, they have assisted in the rebirth of the influence forgotten during the storm .

Wait's response to the crew's brave action is typically arrogant. He reproaches the sailors for not coming sooner. The crew members suspect that Wait "was shamming sick, had been malingering heartlessly in the face of our toil, of our scorn, of our patience—and now was malingering in the face of our devotion—in the face of death." (72-73) They are anguished at the influence Wait exercises on them but they mean to stick on to him. They do not let him go, for now it has become a personal matter between them and the sea. As they pass Wait from hand to hand towards the safety of the poop, the men draw together. They unite in the struggle against the onslaught of the storm. But vulnerable to Wait's influence, they become uncertain once again: "The secret and ardent desire of our hearts was the desire to beat him viciously with our fists about the head; and we handled him as tenderly as though he had been made of glass." (73) They feel helpless in the face of threat of Wait because they are not sure as to how to react to this inscrutable figure.

In this situation, the cook amazes everyone by tenaciously working to produce hot coffee which helps the crew through the hours to dawn. The cook's feat is pronounced "meeraculous" (83) by the men on board. It lifts the low morale of the wretched crew. Podmore's devotion to duty makes him a hero: "He remained heroic. His saying—*the* saying of his life—became proverbial in the mouth of men as are the sayings of conquerors or sages. Later, whenever one of us was puzzled by a task and advised to relinquish it, he would express his determination to persevere and to succeed by the words: 'As long as she swims I will cook!'" (84)

As the storm begins to subside, the ship jerks violently "as though she had torn herself out from a deadly grasp." (88) And the crewmen feel that they have started their life afresh as if they had died and had been resuscitated. They resume their work. Though they have emerged victorious in their struggle against the storm, they are not happy with their lives: "They seemed to hate one another with a deadly hate. The longing to be done with it all gnawed their breasts, and the wish to do things well was a burning pain. They cursed their fate, condemned their life, and wasted their breath in deadly imprecations upon one another." (93)

The ordeal of the furious storm awakens Singleton to his weakening age. He has proved his worth during the storm by remaining at the wheel for thirty hours. However, he feels agonized at the truth of his mortality and faces it in the eye of the eternal sea. He copes with the thought of death as a personal experience.

Conrad presents Donkin as a man who knows all about his rights, but nothing of his duties. Consumed by a feverish destructive energy, Donkin encourages the men to rebel against the captain because he makes them work. He tries to move the crew by emphasizing social and political inequality: "'E said'e would brain me—did yer 'ear? They are goin' to murder us now for the least little thing" and "Didn't we lead a 'dogs's loife for two poun' ten a month'?" (100) He is successful in convincing the crew that their work is too hard. Exploited by the cowardly bluffer Donkin, the seamen decry their officers. They are led to believe that their devotion and perseverance has not been aptly rewarded. They "could not deny the luminous truth of his contentions. . . . Our deserts were great and our pay small. Through our exertions we had saved the ship and the skipper would get the credit of it. What had he done? We wanted to know." (101-2) As the row breaks out between the crew and the officers, the helmsman lets go the wheel to find out the matter with them.

The crew members suspect Wait of feigning illness but only Donkin has the courage to ask him directly whether he is sick or not. Donkin admires Wait for being so successful in his malingering. And for the first time in the novel we definitely learn that Wait believes he is not sick and that he has done this malingering on the last ship also; he has chosen this role on his own initiative. But soon Conrad shows that the man is not well and this he does by describing Wait's feverish hallucinations. Wait's act of self-deception that he is not dying is, in Sartrean terms, an instance of bad faith.

Podmore's talk of hell-fire and death makes Wait protest against his solitary confinement. Claiming to be well, he seeks the captain's permission to return to duty. The captain refuses to meet the demand because he feels sorry for James Wait and wants him to die in peace. Donkin stirs an angry reaction amongst the men who feel this disciplinary action to be excessively harsh. There is a near-mutiny on board the ship. The crewmen gather near Wait's cabin, rave at the injustice done to Wait and denounce the captain. Donkin caps it all by assaulting the captain with a belaying pin. In this tense situation, the captain keeps his balance of mind and orders Baker to come back when the latter advances to stop the crew members. Very calmly he tells Creighton and Baker that the object thrown on him was a belaying pin. Later, when the officers discuss the events, Baker is bewildered and Creighton is calmly furious, but Captain

Allistoun remains composed and thoughtful.

Allistoun is presented as Conrad's most exemplary ship's master. He has depth of insight into human nature and handles Donkin, Wait and the remainder of the ship's company in a very expert manner. He is "one of those commanders who speak little, seem to hear nothing, look at no one—and know everything, hear every whisper, see every fleeting shadow of their ship's life." (125) Aware of his responsibility to the ship, he adheres to routine. His confident behaviour leaves the mates "more impressed than if they had seen a stone image shed a miraculous tear of compassion over the incertitude of life and death." (127)

The crewmen become aware of their responsibility to the ship when Captain Allistoun asks them the next morning what they want. They are unable to give a single conceivable reason for their rebellion and forget even Wait. The captain shows firm leadership when anarchy is imminent. He finally subdues the whole crew by forcing Donkin to take back his murderous weapon and restore it to its hole in the forerigging.

The question of Wait's fate still looms large before their eyes and the crew members keep discussing it. They turn to Singleton for a definite answer, "expectant and appeased as if that old man, who looked at no one, had possessed the secret of their uneasy indignations and desires, a sharper vision, a clearer knowledge." (129) And like an oracle, Singleton predicts that the black man will die when the ship gets in sight of land. The prediction assuages the feelings of the crew.

Wait's influence on the crew now becomes more apparent than ever. His demoralizing effect turns the crewmen into obsequious sychophants who can see the death approach: "He was demoralizing. Through him we were becoming highly humanized, tender, complex, excessively decadent: we understood the subtlety of his fear, sympathized with all his repulsions, shrinkings, evasions, delusions—as though we had been over-civilized, and rotten, and without any knowledge of the meaning of life." (139) The rough kindliness of the crewmen gradually loses its positive and humane quality. Singleton has shown them the illogicality of their position and they begin to regain control.

Wait also has the growing awareness of his approaching death. The slightest gesture that he makes discloses to him his bodily weakness and causes a pang of mental suffering. He is so weak that he cannot stand on his feet without support. Everyone is moved by the sight of Wait wrestling with the shadow of death. Belfast spends every moment of his spare time in Wait's cabin and nurses him tenderly. However, he becomes increasingly irritable with his mates; "With him it was a tear and a blow: a tear for Jimmy, a blow for any one who did not seem to take a scrupulously orthodox view of Jimmy's case." (140) With their obsession to keep Wait alive to the end of the journey, the crew members talk about nothing else. In the evenings, they crowd Wait's cabin. Singleton as usual remains aloof and visits Wait only once. Not taken in by the dying man, he is convinced that Wait would die as soon as they approach land: "Mortally sick men—he maintained—linger till the first sight of land, and then die; and Jimmy knew that the very first land would draw his life from him. It is so in every ship." (142)

Ignored by all except the cook, Donkin feels bitter and spiteful. Even the sighting of the land does not cheer him up, for it means more hard work. He visits Wait hoping him to be already dead and his money left for the taking. Wait, however, is alive and reminisces to Donkin. Donkin keeps him company throughout the night and hastens his death by unrelentingly tormenting him with the prospect of his imminent death.

All through the voyage, Wait has deluded himself about the seriousness of his illness. Now, however, he is in a state of absolute terror at the idea of death:

> His eyes were terrified as though he had been looking at unspeakable horrors; and by his face one could see that he was thinking of abominable things. Suddenly with an incredibly strong and heartbreaking voice he sobbed out:
>
> "Overboard! . . . I! . . . My God!" (153)

Wait's fear draws a sympathetic response from Donkin who realizes that he too might end this way. He sees a large tear drop to Wait's pillow and feels sad: "And Donkin, watching the end of that hateful nigger, felt the anguishing grasp of a great sorrow on his heart at the thought that he himself, some day, would have to go through it all—just like this—perhaps!" (153-54) Evidently, Donkin is not free from this fear of death.

Donkin, the sole witness of Wait's death, is in a daze as he comes out of the cabin. He looks upon the scene outside and wonders at the absurdity of life: "He stood motionless and perfectly astounded to find the world outside as he had left it; there was the sea, the ship—sleeping men; and he wondered absurdly at it, as though he had expected to find the men dead, familiar things gone for ever." (155)

Wait seems reluctant to leave even after his death. He clings to the plank until Belfast cries: "Jimmy, be a man! . . . Go, Jimmy!—Jimmy, go! Go!" (160) Although the crewmen have been expecting Wait's death, it comes as a shock: "A common bond was gone; the strong, effective and respectable bond of a sentimental lie." (155) They have supported Wait's self-deception till the very end.

As Wait's body is consigned to the deep, the crewmen let out a united sigh—feeling quite sure that they have not been fooled. Wait's death releases them from the unwelcome spell cast over them. Purged of the evil influence, they face the fact of death and feel relieved that the burden is off. Death loses its terror. Immediately a favourable breeze springs up, proving right Singleton's belief in the old superstitions: Wait had kept the ship under its spell and as soon as she gets rid of him, she moves quickly to port.

As the *Narcissus* reaches the shore, it ceases to live. The voyage has ended and the crew members disperse. Only Baker stays on, ordered by Captain Allistoun not to forget to wind up chronometers the next morning. He moves about solitary and grunting. It is an ironic portrait that we have of a model chief mate. No one waits for him ashore. He has given up everything for this life and yet, there is no chance of his being appointed a skipper: "The darkness of a misty evening fell, cold and damp, upon the deserted decks; and Mr. Baker sat smoking, thinking of all the successive ships to whom through many long years he had given the best of a seaman's care. And never a command in sight. Not once!" (167) The crewmen reassemble the next day at the shipping office. They are paid off, and before dispersing, they gather on the shore for a last drink. We have a last look at Old Singleton who can hardly find the small pile of gold in the profound darkness of the shore. He goes out "unsteadily, without as much as a glance at any of us." (169)

At the end, Conrad shows the crewmen as a dark knot drifting in the sunshine. They have forgotten the ordeals of the storm and James Wait as they reach the shore. The narrator ends the story by posing a question, "haven't we, together and upon the immortal sea, wrung out a meaning from our sinful lives?" and then answering it by paying a tribute to the crew who "gave back yell for yell to a westerly gale." (173) The narrator's last apostrophe to the crew is a final good-bye. In a letter to Henry Canby, written some time before his death, Conrad insists that the central presence of the ship does not make the novel a sea story. Conrad is indeed more concerned with analyzing human condition: "In the *Nigger* I give the psychology of a group of men and render certain aspects of nature. But the problem that faces them is not a problem of the sea, it is merely a problem that has arisen on board a ship where the conditions of complete isolation from all land entanglements make it stand out with a particular force and colouring."[13]

V

Conrad wrote *Youth* while taking respite from the writing of *Lord Jim*. The facts of the narrative are based on the author's experience aboard a sinking ship and the ensuing adventure in an open boat. Marlow begins the narrative by warning his audience that the story be construed as "a symbol of existence." (4)[14] He introduces his first voyage to the Eastern Seas twenty-two years ago as one of those voyages which should be taken as an illustration of life: "You fight, work, sweat, nearly kill yourself, sometimes do kill yourself, trying to accomplish something—and you can't. Not from any fault of yours. You simply can do nothing, neither great nor little—not a thing in the world." (4) An undercurrent of profound melancholy creeps in when Marlow says that in spite of all fighting, working, sweating, it was not possible to get a wretched 600-ton cargo of coal to its port of destination. The crew's heroic efforts were of no avail. Realizing the existential absurdity, Marlow expresses the disillusionment of middle age and the futility of much that life offers to men.

Marlow describes his ill-fated voyage on the *Judea* as a memorable affair. He relates how youth had enabled him to respond heroically to the challenges of life. Brimming over with excitement at the prospect of travelling to the Far East, the young Marlow had overlooked how somewhat grudgingly he was appointed by Captain Beard as a second mate to the *Judea*. It was an old, dirty vessel of four hundred tons and had long been laid up in a London dock. At the time of Marlow's appointment, the ship was about to take a cargo of coal from Tyneside to Bankok in Siam, entailing a prior journey from London to Tyne for loading. Below her name in big letters was painted the motto: "Do or Die." The inscription had appealed to young Marlow's imagination and he started loving the old ship.

Full of unconquerable optimism and romance of life, Marlow had undertaken the voyage without any depression. His comment on life and its end smacks of pessimism: "Mrs. Beard is dead, and youth, strength, genius, thoughts, achievements, simple hearts—all dies." (7) But Marlow tones down this talk of death with the remark, "No matter." (7) He introduces us to the members of the crew who were strangers to one another since the ship was newly commissioned. Captain Beard was a veteran mariner, some sixty years of age; the *Judea* was his first command. The candid expression of his eyes bespoke his simplicity, honesty and tenacity of character. The first mate, Mr. Mahon, is likewise an elderly man of long experience and in their presence Marlow feels "like a small boy between two grandfathers." (5) Though surrounded with images of age, the young Marlow is not depressed; his youthful zest and exuberance are not dampened. He, however, hates Jermyn, the pilot, because he "mistrusted my youth, my common-sense, and my seamanship." (6) He does not expect such criticism after being at sea for six years. His hatred is also the result of the gloomy atmosphere that Jermyn spreads on the ship.

Conrad depicts how a young man of just twenty could face and even exult in the innumerable hardships and inconveniences that drive his seniors to despair.[15] It seems that a succession of material disasters had cursed the voyage of the *Judea*. She leaves London in ballast and takes a week to reach Yarmouth Roads where she is hit by an October gale that lasts for three days. Due to wind, lightning, sleet, snow and a terrific sea, the ship's bulwarks are smashed, her decks flooded, and the violent movements of the ship shift the sand ballast to the lee bow. All the crewmen work desperately to move the ballast to the opposite side of the ship, as she is tossed about by the heavy seas. Marlow reports the men's difficulties as a sort of adventure. Engaged in "that gravedigger's work," (6) the men toss shovelfuls of wet sand up to windward. On the third day, the gale subsides and a tug is secured to tow the ship to its destination. When the *Judea* eventually reaches Tyneside, sixteen days after she had left London, she has lost her turn for loading and is hauled off to a tier where it has to wait for a month.

When the *Judea* is finally loaded and about to set sail, a serious hitch occurs. While Captain Beard is below supping with his wife and the first mate, a steamer having a woman's name—*Miranda* or *Melissa*— comes out of the fog at night and hails Marlow before ramming against the *Judea*. The result of this accident, to quote Mahon the first mate, is "another month in this beastly hole." (8) The bows of the unfortunate *Judea* are stoved in and the repairs take three weeks.

The whole incident seems absurd with the captain making an attempt to save his wife, but finding himself incapable to do so. In retrospect, the heroic action looks pathetic and ludicrous. The captain's first thought on hearing Marlow's call was to ensure the safety of his wife; accordingly he had picked her up and put her in an oarless skiff at the stern of his ship. Only after casting off does he realize the absurd situation that he is adrift without oars. Eventually, a passing waterman is hired to tow the captain and his wife alongside. When at last the captain returns to his post, he is most embarrassed, feeling that he has been remiss in his duty. He is apologetic for being absent from his post in time of danger which constitutes a serious breach of the ship officer's code. Like Lord Jim, he jumps the ship in a crisis though here it does not lead to any serious repercussions.

Three weeks after the accident, the *Judea* makes a start for Bankok in bright January sunshine. The unusually fine weather continues all through the North Sea and the English Channel. It is not until the ship is some three hundred miles to the westward of the Lizard Head that the weather changes for the worse. In existential terms, it is man's struggle against the hostile universe. A violent gale springs up which blows "with spite, without interval, without mercy, without rest." (10) Day after day, and night after night, there is nothing round the ship but the howl of the wind, the tumult of the sea, the noise of water pouring over her deck. There is no rest for the *Judea* and no rest for the crew: both struggle to overcome the furious storm. The terrific gale batters the ship: "She tossed, she pitched, she stood on her head, she sat on her tail, she rolled, she groaned," (10) and the crewmen have to keep their balance of mind amidst all this.

The traditions of the sea which pervade the atmosphere on the *Judea* bring out the best in the men aboard her. Marlow and the other crewmen understand the value of doing one's work well. Mahon's discovery that the old ship has sprung a leak leads to a grim struggle on the part of the crew. To prevent the ship from foundering, the officers and the seamen work desperately at the pumps; they pump all day, all night, all the week. They face the cruel and indifferent universe of "angry clouds and an infuriated sea" (11): the sea is white like a sheet of foam, like a caldron of boiling milk; there is no sign of break in the clouds, not even for ten seconds. The crewmen make superhuman efforts to save the ship. They man the pumps and pumping becomes their whole existence: they forget the day of the week, the name of the month. There is not a dry spot on the ship and they seem to have forgotten how it felt to be dry—their days filled with endless, backbreaking pumping.

Amidst all this hostility of nature, Marlow has feelings of exultation. Faced with enormous physical discomfort, danger and hard work, he considers the storm to be the deuce of an adventure, a golden chance to prove his physical strength, his ability to stand hardships as well as any other man. At this moment, he makes another comment on youth: "O youth! the strength of it, the faith of it, the imagination of it! To me she was not an old rattletrap carting about the world a lot of coal for a freight—

to me she was the endeavour, the test, the trial of life." (12) In his later years, Marlow thinks of the defiant old *Judea* with pleasure, with affection and with regret.

In this mood of exultation, the older Marlow does not forget to mention the hardships and perils of the voyage. The cruelty of the sea, which shows utter disregard to men's lives, surfaces. The concept of a friendly universe is shattered as he remarks: "One would think that the sole purpose of that fiendish gale had been to make a lunatic of that poor devil of a mulatto." (14) The cook's galley, which was above deck, has been swept away, leaving the mulatto steward trapped in his bunk. Though he is rescued but he goes "out of his mind; completely and for ever mad, with this sudden shock coming upon the fag-end of his endurance." (13) In spite of emerging victorious in this war with the unfavourable weather, the crewmen are not happy. The exhausted and disgruntled crew demand a return to Falmouth for repairs and Captain Beard cannot do otherwise than acquiesce.

The *Judea*'s misadventures do not end here. She sets sail once again after the repairs with a new crew on board but is again put back within a week as the crewmen refuse to serve for a hundred and fifty days on an unseaworthy ship which needs pumping eight hours a day. The next crew, acquainted with the history of the old ship, refuses even to take the ship out of the harbour. The *Judea* has already spent six months at Falmouth, either waiting for or undergoing repairs. Overcome by a sense of nothingness, Marlow too becomes despondent and describes the absurd situation thus: "It was horrid. Morally it was worse than pumping for life. It seemed as though we had been forgotten by the world, belonged to nobody, would get nowhere." (16)

After the *Judea* is thoroughly examined and repaired, and rendered entirely seaworthy, the innumerable rats infesting the ship desert her and take refuge in an empty hulk berthed alongside. Mahon, the first mate, opines that the event proves that the popular superstition about rats deserting a sinking ship is grossly exaggerated. He doubts the wisdom of the rats for they had not left the old ship when it had had a narrow squeak from foundering, and he calls them fools for now leaving a good ship for an old rotten hulk. Man's ignorance on the subject becomes evident when Mahon says: "I don't believe they know what is safe or what is good for them, any more than you or I." (17) The statement is ironical as we know that the ship ultimately did catch fire and founder, and the rats were right in leaving her.

The *Judea*'s repeated attempts to get a new crew and start the journey can be compared to the unsuccessful labours of Sisyphus, Camus's hero in *The Myth of Sisyphus*. Sisyphus was condemned by gods to roll a rock up a hill, only to see it roll down, and start the labour all over again. However, Sisyphus keeps on trying and does not give up hope. Similarly Marlow remains hopeful despite successive failures. To his unrestrained enthusiasm, the *Judea* remains "the endeavour, the test, the trial of life." (12)

An unsuspecting crew is eventually recruited in Liverpool for *Judea*'s final, ill-fated journey. The first part of the voyage is quite uneventful. Marlow, though not complaining, seems to feel frustrated by the ship's leisurely progress: "To us aft, at least, it seemed as though we had been born in her, reared in her, had lived in her for ages, had never known any other ship." (18) His enthusiasm is by no means dampened by the interminable delays and mishaps. He remains quite hopeful and gives expression to this imagination: "And for me there was also my youth to make me patient. There was all the East before me, and all life, and the thought that I had been tried in that ship and had come out pretty well." (18) To Marlow's romantic fancy, the decrepit *Judea* seems to forge a link with the past when other similarly inefficient craft traded with the gorgeous East.

In spite of the romantic hopes of the young Marlow, the *Judea* is doomed. When she at last seems to be within reach of her goal, Marlow discovers fire in the hold of the ship. Captain Beard, anxious to carry out his first command successfully, decides to continue the journey to Java, although the coast of Western Australia is nearer. In their superhuman efforts to overcome the absurd situation, the members of the crew try to stifle the combustion by sealing it off. But the fire cannot be quenched and smoke keeps rising to the deck. Disheartened to find that the combustion refused to be stifled, the crewmen make an attempt to douse the fire with water. Conrad here presents man against the uncongenial environment. The main hose, rotten with age, is brought along but it soon bursts. A smaller pump and buckets of water are then used in an effort to quell the fire. Marlow emphasizes the absurd aspect of the crew's labour: they had previously worked at the pumps of the leaky *Judea* to the point of uttermost exhaustion; now, with equal desperation, they pump water into the hold to quench the fire: "It was our fate to pump in that ship, to pump out of her, to pump into her; and after keeping water out of her to save ourselves from being drowned, we frantically poured water into her to save ourselves from being burnt." (20)

The crewmen face the utter unreason of existence and absurdity of life. The work that takes place on the disastrous *Judea* is hopelessly absurd. In a world characterized by lack of significance and coherence, Mahon even suggests that it would be fortunate for them if the ship once again sprang a tidy leak. Finally, despite the great quantities of water flung down the hatchways by the crew of desperate seamen working in relays, it becomes clear that the fire is still burning vigorously.

The crewmen finally attempt to dig down to the fire but all in vain, for nobody could remain below more than a minute. And then, after a fortnight of grim struggle, the smoke suddenly vanishes. The men wash and have a special dinner. They rest for a day, having fought the fire for two weeks. Everyone rejoices, including Marlow who feels pleased and proud as though he had helped to win a great naval battle.

The very next day a devastating explosion shakes the ship. As Marlow is leaning against the carpenter's bench, sucking at his pipe, he has the absurd impression that the carpenter is tilting it. He becomes "aware of a queer sensation, of an absurd delusion" (22) that he is in the air. A terrific explosion has blown the deck away and propelled him off it. He realizes in mid-air that he is falling into the burning cargo. When he scrambles out after his perilous descent, he finds the deck a wilderness of smashed timber, lying crosswise like trees in a wood after a hurricane.

Vibrated with the nearly fatal experience, Marlow experiences a moment of uncertainty: "I wasn't quite sure whether I was alive." (24) First, he and the mate gape at each other in an open-mouthed amazement. Mahon stares at Marlow with a queer kind of shocked curiosity for the latter is hairless, blackened and his shirt is in ribbons. The effect of the explosion is presented by Marlow in an ordered catalogue: "I had no hair, no eyebrows, no eyelashes . . . my young moustache was burnt off . . . my face was black, one cheek laid open, my nose cut, and my chin bleeding. I had lost my cap, one of my slippers, and my shirt was torn to rags." (23-24) Marlow's neat list achieves the effect of imposing an order on this absurd explosion.

The captain was in his berth when the explosion occurred. The concussion sends him spinning and he goes temporarily out of his mind. He does not respond to the devastation and is worried most of all by the disappearance of his table. As Marlow and Mahon turn to him, the captain angrily asks where his cabin-table has gone to. Though Mahon protests at this absurd question, Marlow, as if conscious of some gross neglect of duty, stammers out that he did not know where the cabin-table was. In retrospect, the whole thing seems to Marlow "an absurd dream." (24) The captain then very placidly gives orders for the foreyard to be trimmed, in spite of the fact that all is still confusion, and that many of the crew are probably missing or injured. Despite his dazed condition, the remarkable old man is still obsessed with his determination to get "that miserable, stripped, undecked, smouldering shell of a ship" (25) to its destination.

The traditions of the sea pervade the atmosphere on the *Judea* and bring out the best in the men aboard her. Devoted to their duty, the crewmen know that the disaster must be treated with patient toil. As Marlow says: "That crew of Liverpool hard cases had in them the right stuff. It's my experience they always have. It is the sea that gives it—the vastness, the loneliness surrounding their dark stolid souls." (25) This fidelity to the ship and sea is essential to overcome the absurdity of the situation.

The ship itself is in sorry plight, the decks being a tangle of wreckage and splintered timbers. Marlow notices one of the boards protruding overboard, "like a gangway leading upon nothing, like a gangway leading over the deep sea, leading to death." (26) He has the absurd idea that it was inviting them "to walk the plank at once" and be done with their "ridiculous troubles." (26) The knowledge of a hostile annihilating force at the centre of existence brings to Marlow a feeling of the impending death.

In this utter confusion, the helmsman totally forgets himself and jumps overboard. He regains control on himself and swims lustily to keep up with the ship. Anxious to come back, he yells and is successfully rescued. Fortunately, none of the crew is killed or even disabled. Though all are in rags, with black faces, like coal-heavers, like sweeps, they do not stop the work. Through devotion to work only can they hope to triumph over the enigmas and insecurities of existence.

In a world ruled by absurdity and irrationality, the efforts of the crew come to nothing. Ultimately they give out a signal for assistance. Responding to this signal, the steamer *Somerville* heaves in sight. Marlow and the rest yell in excitement but *Somerville*'s mate remains unperturbed. Marlow is struck by the apathy of the Malay seamen who do not even deign to lift the heads for a glance. He feels that people who had been blown up deserved more attention.

The chief mate of the *Somerville* comes aboard the *Judea* and advises abandonment of the damaged, burning ship. Captain Beard does not agree to this proposal, but accedes to the suggestion of being towed to Batavia in Java, where it may be possible to quell the fire after which they could proceed on their voyage. The captain seems excited and tells Mahon: "We will do it yet." (27) But the troubles of the *Judea* become more and more critical. Once under tow, the accelerated movement furnishes air to the smouldering cargo, and flames break out. The towing rope is then cut with an axe, an action which causes the *Somerville* to return, and to offer the captain and the crew of the *Judea* passages to Singapore. However, Captain Beard refuses to abandon the ship. Like an ideal sea captain, he is determined to "see the last of the ship." (29)

The *Somerville* departs, her captain promising to report the matter at Singapore. Disaster looms everywhere but the crewmen appear unperturbed. Every man had saved a little bundle or bag but when the captain refuses to abandon the ship, they "dropped their bundles quietly" (30) although they know that their ship will sink soon. They not only work, but also obey orders which endanger their lives. A few minutes ago, Marlow had just wondered why these people did not mutiny:

> And, mind, these were men without the drilled-in habit of obedience.... What made them do it—what made them obey me.... They had no professional reputation—no examples, no praise. It wasn't a sense of duty; they all knew well enough how to shirk, and laze, and dodge—when they had a mind to it—and mostly they had. Was it two pounds ten a-month that sent them there? They didn't think their pay half good enough. No; it was something in them, something inborn and subtle and everlasting. (28)

Out of the sheer absurdity of the voyage comes the young Marlow's greatest moment—the opportunity of his first command. Captain Beard, disappointed over losing his first command, orders Marlow to mind the boats. Marlow is ecstatic at the opportunity of being placed in command of one of the *Judea*'s boats; for now he would reach the East by his own efforts: "I thought it fine." (30) He is not bothered by the flames that gut the ship; rather he gives expression to his illusions as a young man: "Oh, the glamour of youth! Oh, the fire of it, more dazzling than the flames of the burning ship, throwing a magic light on the wide earth, leaping audaciously to the sky, presently to be quenched by time, more cruel, more pitiless, more bitter than the sea—and like the flames of the burning ship surrounded by an impenetrable night." (30) Marlow remarks on the glamour of youth and his own youthful impulses.

After the departure of the *Somerville*, Captain Beard is determined to salvage as much of the ship's gear as possible for the ship's underwriters. Making fun, Marlow says: "One would have thought the old man wanted to take as much as he could of his first command with him." (30)

The captain is very quiet and seems to be off his balance. Marlow takes his place with two seamen, and awaits Captain Beard who will be in command of the little flotilla. The captain, however, remains on the *Judea* and Marlow grows impatient, fearing that the burning ship may explode at any moment.

Returning to the *Judea*, the sheet of fire facing Marlow is a terrifying sight; the heat seems hardly bearable. In the midst of such a chaos, Marlow is shocked to find the captain peacefully asleep on a settee cushion and the crew regaling themselves on bottled stout and bread and cheese. The first mate announces that it is their last chance to have a meal on board, and that it would be senseless to leave good food behind. He goes on to point out to Marlow, who is incredulous at the captain's apparent unconcern, that the old man has had no sleep for days and that there will be little damn sleep in the boats.

Acting again according to the tradition which requires a man to put the lives of others before his own, the captain orders: "Youngest first." (33) One after the other, the seamen leave the ship. Only the skipper lingers on disconsolately, and the crewmen leave him "to commune alone for a while with his first command." (34) Sixteen hours after the explosion, they finally abandon the ship. The captain takes charge of the long-boat while Mahon takes the second boat, and Marlow the third. The boats drift about in the vicinity of the *Judea*, which burns furiously against the background of the night sky and a tropical sea. According to the maritime code, they await her end. Just before daybreak, she goes down, head first, to the accompaniment of a great hissing of steam.

Marlow remains undaunted even when the ship sinks. He does not despair; rather he feels triumphant; he has overcome the dread of death: "A magnificent death had come like a grace, like a gift, like a reward to that old ship at the end of her laborious days. The surrender of her weary ghost to the keeping of stars and sea was stirring like the sight of a glorious triumph." (35)

The abandoning of the ship provides Marlow an opportunity for further adventure. He is overjoyed at the prospect of seeing "the East first as commander of a small boat." (30) An existential hero, we know, defines himself in his action and thus gains authenticity. Marlow, in order to have his first command all to himself, decides to part company: "I wasn't going to sail in a squadron if there were a chance for independent cruising. I would make land by myself. I would beat the other boats. Youth! All youth! The silly, charming, beautiful youth." (34) He receives his final instructions from the captain which are to sail northwards and to keep together as much as possible. But Marlow, as per his earlier decision, overtakes the other boats and is well out of sight by the next morning.

During the course of the day, Marlow espies a passing sail, but does not inform the sailors, afraid that the ship might be homeward bound: he "had no mind to turn back from the portals of the East." (36) In spite of the rain squalls and fierce heat that they have to face, Marlow does not feel dejected. He attributes this to his youth:

> I remember my youth and the feeling that will never come back any more—the feeling that I could last for ever, outlast the sea, the earth, and all men; the deceitful feeling that lures us on to joys, to perils, to love, to vain effort—to death; the triumphant conviction of strength, the heat of life in the handful of dust, the glow in the heart that with every year grows dim, grows cold, grows small and expires—and expires, too soon, too soon, before life itself. (36)

Marlow's boundless enthusiasm is in direct contrast to Captain Beard who seems to be a victim of the incomprehensible fate which keeps a competent man from success. Our last view of the captain is quite depressing: he is sitting "a broken figure at the stern, wet with dew, his hands clasped in his lap" and complaining "I had a terrible time of it." (38)

The culmination of the voyage is Marlow's vision of the East. It is the promised fulfilment of the young Marlow's striving. He is thrilled to see the Eastern beauty and describes the magic of the orient as it looks from his lifeboat on a quiet sea, "a high outline of mountains, blue and afar in the morning; like faint mist at noon; a jagged wall of purple at sunset." (37) He watches everything in sight: "The mysterious East faced me, perfumed like a flower, silent like death, dark like a grave." (38) And he sits there "exulting like a conqueror, sleepless and entranced as if before a profound, a fateful enigma." (38)

In his narration, the older Marlow recaptures the mood of a first marvelling glance of the longed-for East. His enthusiastic dreams of the East are realized. He is excited to see "the East of the ancient navigators, so old, so mysterious, resplendent and sombre, living and unchanged, full of danger and promise." (41) He is completely captivated by the erotic sights that meet his eager eyes—the wide sweep of the bay, the glittering sands, the blueness of the sea. His intense experiences are not shared by the rest of the crewmen who are fast asleep due to physical exhaustion: "The East looked at them without a sound." (41) The triumph is his and his alone.

Marlow protests against the inability of adulthood to preserve younger fantasies of success. Since that first arrival, he has known the East. He has seen the evil of the world, "the mysterious shores, the still water, the lands of brown nations, where a stealthy Nemesis lies in wait, pursues, overtakes so many of the conquering race, who are proud of their wisdom, of their knowledge, of their strength." (41-42) But Marlow refuses to surrender the illusions of the past. The actual East that he cherishes is "contained in that vision of my youth . . . when I opened my young eyes on it." (42)

The narration evokes a mood of nostalgia and wistfulness for the lost illusions and a regret for the passing of youth. The time when a sailor is young at sea is the best period of his life.[16] Marlow concludes his narrative with a positive approach: "I came upon it (the East) from a tussle with the sea—and I was young—and I saw it looking at me. And this is all that is left of it! Only a moment; a moment of strength, of romance, of galmour—of youth! . . . Ah! The good old time—the good old time. Youth and the sea. Glamour and the sea! The good, strong sea, the salt, bitter sea, that could whisper to you and roar at you and knock your breath out of you." (42)

The significance of Marlow's story is not lost to the group of middle-aged men, sitting around a mahogany table and reminiscing over a bottle of claret. Between the five of them, there is "the strong bond of the sea" and "the fellowship of the craft" (3); all of them began life in the merchant service. When the story is told, only Marlow is pursuing life at sea, others having drifted to a life of security and routine. But still they share Marlow's feelings. The unidentified narrator gets in a similar mood and concedes that with their "faces marked by toil, by deceptions, by success, by love," their weary eyes are still "looking anxiously for something out of life, that while it is expected is already gone—has passed unseen, in a sigh, in a flash—together with the youth, with the strength, with the romance of illusions." (42) They still expect "something out of life." These lines are a comment on the existential man's determination that he will not reconcile his personal aspirations to the merciless limitations of temporal existence.

The sole purpose of Marlow's voyage on the *Judea* was to visit the East. He is not disturbed when, in spite of all the heroic efforts of the crew, the *Judea* sinks. He takes the command of a small boat and overlooks the other ships crossing him. And he is rewarded by a moment of triumph when he brings his own boat ashore in the East. Marlow's victory is also man's. The novel depicts the romance of youth and illimitable optimism in face of a hostile, indifferent, absurd universe. Marlow is not a victim of lost opportunities. His enthusiastic dreams of the East and of heroism at sea are realized beyond expectations. His experience has approved his great faith in potentiality of human action. The final impression that emerges from reading *Youth* is that man must heroically and necessarily struggle against the indifferent environment.

NOTES

1. Jean-Aubry, *Joseph Conrad: Life and Letters*, I, p. 96.
2. Edward Garnett, ed., *Letters from Joseph Conrad:* 1895-1924, p. 142.
3. Jean-Aubry, *Joseph Conrad: Life and Letters*, II, p. 342.
4. *The Nigger of the "Narcissus"* (Garden City, New York, Doubleday, Page, 1925).
5. *Almayer's Folly* (Garden City, New York: Dobleday, Page, 1925), p. viii.
6. John H. Hicks, "Conrad's *Almayer's Folly:* Structure, Theme, and Critics," *Nineteenth-Century Fiction*, XIX (1964), p. 28.
7. Likewise, Susan Lundvall Brodie holds the view that the birth of a son suggests "Nina's success and the validity of her creative response to love." "Conrad's Feminine Perspective," *Conradiana*, XVI (1984), p. 147.
8. *An Outcast of the Islands* (Garden City, New York: Doubleday, Page, 1925).
9. Jean-Paul Sartre, *Existentialism and Humanism*, p. 29.
10. Edward Garnett, ed., *Letters from Joseph Conrad: 1895-1924*, p. 42.
11. Jean-Aubry, *Joseph Conrad: Life and Letters*, I, pp. 214-15.
12. It is hard to agree with R.D. Foulke who argues that the captain unnecessarily risks the ship in his preoccupation with his own fame. "Creed and Conduct in *The Nigger of the 'Narcissus'*," *Conradiana*, XII (1980), pp. 105-28.
13. Jean-Aubry, *Joseph Conrad: Life and Letters*, II, p. 342.
14. *Youth* in *Youth: A Narrative and Two Other Stories* (Garden City, New York: Doubleday, Page, 1925).
15. David Daiches very aptly points out that the whole point of the story

is that "youth can and should be immature, can and should have illusions, can and should see disaster as adventure and mishap as opportunity." "Joseph Conrad," *The Novel and the Modern World* (Chicago and London: Chicago Univeristy Press, 1967), p. 31.

16. Walter F. Wright points out, "With Conrad as with Lamb, there was a pining for that was gone, but there was a recognition that youth was a precious time." *Romance and Tragedy in Joseph Conrad* (New York: Russell and Russell, 1966), p. 10.

The Middle Phase: Philosophic Maturity

The novels written during the middle phase of Conrad's career—*Heart of Darkness*, *Lord Jim* and *Nostromo*—are the most explicit exponents of existential humanism and represent the culmination of Conrad's genius. In these novels, the themes are treated more fully and more maturely than in the works of the early phase. Indeed as Conrad's awareness progresses, his technical ingenuity keeps pace.

Heart of Darkness signals the advent of Conrad as a mature artist. It was serialized in *Blackwood's Magazine* from February to April 1899 and marks the end of Conrad's apprenticeship as a writer. *Lord Jim*, like *The Nigger of the "Narcissus"* earlier, was originally planned to be a story only. However it became too long to be included in a volume of short stories and was published in book form in 1900. *Nostromo*, his masterpiece, was published in 1904 when Conrad was at the height of his powers.

In the novels of the early phase, Conrad had viewed man in relation to others. But in *Heart of Darkness* and *Lord Jim*, he focuses his attention on man in relation to his own self. A preoccupation with the self inevitably takes precedence over commitment to others; Conrad begins the search of the dark interior of the self and expresses his concern for human predicament in terms of character. In *Nostromo*, however, Conrad moves away from the exploration of purely individual catastrophes to a world in turmoil. These three novels thus represent Conrad's most intensive efforts to extend and deepen the significance of his existential themes.

II

A close examination of *Heart of Darkness* amply reveals the profundity of Conrad's comment on the human predicament. Marlow, the key figure, yearns for a meaning in the ineluctable conditions of existence. In the course of the story, Marlow affirms some basic concepts of existentialism. He realizes that man is isolated in an alien universe. Man is, no doubt, a part of the universe, but he is alone in it. Search for security which is basic to human nature compels man to understand the human situation through conscious decisions. He has to choose his values and commit himself. The universe however does not reassure man that his beliefs are always the right ones or that they can be depended upon for strength in a time of crisis. When Marlow makes judgment about Kurtz, he seeks proof that his judgment is correct. From the actions of Kurtz with whom he thinks he has values in common, Marlow attempts to measure himself and his ideals. He makes his choice of nightmares and affirms faith in the human condition, despite the potentiality of evil present in man.

It is significant to note that *Heart of Darkness* follows very closely the actual events of Conrad's trip to Stanley Falls on the Congo in 1890. Conrad got this appointment when the Company learnt that one of its captains, Friesleben, was killed. In the novel, the name of the captain becomes Fresleven. The Brussels headquarters of the Belgian Congo Trading Company had promised command to Conrad but he had to remain satisfied with being mate of the small river steamboat *S.S. Roi des Belges*. He was given only temporary command when the captain fell ill. The complete breakdown of Conrad's health through fever and dysentery caused him to resign his post and return to Europe. The malarial gout which troubled him for the rest of his life became special source of vexation by affecting the wrist of his right hand. His natural vitality was undermined by the Congo and he became highly speculative. With no particular occupation, he had plenty of time on his hands. Feeling restless and dissatisfied with the seeming emptiness of his existence, Conrad was in a state of mind which is often the prelude to creative activity. There is a hard core of truth in Aubry's statement that while the excursion ruined Conrad physically, it nonetheless matured him as a novelist. It is the depth of meaning and philosophical content that sets *Heart of Darkness* apart from Conrad's earlier novels *Almayer's Folly* and *An Outcast of the Islands*.

Despite the disclaimer, "I don't want to bother you much with what happened to me personally," (51)[1] we know it too well that Marlow is the narrator as well as the protagonist of the novel. Kurtz on the other hand functions only as a pivot. It is Marlow who faces the predicament of an existential protagonist. The story is concerned with the effect of the country and of Kurtz on Marlow. Hewitt rightly points out that Marlow's journey is "both into the impenetrable darkness of Africa and into the darkness of Marlow's thoughts."[2]

Marlow narrates his story sitting on the deck of the ship *Nellie*, anchored in the Thames. Physically immobilized by the tide, Marlow and his audience are isolated from all else. The physical isolation is coupled with the closeness of the group. Although part of the group to which he is narrating his tale, Marlow is alienated from them in one respect: he is the only member of the group who still follows the sea. The reader's attention is focused on the physical immediacy of Marlow's presence as he sits cross-legged with the ascetic aspect of a Buddha-like idol. "Marlow's lotus posture," points out W.B. Stein, "shows that he is ready to contemplate the chaos out of which order or chaos comes."[3] The Buddha postures that Marlow assumes accentuate the deeply introspective atmosphere of extreme contemplation on the *Nellie*. The journey into the self has to be made in isolation. To perceive the truth of Kurtz, the readers also have to detach themselves from the inherited experience. Marlow's internal isolation at this point parallels the external isolation later, when he reaches the Inner Station and confronts Kurtz.

After finishing the tale, Marlow once again sits isolated from his friends aboard the *Nellie*. He sits "apart, indistinct and silent, in the pose of a meditating Buddha." (162) He looks thoughtfully concerned with the truth of what happened to him. He sits detached from the world dominated by the safety of policemen. He has seen beneath the illusion which generates a view of history as progressive and colonization as a power for good. Completely detached like an ascetic, he sits purged by the re-living of his introspective descent into the self.

Marlow starts out on the journey as a young, idealistic man but his collision with the truth about Kurtz alters his perspective to the tragic. The older Marlow, as he tells the story, has been strengthened by the experience. He tells it after he has experienced and digested the whole of it. The tale is filtered through the narrator who has changed mentally and morally as a result of that experience. He has found the extent to which one can go without being overcome by the dark forces of nature.

The anonymous frame-narrator makes it clear that Marlow is no ordinary seaman. Unlike other seamen, Marlow works at deep mysteries. The meaning of his tales is not inside the facts but outside like a mist lit up by a light:

> The yarns of seamen have a direct simplicity, the whole meaning of which lies within the shell of a cracked nut. But Marlow was not typical... and to him the meaning of an episode was not inside like a kernel but outside, enveloping the tale which brought it out only as a glow brings out a haze, in the likeness of one of these misty halos that sometimes are made visible by the spectral illumination

of moonshine. (48)

A sensitive individual capable of using his experiences to expand his knowledge of himself and humanity, Marlow spends his life seeking the meaning of episodes. The frame-narrator prepares the reader for Marlow's unique method of yarnspinning. That is precisely why he comments thus about the tale: "we knew we were fated . . . to hear about one of Marlow's inconclusive experiences." (51) The inconclusiveness of the tale hints at ambiguity of life itself. Marlow's mission in narrating the story is to preach the meaning of his descent into the heart of darkness of the self and there to confront Kurtz, symbolic of the evil that lurks in every man. The story shows the consequences of unbridled egoism. While narrating, Marlow once again goes through every step of his journey and the ordeal of looking into himself. In telling the story, Marlow reinvades the wilderness while remaining in Europe and thus reenacts Kurtz's act of recognition by causing his comfortable audience to question the grounds of their comfort.

Marlow is appalled by the civilized hypocrisy involved in the establishment of a trading station which is set up in the name of progress and civilization but which serves only to exploit the natives in the acquisition of ivory. The white men work under the mistaken notion that the forces of imperialist commerce will bring civilization to the dark continent. Marlow is highly critical of the Belgian empire in the Congo. He expresses indignation at the folly and greed of the Europeans who are lured to the Congo by the vision of immense riches. Reacting to the pretensions of the looters, Marlow observes that the process of colonization lacks humanitarian ideals: "The conquest of the earth, which mostly means the taking it away from those who have a different complexion or slightly flatter noses than ourselves, is not a pretty thing when you look into it too much." (50-51) Conrad himself was deeply affected by the sight of human baseness and degradation there. His Congo experience had devastatingly exposed the cleavage between human pretensions and practice. Disgusted with the European exploitation of Africa, he castigated the systematic looting of a continent and the men responsible for this looting. In *Last Essays,* he calls it "the vilest scramble for loot that ever disfigured the history of human conscience and geography."[4]

The suppression and exploitation of savages can be justified by a redeeming idea and its saving power: "What redeems it is the idea only. An idea at the back of it; not a sentimental pretence but an idea; and an unselfish belief in the idea—something you can set up, and bow down before, and offer a sacrifice to." (51) Even the most abject horror can be idealized thus. Kurtz has idealistic dreams about what the Europeans can accomplish in Africa. But the ideals that Kurtz has are wrong and that is why he fails. Ideals must after all never work to the detriment of one's fellow creatures. Kurtz's possession of the idea serves to intensify his conversion to savagery. The ideal is complicated with impure ambition.

Marlow begins his narrative by methodically announcing that to understand his experience and its effect on him fully, his listeners would have to know all the details: "how I got out there, what I saw, how I went up that river to the place where I first met the poor chap (Kurtz)." (51) The experience of knowing Kurtz is the culminating point for Marlow: "It seemed somehow to throw a kind of light on everything about me—and into my thoughts." (51)

The Congo journey that Marlow undertook largely on a boyish whim proved an almost devastating experience for him: it transformed him profoundly. He recollects his youthful passion for maps and his boyhood ambition to visit exotic places—the blank spaces on the earth. Over the years, the most blank space that he hankered after has ceased to be "a blank space of delightful mystery—a white patch for a boy to dream gloriously over. It had become a place of darkness." (52) He meaningfully introduces the river as "an immense snake uncoiled, with its head in the sea, its body at rest curving afar over a vast country, and its tail lost in the depths of the land. And... it fascinated me as a snake would a bird—a silly little bird." (52)

From the very beginning we see Marlow confronted with the existential predicament to choose. His decision to go to the Congo is his first conscious choice, resulting from his desire to travel to the centre of the earth. Once decided, Marlow, through the influence of a doting aunt, secures a position as captain of one of the Company's steamboats plying the Congo. One of the purposes of his voyage is to relieve Kurtz, an agent of the Company. Conrad had similarly undertaken the trip to Stanley Falls to bring back Georges Antoine Klein, the inner station agent, then close to death. Like Kurtz, Klein also died on the way back.

In the steamboat, Marlow is to take the place of Fresleven, a Dane, who, he learns later, has been killed in a scuffle with the natives. The reason of his death emphasizes the theme of the futility and utter trivialization of human existence. Thinking himself wronged in a transaction involving two black hens, this "gentlest, quietest creature" (54) felt the need to assert himself. The result is that he is speared to death by the Chief's son. The tragedy leads to the destruction of the whole village community. The natives desert the village in terror and Fresleven's body is left there to rot amid the grasses that grow up through his ribs. Marlow, a replacement for the dead man, starts feeling as if he is not alive.

Marlow's confrontation with the dark forces begins as he visits the company headquarters to sign a contract. His enthusiasm is tempered by this visit. The city reminds him of a whited sepulchre. The company offices are situated in a narrow deserted street and overall it looks a dreary forbidding place. In an outer room, Marlow meets two women, one fat, the other slim, both knitting black wool feverishly. It seems to him that they are knitting his fate in black wool. They resemble the shadowy Fates who guard the gate between the world of civilized conventions and the uncivilized world. Marlow sees an unconcerned wisdom in their scrutinizing gaze. The whole atmosphere seems eerie and fateful to Marlow.

Marlow begins to feel uneasy, as he signs the necessary documents. He encounters a shabby-looking clerk who takes him to the company doctor for a check-up. To pass time as they wait for the doctor, Marlow invites the clerk to have a drink. As they chat, the clerk glorifies the company's business. When Marlow notes his surprise at the clerk's not going out to the Congo, the clerk replies that he is not such a fool as he looks.

It is the macabrely facetious doctor who establishes Marlow's initial concern with internal changes. Marlow is pronounced physically fit after a medical examination. But the doctor's query about there being an insanity in his family irritates Marlow. In the course of his talk, the doctor expresses a morbid interest in the fate of those persons who go to the Belgian Congo. We get a foreboding of the future events as the doctor, after measuring Marlow's cranium, hints that Marlow will be a changed man when he returns, adding that the changes will take place inside his skull. Later, during his journey to the Congo, Marlow does recall the apparently foolish but actually wise doctor: "I felt I was becoming scientifically interesting." (72) The doctor's parting advice to Marlow to avoid irritation and to keep calm is quite meaningful: "*Du calme, du calme*, Adieu." (58) If Marlow is not able to exercise restraint in seeking to accomplish his ends, he will, in doctor's opinion, become mad. Marlow leaves the office totally disillusioned about the value of his trip and with a feeling that he has been led into some conspiracy.

Before setting out, Marlow goes to say good-bye to his aunt. As he goes there, he finds his aunt quite elated and under the mistaken notion that he is "something like an emissary of light, something like a lower sort of apostle." (59) His aunt spouts idealistic words about missionary work which make Marlow quite uncomfortable. She believes that he is going to Africa as the envoy of a society that would wean "ignorant millions from their horrid ways." (59) Marlow, who has a balanced view of the Belgian venture, reminds her that things are run for profit. He ruminates how out of touch with truth women are, living in a world of their own. As he leaves his aunt, Marlow experiences a queer feeling that he is an impostor. This sense of being not himself strikes Marlow ominously and the feeling remains with him throughout the journey. He further feels that "instead of going to the centre of a continent, I were about to set off for the centre of the earth." (60) His trip is a journey into the unconscious or to the end of the world.

Marlow's journey to the mouth of the Congo establishes the tone of heartless rapacity and nightmare absurdity. The journey is an ordeal and seems to Marlow to be "like a weary pilgrimage amongst hints for nightmares." (62) He is puzzled by the enigmatic appearance of the coast that invites him to come and find out—to undertake the journey within. The slow-moving French steamer in which Marlow travels has an apparently absurd purpose of transporting soldiers and customhouse officers to foreign ports. It proceeds along the uninhabited coast which every day looks the same as if it has not moved. Everything seems unreal and nightmarish. They cross places with names that seem "to belong to some sordid farce acted in front of a sinister back-cloth." (61) Marlow's enforced idleness, his isolation, the sombreness of the coast produce the effect of "a mournful and senseless delusion" and keep him away from "the truth of things." (61) Marlow feels isolated despite the presence of others on the French vessel. He has no point of contact with the men aboard the steamer.

The occasional sight of a boat paddled by intensely vital blacks brings Marlow into "a momentary contact with reality" and reassures him that he still belongs to "a world of straightforward facts." (61) This momentary feeling of comfort is quickly dissipated by experiences of the absurd. Marlow sees the anchored warship firing aimlessly into the wilderness. It seems to him to be an insane enterprise: "nothing happened. Nothing could happen." (62) The emphasis on "nothing" expresses a personal vacuum.

The dark and sombre journey makes Marlow increasingly aware of his state in the world. He is alone in an indifferent universe. His alienation is further increased by the absurd and entirely irrational behaviour of his fellow Europeans. Marlow realizes the uselessness of the white presence in Africa. The more he learns of their corruption, the more he is estranged from them. He rejects the principles which govern their behaviour and tends to rely more and more on the values which he has acquired as a seaman: the values of duty, discipline, and order.

Marlow's feeling of isolation deepens as he leaves the sea. He feels a stranger to the land and finds it dark, grim, and forbidding. He is at once struck by the atmosphere of decay and death. He meets with more rapacity, more irrational activity, and more inhumanity at the company station. The work the company professes to do is shown to be an absurdity of inefficiency as well as a callous, heartless enterprise. Marlow is quick to observe every intimation of the absurd which he finds everywhere. Nothing is achieved by the objectless blasting of cliffs going on there. It is not needed: "The cliff was not in the way or anything." (64) The sense of meaninglessness is intensified by the sight of a wasted landscape of industrial junk, a discarded boiler and an undersized railway truck lying on its back with its wheels in the air—like a dead carcass. Unused pieces of machinery lie decaying and stacks of nails rusting.

During his journey, Marlow observes the racial discrimination being practised in society. The civilized deal with the natives of the African Congo in cruel and inhumane ways. Marlow confronts six manacled negroes who perform their job with a deathlike indifference. He finds the group of emaciated negroes dying of hunger and starvation. It is a scene of eternal misery. The welcome by a uniformed native guard makes Marlow realize that he too is "a part of the great cause of these high and just proceedings." (65) He experiences a sense of guilt in being a partner to the passive agents of heartless exploitation being carried on there. It seems to him that he has entered the gloomy circle of some inferno, an unnatural and absurd world where men have become inhuman.

At the station, Marlow meets an elegantly attired white man, the company's chief accountant, and admires him for keeping up his appearance in the midst of the great demoralization. Marlow finds his books in apple-pie order and feels that this man understands the meaning of restraint. By contrast, everything else in the station is a muddle, a veritable chaos of heads, things, buildings. Disorder, waste, and exploitation of the natives are the salient features of the place.

The disparities that exist in the standards of living of the white men and the natives are brought out in Marlow's description of the chief accountant's dress and the misery of the natives:

When near the buildings I met a white man, in such an unexpected

> elegance of get-up that in the first moment I took him for a sort of vision. I saw a high starched collar, white cuffs, a light alpaca jacket, snowy trousers, a clear necktie, and varnished boots. No hat. Hair parted, brushed, oiled, under a green-lined parasol held in a big white hand. He was amazing, and had a penholder behind his ear. (67)

> Black shapes crouched, lay, sat between the trees leaning against the trunks, clinging to the earth, half coming out, half effaced within the dim light, in all the attitudes of pain, abandonment, and despair . . . black shadows of disease and starvation, lying confusedly in the greenish gloom. Brought from all the recesses of the coast in all the legality of time contracts, lost in uncongenial surroundings, fed on unfamiliar food, they sickened, became inefficient, and were then allowed to crawl away and rest. (66)

On one of his visits to the accountant's office, Marlow finds him perched on a high stool attending to his books and exhibiting annoyance at his having to put up with a sick agent temporarily quartered in the office: "In the steady buzz of flies the homeward-bound agent was lying flushed and insensible; the other, bent over his books, was making correct entries of perfectly correct transactions." (70)

Marlow's report of the accountant's working with strict discipline, however, has an ironic touch. He feels that the accountant is keeping irrelevant accounts at the price of an obliviousness to life and death. The man has no moral imagination whatsoever and hence can stick to the observance of rules. Through devotion to his books, he is only avoiding the realities of the Congo. That is why Marlow cannot identify himself with the accountant. He realizes that clothes do not make a man. In being particular about his dress, the accountant has become inhuman to the people around him.

On his way to the Central Station, Marlow suddenly comes upon a negro with a bullet-hole in his forehead. Furthermore, there is the absurdity of Marlow's fat companion, continually fainting, who has come out to make money. Another of his companions dies on way. Subjected to the test of the wilderness, Marlow wonders: "Could we handle that dumb thing, or would it handle us?" (81) Marlow's journey is a journey into the abyss of the mankind. He is anxious to uphold the white man's role among the primitives. However, when he reaches Africa, he sees no evidence of restraint. Everything seems meaningless.

Marlow feels himself a victim of incomprehensible and uncontrollable happenings. His arrival at the Central Station brings him further into the absurd world of colonialism. A glance is sufficient to tell him that a flabby devil is in charge. He is rudely shocked to discover that his steamer lies sunk at the bottom of the river: "I did not see the real significance of that wreck at once. I fancy I see it now, but I am not sure—not at all. Certainly the affair was too stupid—when I think of it—to be altogether natural. Still. . . . But at the moment it presented simply as a confounded nuisance." (72)

Marlow is interviewed by the manager who inspires immediate uneasiness in him. The hostile relationship is set at first sight. Without considering Marlow's condition after his long journey, the manager begins to speak of his own problems. Marlow feels alienated from the manager who is a hollow man: "Perhaps there was nothing within him." (74) He lacks the restraint necessary for leadership. Being a representative of colonizers, he should have a feeling of superiority to the natives whom he is to rule. Through his lack of restraint, he upsets the balance between colonizer and native.

Marlow's decision to work sets him apart from the inefficient white men by whom he is surrounded at the station. Repelled by the circumstances, Marlow takes refuge in the work of retrieving his wrecked steamer and repairing it. He throws himself enthusiastically into work because he feels that work is the only way to keep his hold on the redeeming facts of life. He condemns the white agents of the company who do no work and while away their time awaiting assignments to lucrative posts. They plot and speak of future prospects and careers, saying that one can go far in an obviously futureless land where there is only a primal timelessness. Marlow sees the degradation of men whose only aim in life seems to be accumulation of wealth.

The station is full of men strolling aimlessly with their absurd long staves in their hands, like a lot of faithless pilgrims. Marlow dissociates himself from the pilgrims who look unwholesome to him. He feels alienated from them and they, in turn, look upon Marlow with dishonour. Marlow detects the taint of corruption in the very air which breathes the word ivory. Everything seems unreal; the only reality is work. Engrossed in work, Marlow does not bother much about the pilgrims. He responds deeply to the task as a value in its own right.

Work gives man a chance to find out what he is capable of doing. Man can discharge his obligation to society through devotion to duty. In a letter to Mme. Poradowska, Conrad holds:

> One becomes useful only on realizing the utter insignificance of the individual in the scheme of the universe. When one well understands that in oneself one is nothing and that a man is worth neither more nor less than the work he accomplishes with honesty of purpose and means, and within the strict limits of his duty towards society, only then is one the master of his conscience, with the right to call himself a man. Otherwise, were he more attractive than Prince Charming, richer than Midas, wiser than Doctor Faust himself, the two-legged featherless creature is only a despicable thing sunk in the mud of all the passions.[5]

The necessity of doing work, in fact, lends dignity to many of Conrad's seamen. Marlow's profound disillusionment with the situation makes him realize that there is an inherent private value in work, a reality that is ineffable and unknowable by others. Marlow thinks of the unreality of his new environment as a new kind of reality, a dream reality that he finds difficult to communicate: "We live, as we dream—alone." (82)

There are various instances in the novel where we are told of the futility and hopelessness of our existence. Marlow relates how one evening the routine is upset as a grass shed is suddenly consumed by fire. He sees the natives trying to douse the flames. The whole thing seems totally absurd with the stout, black-moustached trader trying to extinguish the flames with water in a pail having a hole in the bottom. Such sights are emotionally disturbing. The act symbolizes the essential futility and purposelessness of the work being done by these white traders. Marlow realizes that no activity of any kind is going on there—not even waste and exploitation. The brickmaker has not produced a single brick during his stay of an entire year. All this while, he has been waiting for materials to make bricks.

The jealous bickering and futile intriguing at the station awakens Marlow's interest in Kurtz. Marlow overhears the manager talking to the brickmaker about Kurtz and then something like taking advantage of this unfortunate incident. The brickmaker is the manager's consort and informant. Together they represent everything that Marlow detests. There is not a drop of honesty in them. Marlow has only contempt for the brickmaker and terms him a "papier-mache Mephistopheles." (81) He also feels that the manager and the brickmaker resent Kurtz because he represents a threat to their ambitions. Marlow senses the malignant air of plotting in the very air, as unreal as everything else about the station and its traders. He experiences moral nihilism.

At the brickmaker's place, Marlow is attracted by a small oil painting in the room, "representing a woman, draped and blindfolded, carrying a lighted torch. The background was sombre—almost black. The movement of the woman was stately, and the effect of the torch-light on the face was sinister." (79) He is informed that Kurtz has painted the picture while awaiting assignment. The figure in the sketch represents Kurtz's original conception of his mission. The portrait presents Kurtz's initial idealism: he had come to Africa armed with grandiose ideals and intended to be a bringer of light to Africa. Dowden very rightly points out that the painting "symbolizes mankind, groping blindly through the darkness of his existence, seeking his way, with what light civilization can offer."[6]

The painting increases the mystery of Kurtz and prompts Marlow to make further inquiries about him. The brickmaker tells Marlow sarcastically that Kurtz is an emissary of science and progress. He displays interest in Marlow, revealing finally that in his mind Marlow is connected with the legendary Kurtz. Marlow is lumped together with Kurtz by the brickmaker: "The same people who sent him (Kurtz) specially also recommended you (Marlow)." (79) The brickmaker feels alienated from Marlow because he thinks that Marlow can use his connections in Europe to his disadvantage. Marlow does not correct him hoping that this false impression would help Kurtz.

Malrow is aware that it is not possible to find a solution to the problems of existence. He finds it difficult to define to his audience the feelings that he had towards Kurtz at that moment. He interrupts himself with the interjection, "Do you understand?" for, throughout the tale, his attempt has been to convey it to the very spirits of his listeners. As he was invaded by Kurtz, Marlow tries in turn to invade his listeners:

> He was just a word for me. I did not see the man in the name any more than you do. Do you see him? Do you see the story? Do you see anything? It seems to me I am trying to tell you a dream—making a vain attempt, because no relation of a dream can convey the dream-sensation, that commingling of absurdity, surprise, and bewilderment in a tremor of struggling revolt, that notion of being captured by the incredible which is of the very essence of dreams. (82)

The necessity of self-knowledge is linked with the value of toil.

Disgusted with the atmosphere at the Central Station, Marlow gets on with the job of repairing his steamer. He has enough plates to cover the holes in the side of the steamer, but no rivets are available. The station-master does not heed to his demand. For relief, Marlow turns to the steamboat on which he has expended enough hard work and speaks affectionately about it:

> She had given me a chance to come out a bit—to find out what I could do. No, I don't like work. I had rather laze about and think of all the fine things that can be done, I don't like work—no man does—but I like what is in the work,—the chance to find yourself. Your own reality—for yourself, not for others—what no other man can ever know. They can only see the mere show, and never can tell what it really means. (85)

Kurtz represents the class of traders who have come to Africa with a sense of mission, equipped with moral ideas of some sort. He represents Western ideologies and retains the strength of his faculties to the end. Kurtz hopes to improve the human condition—an altruistic idea that is certainly in keeping with Conrad's notion of man's obligation to the human bond. As the manager tells his uncle, Kurtz wants each station to be "like a beacon on the road towards better things, a centre for trade of course, but also for humanizing, improving, instructing." (91) Kurtz is an idealist who sets out to civilize Africa, although he was to serve the colonial exploitation as an agent. Marlow wishes to meet Kurtz and know what has happened to the man of principles. He is curious to know how Kurtz's idealism has fared in Africa. Kurtz will show how man's idealism stands the test of reality.

Quite in contrast to Kurtz's idealistic trip is the Eldorado Exploring Expedition, led by the uncle of the manager. This is certainly exploitation at its worst: "To tear treasure out of the bowels of the land was their desire, with no more moral purpose at the back of it than there is in burglars breaking into a safe." (87)

By their mean enviousness of Kurtz, the manager and his uncle bring Marlow more firmly on the side of Kurtz. Marlow one evening overhears the two conversing about Kurtz. The manager is worried because Kurtz is exporting enormous and excellent quantities of ivory. He fears that Kurtz, if promoted, would replace him. Both agree that Kurtz's popularity and influence are frightful. The uncle hopes that the climate will do away with this problem of Kurtz. He foreshadows Kurtz's death when, pointing to the jungle, he exclaims to his nephew: "Ah! my boy, trust to this—I say, trust to this." (92)

From their conversation, Marlow comes to the conclusion that Kurtz also believes in fidelity to work. He learns that about a year ago, Kurtz and a half-caste clerk had come down-river with a fleet of canoes bearing ivory which he intended to deliver. But after travelling three hundred miles, Kurtz had decided to go back, letting the clerk continue without him. This is an incomprehensible act to the manager and his uncle who are at a loss to find an adequate motive for it. As for Marlow, he seems to have for the first time a distinct glimpse of the lone white man in a dugout canoe, his back turned on the headquarters, and his face set towards the wilderness. Marlow himself is unsure of a possible motive for such an act. "Perhaps he was just simply a fine fellow who stuck to his work," speculates Marlow, "for its own sake." (90) This speculation is another step towards Marlow's identification with Kurtz.

Eventually, despite all the absurdity surrounding him, Marlow is able to repair his ship and proceed up the river. He is accompanied by the manager, three or four pilgrims, and a crew of thirty cannibals. The trip of two months's duration seems to take Marlow "to the earliest beginnings of the world." (92) It seems to him that he is travelling into his own past or into his dreams. Silence, emptiness, and an impenetrable forest greet them. The landscape is brooding, mysterious and sinister: "It was the stillness of an implacable force brooding over an inscrutable intention. It looked at you with a vengeful aspect." (93) The weather is hellish and the river full of hidden snags and reefs. Marlow feels the power of the wilderness when confronted with the jungle humanity. He feels cut off from everything familiar. At the same time, he is thankful that he is kept occupied.

Conrad believes that emptiness and inanity can be overcome by an active engagement in work. By concentrating on the work that is at hand, one can perceive a meaning in life. Keeping the steamer afloat past all the snags is an impressive testimony of Marlow's concern for work. The sense of responsibility maintains his sanity. He busies himself in piloting the boat, in attending to the surface reality. His preoccupation with these mundane surface-truths saves him as well as his steamer from destruction. Against an obvious purposelessness and aimlessness, Marlow creates the illusion of purpose.

Life can acquire meaning through the search for truth. When Marlow pilots his barque up river on the Congo, he makes a comparison: "When you have to attend to things of that sort, to the mere incidents of the surface, the reality—the reality, I tell you,—fades. The inner truth is hidden—luckily, luckily." (93) The almost totally hidden tree-trunks symbolize truth which similarly remains invisible.

The earth seems unearthly. The steamer moves on towards its destination, for Marlow it moves "towards Kurtz—exclusively." (95) In the silence, it seems that Marlow and his crew are wandering "on prehistoric earth, on an earth that wore the aspect of an unknown planet." (95) As they penetrate deep into the heart of darkness, Marlow hears the nerve-tearing sounds of the drums, sees savages engaged in primitive dances, and is attracted towards them. Although he has a dim suspicion of there being a meaning in their acts, Marlow cannot participate in that meaning. The thought of a heritage in common with the savages makes Marlow question: "And why not? The mind of man is capable of anything—because everything is in it, all the past as well as all the future." (96)

On symbolic level, the cries call on a man to act in response to his emotions, to break his bonds with the rules imposed artificially. Man is capable of any sort of action, he has no innate limitations. The brutal and savage instincts are buried within each man. But in the civilized world, man must restrain himself from certain acts and must impose his own limitations upon himself. Conrad had a strong belief in the existence of a so-called inner order or conscience. The inner strength is to serve as man's guide in every situation. In the howling natives, Marlow glimpses truth which man must meet "with his own true stuff—with his own inborn strength." (97) He quenches his savage instincts to join these natives by immersing himself in his job of keeping the steamer afloat, in performing his duty as a captain. The necessity for inner strength restrains him. In a world where things happen without logic or meaning, Marlow is forced to choose between reality and attention to objective matters. Watching the steering, he realizes that there is "surface-truth enough in these things to save a wiser man." (97)

Marlow feels that the cannibals, who help him aboard the steamer, are "fine fellows . . . men one could work with." (94) There is the savage fireman who, under a superstitious belief, keeps the steamer moving up the river very efficiently: "what he knew was this—that should the water in that transparent thing disappear, the evil spirit inside the boiler would get angry through the greatness of his thirst, and take a terrible vengeance." (98) The fireman does not understand his work, but he is useful to the ship.

Some fifty miles away from the Inner Station, Marlow's party comes upon a deserted hut where he finds a sixty-year-old book entitled *An Inquiry into Some Points of Seamanship.* This manual is another symbol of restraint, the fidelity that binds the British seaman and the British Empire to a spirit of service—the spirit of service that Marlow finds lacking in deepest Africa. He handles the tattered book with great tenderness, for it has "an honest concern for the right way of going to work." (99) Mystified by the presence of the manual in this lonely place, Marlow slips it into his pocket, feeling that to tear himself away from the book is like being torn from an old relationship. He feels that his profound discovery has something unmistakably real in it.

All Marlow's impressions of the hut's inhabitant are diametrically opposite to those so far gathered about the people at the Company Station. It is a tangible manifestation of the honour which Marlow has been able to salvage from the chaos of Africa. While he peruses the pages of the book, the pilgrims get busy in hauling the wood-pile aboard. The sight of the wood-pile, stacked neatly, fortifies Marlow's conviction of the decency which is there in good, efficient work done from a sense of solidarity. What strikes him is the efficiency of the workmanship, the ready helpfulness of which it speaks, and the brisk vital energy it reflects.

As they resume their journey, Marlow and the crew realize that the boat has to fight the swift current. In this situation, the manager displays a commendable resignation and advises Marlow to watch the night out. Marlow, by contrast, is impatient to proceed. He frets and fumes, wondering whether he is ever to reach Kurtz. But suddenly he experiences a flash of insight: "it occurred to me that my speech or my silence, indeed any action of mine, would be a mere futility" because "the essentials of this affair lay deep under the surface, beyond my reach, and beyond my power of meddling." (100)

Marlow anchors midstream and the company passes the night in what seems like a trance instead of sleep. Dusk sets in quickly and the landscape seems immobile. The thick fog which envelops them also cuts them off from the outside world. Suddenly, a very loud cry, as of infinite desolation, rends the air, making Marlow's hair stand on end. The whites are white-faced, fearful of attack, and certain that they will be butchered. By contrast, the blacks are essentially quiet. One or two even grin as they work.

Conrad presents the primary, unadorned realities of existence in describing the remarkable restraint displayed by the cannibals. Their only food, the foul-smelling meat, has been thrown overboard. Marlow realizes that they must be very hungry and wonders why these men do not "go" for the whites. Their restraint, exhibited under the pressure of extreme hunger, is incredible and inexplicable. It is all the more amazing in view of the fact that they outnumber the whites six to one. They represent an "unfathomable enigma" to Marlow. Their restraint is "one of those human secrets that baffle probability." (104) Impressed by their restraint, Marlow sees them in a new light now. He concludes that what controls them is their primitive honour.

Marlow feels that the approach to the Inner Station is "beset by as many dangers as though he (Kurtz) had been an enchanted princess sleeping in a fabulous castle." (106) As the pilgrims quarrel over the location of the howling natives, the manager declares that he will be desolated if anything happens to Kurtz before they reach him. The manager's concern seems genuine to Marlow. However, the manager is just the kind of man who wishes to preserve appearances.

Marlow's growing anticipation of meeting Kurtz suffers a severe setback when the steamboat is attacked by the savages. The helmsman meets the challenge heroically and steers the ship "lifting his knees high, stamping his feet, champing his mouth, like a reined-in-horse." (110) Hit by a spear that mortally wounds him, the helmsman looks at Marlow in an "extraordinary, profound, familiar manner." (111) Marlow acknowledges his personal tie to his helmsman, a claim of distant kinship that he still remembers. The hysterical behaviour of the whites on board confirms Marlow's loathing of them. He prefers the savages on board and in the bush to these whites. After the blacks are chased off by his tugging at the line of the steam-whistle, Marlow looks down at his dying black helmsman. In his very last moment, the helmsman frowns heavily and his eyes reveal an accusation. The recognition of kinship has disappeared from his glance and it seems to league Marlow with the other whites on board.

Marlow's shoes are drenched by the dying helmsman's blood. Pulling his bloody shoes from his feet, Marlow throws them into the river. Marlow, who had stepped into Fresleven's shoes when he accepted the job, now casts off these shoes. As Ted E. Boyle points out: "He is no longer merely Fresleven's replacement, but a new sort of adventurer who will progress even further into the heart of darkness."[7]

As the helmsman collapses, Marlow presumes that Kurtz is dead too. The thought almost overwhelms him, as if the sole purpose of his expedition had been to meet Kurtz. He discovers that in his imagination he has never envisaged Kurtz as doing something but only as discoursing. His controlling passion, from the time he hears of Kurtz, is to converse with him. To Marlow, Kurtz has become a voice rather than a man of action, though Marlow knows that Kurtz has "collected, bartered, swindled, or stolen more ivory than all the other agents together." (113) What looms largest in Marlow's imagination is Kurtz's "ability to talk, his words—the gift of expression, the bewildering, the illuminating, the most exalted and the most contemptible, the pulsating stream of light, or the deceitful flow from the heart of an impenetrable darkness." (113-14) Marlow, fearing that it is too late to hear Kurtz speak, experiences a sense of extreme disappointment: "I couldn't have felt more of lonely desolation somehow, had I been robbed of a belief or had missed my destiny in life." (114) He fears at this time that he will never succeed in delving into himself to whatever lay inside him—would never confront the possibility of evil in Kurtz and overcome it, as he does.

Marlow's commitment to Kurtz occurs unconsciously at this moment as he defends his feelings at that point in time to his audience. His manner has offended his listeners and made one of them utter "absurd." Marlow reacts sharply to this utterance: "Why do you sigh in this beastly way, somebody? Absurd? Well, absurd. Good Lord? Mustn't a man ever—" (114) He condemns his auditors's failure to understand his feeling of desolation at the prospect of never hearing Kurtz, and how this feeling echoes in the natives's lament from shore. It is difficult for his listeners to understand a situation they have never experienced. Safely anchored within society, with bodily sustenance and protection nearby, living a so-called normal, civilized life, they cannot appreciate Marlow's position. They live in a society where restraint has been institutionalized and is no longer a matter of individual responsibility. They have never felt as Marlow did about the need to discover who and what he is. They seem oblivious of the fact that in the wilderness, in unfamiliar circumstances, men suffer emotional collapse. It is easy to act in a civilized manner on the streets of London and Paris. The society with its laws and policemen protects us. Acting in a civilized way in other regions of earth is a different matter. In the lawless world of the Congo, Kurtz and Marlow needed personal restraint. In fact, looking back, Marlow praises his own fortitude at that time.

Communication is pictured here as a highly problematic process. Marlow realizes the absurdity of his attempt to communicate but still he continues. He assures his listeners that Kurtz was not dead and that he had the privilege of meeting him later.

Marlow describes his meeting with Kurtz's Intended and exclaims that he "laid the ghost of his (Kurtz's) gifts at last with a lie." (115) He takes this opportunity to relate the essentials of Kurtz's experience. He uses a flash-ahead to describe and comment on Kurtz's appearance and behaviour. When Marlow meets Kurtz in the jungle, the latter is just a disinterred body. Kurtz enters the heart of Africa with the explicit intention of spreading the light of civilization in its dark regions. His dream, however, ends in a nightmare. A solitary, depraved by extreme circumstances, Kurtz raves about "My Intended, my ivory, my station, my river." (116) He thinks himself lord of all he surveys. Ivory plays an important role in the corruption of Kurtz. Marlow recalls that there were heaps of ivory in Kurtz's station.

Kurtz suffers a possession by the powers of evil: the wilderness has absorbed him, "got into his veins, consumed his flesh, and sealed his soul to its own by the inconceivable ceremonies of some devilish initiation." (115) He has literally made himself a kind of devil-god, "taken a high seat amongst the devils of the land," (116) and allowed the natives to deify him. Once humanistic mastermind of inordinate personal energy and intelligence, whose burning idealism has been lost to festering empathy with the jungle, Kurtz now has been installed as a kind of ruthless godhead among cannibals. The fact that he has presided at certain midnight dances where unspeakable rites are offered to him suggests that Kurtz has succumbed to the savagery. The jungle has debilitated the moral fibre of Kurtz, who wants his domination over the natives to continue. The mystery to Marlow is not what belonged to Kurtz; he wants to know the thing that Kurtz belonged to, "how many powers of darkness claimed him for their own." (116) Isolated from the surface routine of organized society, Kurtz has succumbed to the disintegrative powers of the jungle. Marlow emphasizes his own view that man in solitude has only himself to rely upon. Marlow feels that Kurtz's disintegration is the result of his loneliness.

Most of mankind faces the existentialist test of character in lives of action. Marlow confronts his audience directly again. He fears that they cannot comprehend his state of mind. How can they who live so securely and contentedly, with solid pavement under their feet, understand Kurtz and imagine the particular region of first ages a man may wander into by way of solitude and of silence, where no warning voice of a neighbour can be heard ? His listeners cannot understand that isolation robs certain men of those stays of conduct which allow him to survive in civilized society. In the absence of policemen and public opinion, a man must rely on his own innate strength, his own capacity for faithfulness. That is the only way to resist the powers of darkness. Kurtz has failed this test; Marlow will now face it. Solitude without a policeman is the man's testing ground where he must create his own values.

Kurtz is a kind of Everyman; the Kurtzian possibility of evil is universal; the devil is everywhere. Before he dies, Kurtz confides in Marlow something of his background. He is a universal genius and has an international background: all Europe has contributed to his making. His mother was half-English, his father half-French. "Whatever he was, he was not common," (119) is Marlow's verdict on him. Later Kurtz's Intended testifies: "He drew men towards him by what was best in them." (159)

The seventeen-page report that Kurtz has written on a request from the "International Society for the Suppression of Savage Customs" is a mirror of his progressive moral deterioration. The eloquent pamphlet is a proof of his intellectual concern with the ethical code and must have been written before he yielded to corruption. The report is a beautiful piece of writing on methods of civilizing the natives and is filled with burning noble words about the possibility of the white man's bringing practically unbounded good to the natives, appealing to every altruistic sentiment. The report intends to help suppress savage customs. Beginning on an idealistic note, Kurtz's supposed humanistic report ends with a brutally simple postscript: "Exterminate all the brutes!" (118)

Marlow considers it impossible to forget Kurtz, a man with the power to charm or frighten rudimentary souls into worshipping him as a deity. He announces himself as Kurtz's devoted friend.

Marlow misses the helmsman awfully and regrets his death. The helmsman, though a savage, had helped Marlow by steering the ship. Marlow recalls once more "the profundity of the look" on the helmsman's face before he died, a look "like a claim of distant kinship affirmed in a supreme moment." (119) For a moment, Marlow affirms a sense of brotherhood with the savage.[8] But the very next moment, he categorically states that the helmsman, like Kurtz, lacked restraint. The savage gets a sea burial because Marlow decides that if the helmsman were to be eaten, it would be the fishes that would have him, not the cannibals on board.

As they reach near the shore, Marlow meets the extremely gay Russian harlequin, having beardless boyish face and wearing clothes covered with brightly coloured patches. In his initial exchanges, the youth expresses alternate cheer and gloom in such rapid succession that it seems he lacks substance. He waves to Marlow but immediately feels sorry that he is not English and therefore cannot welcome Marlow with the compatriot's affirmative hail.

It is significant to note that Marlow meets the young Russian just before his encounter with Kurtz. This meeting prepares him for the meeting with the fabulous Kurtz.[9] The Russian gives Marlow direct and reliable information about Kurtz. He serves as a kind of guide: first warning Marlow of possible dangers, then disclosing to him the secret significances hidden within the darkness. The Russian leads Marlow to Kurtz and is, in effect, Kurtz's and Marlow's agent.

Marlow feels that the youth's isolation from the world has exposed him to the devilish influence of Kurtz. He is rather incredulous when the boy claims that his jungle experience has been an enlarging one, that Kurtz has opened up to him splendid vistas of moral inspiration. The harlequin holds Kurtz in extreme exaltation. Like Marlow, he is a victim of Kurtz's idealistic eloquence: "You don't talk with that man—you listen to him." (123) Marlow and the harlequin also have the bond of sea between them. Earlier, replying to the manager's threat that the man must be careful to save himself from getting into trouble, Marlow had said: "no man was safe from trouble in this world." (100) With this remark he had allied himself to the harlequin.

The harlequin represents youth, carelessness, freedom from responsibility, and a kind of unintellectual existence that is neither good nor evil. He makes it explicit to Marlow that the natives's attack on the steamer was a result of their poignant concern about the possible departure of Kurtz. The innocent harlequin considers the natives totally harmless but the fate of Kurtz shows that they represent a very real and very subtle danger to the disillusioned man of moral imagination. An epitome of misguided idealistic youth, the harlequin claims our sympathy by helping out Marlow.

At this juncture in the novel, the Russian's existence seems improbable, inexplicable, and absurd to Marlow. He is an enigmatic figure, an insoluble problem, the seeming embodiment of innocence in the darkness. The man is an incomprehensible to Marlow as were his notes in the margin of the book that Marlow found at the abandoned cabin. Marlow admires the Russian for his possession of youth that urges him on, keeps him unscathed. Ruled by the spirit of adventure, the Russian wants nothing from the wilderness but space to breathe in, to move on at the greatest risk and privation. He is a man of indomitable optimism. His devotion to Kurtz, accepted with eager fatalism, is in Marlow's opinion. the most dangerous thing to have happened in his life so far. Despite momentary admiration, Marlow feels that the Russian's wanderings have been futile. The harlequin has escaped the perils of the Inner Station because he is an adventurer, not a colonialist or an idealist.

The Russian is Kurtz's closest companion in the heart of darkness. He has an intimate knowledge of the mysteries surrounding Kurtz. He tells Marlow how he and Kurtz have spent considerable time in discourse, discussing everything, including love. But normally, the Russian informs Marlow, Kurtz wandered alone, far in the depths of the forest, raiding the country for ivory. Once Kurtz had threatened to kill the Russian for a small amount of ivory. He was pacified only when the Russian parted with his ivory—an act representative of the Russian's surrender to Kurtz. He even ordered the Russian to keep out of his way. But the Russian's uncritical adoration of Kurtz is not affected by this. He has a capacity for solidarity and nurses Kurtz through his two illnesses. The thought of Kurtz's fate saddens his Russian admirer. The recklessly generous Russian defends Kurtz on every point because he feels that this man has suffered much. He tells Marlow that Kurtz, that demon of energy, is seriously ill and is lying helpless.

Marlow focuses his binoculars on Kurtz's house, but finds no sign of life there. He notes the ruined roof, the mud wall in the grass, the odd-sized window holes and is rudely shocked to find that the round knobs in front of the house are the heads mounted on posts. Kurtz has placed the decapitated heads of Africans on the posts of his stockaded camp. The sense of corruption and decay repel and yet fascinate Marlow. Kurtz is the victim of his own hubris, and as Marlow understands the phenomenon, "Kurtz lacked restraint in the gratification of his various lusts, that there was something wanting in him—some small matter which . . . could not be found under his magnificent eloquence." (131)

Kurtz has worked in the jungle in a ruthless way and the jungle in its turn has exacted a terrible vengeance for his having dared invade it. It has whispered to him of things of which he had no conception and this has proved irresistibly fascinating to him. The whisper has "echoed loudly within him because he was hollow at the core." (131) The natives adore him and are his willing followers. According to the harlequin, Kurtz hated all this yet he could not break away.

Kurtz represents civilized man driven mad by the temptations of atavism and the lure of the wilderness which ultimately destroys him. The passion for power on the natives has led him astray. Freedom from outer restraint exposes the absence of inner restraint in him. In the wilderness, Kurtz finds himself faced with evil. The temptation towards evil is to be curbed by the inner strength. Kurtz lives isolated from his fellow-creatures and it is in isolation that he has to assert his choice. Released from the social restrictions of organized society, Kurtz has become a victim of the passions, the hidden weaknesses, and his unconscious desires. His rhetoric seduces himself and others. Kurtz has repudiated traditional checks on human nature without acquiring self-control. He lords over the natives, secure in his knowledge that no outside force will restrain him. He lacked restraint, says Marlow, when the pressing need arose. He has failed the test: the wilderness has found him out, has rendered him as hollow as the ivory he has sought. The enormity of the jungle and its power to find Kurtz out terrifies Marlow.

Kurtz's actions seem morally reprehensible to Marlow. The Russian confirms his doubts about Kurtz's devilish practices. He assures Marlow that he has not dared to remove the skulls because of Kurtz's extraordinary power. Even native chiefs crawl before Kurtz. Furious at this revelation, Marlow feels that the thought of pure savagery is a relief when contrasted with what he has just heard about Kurtz: "I seemed at one bound to have been transported into some lightless region of subtle horrors, where pure, uncomplicated savagery was a positive relief." (132) He is shocked at the Russian's protest that the heads on the poles belonged to the executed rebels. He points out that the white exploiters of the African population had assigned the names of enemies, criminals, workers, rebels to the native population. When the Russian defends Kurtz again, Marlow finds himself unable to understand how such a lifc has tried a man like Kurtz. The Russian is trying to keep Kurtz alive, the Kurtz who has been shamefully abandoned. He is faithful to a person if not an idea. The Russian's existence confirms Kurtz's magnetic existence and influence.

As he works his way towards Kurtz, Marlow does not know what lies ahead of him. But after meeting the Russian, the unreality of Kurtz becomes more real to him. Marlow is now ready to meet Kurtz, the object of his journey. He has the first glance of Kurtz when he comes out of the jungle borne on a litter like a king. Marlow is struck by the fire of Kurtz's eyes and his composed langour. Kurtz looks like "an animated image of death carved out of old ivory." (134)

Kurtz is an isolated person. His homeless existence in the Congo has turned him into a fiend. The isolated Kurtz has surrendered to the forces of darkness. He is estranged from the rest of humanity. Abandoned by the society, he finds himself in the predicament of an outcast. Marlow hears the grave, profound, and vibrating voice of Kurtz and admits his ability to expound his noble ideas. Living far inside the darkness of an evil land, Kurtz resents civilization and is unwilling to return. He promises to carry out his ideas yet, in spite of his illness, in spite of the manager's interference. It is Kurtz's belief in ideals that draws Marlow towards him at the outset.

The manager tries to pull Marlow into agreeing with him that it is his duty to report Kurtz in the proper quarter. He tries to rationalize his action: "We have done all we could for him." (137) He accuses Kurtz of having harmed the Company with his unsound methods and finds the atrocities committed by Kurtz wrong. When he tries to wean Marlow's sympathy in the Company's favour, Marlow turns to Kurtz for mental comfort: "It seemed to me I had never breathed an atmosphere so vile, and I turned mentally to Kurtz for relief—positively for relief." (138) He feels almost nauseated with the manager's amoral judgment of Kurtz's atrocities as merely unsound or bad for company business. On grounds of efficiency, Marlow prefers the nightmare of Kurtz to the perverted reason of the manager. He sympathizes with Kurtz though the latter has succumbed to the evil forces. He points it out to the manager: "Nevertheless I think Mr. Kurtz is a remarkable man." (138) With a cold, heavy glare, the manager replies, "He *was*" (138) and turns his back on Marlow. Marlow's hour of favour is over. He is now allied with Kurtz as unsound.

Marlow sums up for his listeners his final commitment to Kurtz when he consoles himself with the remark: "Ah, but it was something to have at least a choice of nightmares." (138) He rejects the pettiness of the manager for the boldness of Kurtz. The nightmare of Kurtz is preferred to the hypocrisy of the manager. As he says this, Marlow feels a sudden kinship not so much with Kurtz, who is as good as buried, but with the wilderness. And for a moment, Marlow feels buried in a grave full of unspeakable secrets. The Russian's comment at this moment is significant: Marlow is Kurtz's friend—in a way. Marlow identifies with Kurtz, an apostle of light. The reason for Marlow's loyalty to his choice is that evil as Kurtz is, he has at least discovered himself, become fully committed. And when self-knowledge is attained, so is freedom—freedom to do anything, good or evil, away from society's directives.

The Russian decides to go away and borrows from Marlow some tobacco, cartridges and a pair of shoes. One pocket bulging with bullets, the other with Towson's book, he considers himself excellently well-equipped for a renewed encounter with the wilderness. Because of his innocence and ignorance, the harlequin retains his illusion of Kurtz's greatness and escapes scotfree. His last words about Kurtz are: "I'll never, never meet such a man again." (140) In spite of his close association with Kurtz and the evil he embodies, the Russian remains triumphant and indestructible as the wilderness absorbs him. He vanishes in the night after shaking hands with Marlow who stresses his phantom-like unreality when he says: "Sometimes I ask myself whether I had ever really seen him—whether it was possible to meet such a phenomenon!" (140)

Marlow pursues, confronts and wrestles with Kurtz as the latter tries to escape Marlow's ship. Shortly after midnight, Marlow is completely unnerved to discover that Kurtz has disappeared from his cabin. He is shocked as if something monstrous has been thrust on him. He experiences a moment of "sheer blank fright, pure abstract terror, unconnected with any distinct shape of physical danger." (141)

Anxious to deal with Kurtz by himself alone, Marlow does not raise an alarm. He makes it very clear where he stands in the choice between two nightmares—the nightmare of blind illusion or the nightmare of glimpsed darkness. He says that it was preordained he should never betray Kurtz: "It was written I should be loyal to the nightmare of my choice." (141) He admits that to this day he does not know why he was jealous of sharing with anyone the peculiar blackness of his experience.

Marlow sees Kurtz creeping on all fours to the savage fires. His style of movement exhibits his incredible degradation; Kurtz has descended to the animal level. As Marlow nears him, the wilderness becomes more powerful. He imagines he will never get back to the steamer, that he will live in the woods to old age. Ultimately, Marlow reaches near Kurtz and stops him. Kurtz rises unsteadily like a vapour exhaled by the earth. As he actually confronts Kurtz, Marlow senses the danger in its right proportion. Kurtz could have shouted to the natives and Marlow would have been in trouble. Marlow tries to stop his advance and questions him if he realizes what he is doing.

To effect Kurtz's return from the nether world, Marlow has no powers except his inborn courage to support him. Some inspiration makes him say the right thing to Kurtz: "You will be lost . . . utterly lost." (143) His inspired words strike home; the words are meaningful because Kurtz is still intellectually allied to an ethical creed. At this very moment, the foundations of a bond between Marlow and Kurtz are laid to endure even to the end.

Marlow's warning seems to unsettle Kurtz who argues that he had immense plans and was on the threshold of great things. Kurtz feels that his plans would be ruined if he returned to the coast. Although his life in Africa is a nightmare and he is suffering intense anguish, Kurtz does not want to go home. Desperately, Marlow threatens to kill Kurtz if he tries to shout. He tries to mollify Kurtz with an assurance of his success in Europe. What Marlow is attempting all this while is to fight the jungle for Kurtz's soul, to break the spell of the wilderness that has awakened Kurtz's brutal instincts, has beguiled his unlawful soul beyond the boundaries of permitted aspirations.

Unlike Kurtz, Marlow does not succumb and is even able to wrest Kurtz from the grasp of the wilderness. He tries to redeem Kurtz. Marlow realizes the danger of this struggle and experiences the loss of values as a loss of his hold on earth itself: "I had to deal with a being to whom I could not appeal in the name of anything high or low. I had . . . to invoke him—himself—his own exalted and incredible degradation. . . . He had kicked himself loose of the earth. Confound the man! he had kicked the very earth to pieces." (144) To retrieve Kurtz that night, Marlow has to appeal to the evil lurking in the man who stands free from all judgment. Wrestling with the soul of Kurtz, he does not lose his self-possession. Isolated from the society, Marlow confronts the challenge of Kurtz alone and emerges victorious.

The argument rages between Kurtz and Marlow. Marlow struggles with Kurtz's soul to save him. Kurtz's intelligence is clear but it seems that his soul has gone mad. Marlow experiences authentic pain at this moment and tells his listeners: "Being alone in the wilderness, it (Kurtz's soul) had looked within itself, and, by heavens! I tell you, it had gone mad. I had—for my sins, I suppose—to go through the ordeal of looking into it myself." (145) In the process, Marlow sees "the inconceivable mystery of a soul that knew no restraint, no faith, and no fear, yet struggling blindly with itself." (145) Kurtz has transformed into an egoistic and hollow source of darkness rather than light. He owes no allegiance to anything except those animal powers, those various lusts. Marlow also responds to these callings. Indeed he almost becomes their captive. But he does not slip over the edge as Kurtz does. Marlow keeps to the track. Confronted with the ultimate evil, he has the restraint to get on with the job. Marlow is finally able to persuade Kurtz to return to the steamer couch from which he had fled.

As they steam downstream the next day, Kurtz's barbarous and superb native mistress remains on the shore, her bare arms stretched tragically. Racing swiftly out of the heart of darkness, Marlow feels that Kurtz would soon die. After Kurtz's death, Marlow will be the only survivor of the party of unsound method. He has been lumped together with Kurtz as one of the new breed, the breed of idealists. Marlow grudgingly accepts this "unforeseen partnership" (147) forced on him by the pilgrims. With his choice of the nightmare, Marlow has forged a symbolic relationship with Kurtz. So his concern with Kurtz's reputation grows and he does everything possible to protect it.

As they progress seaward, Kurtz discourses. Marlow is hypnotized by his eloquence. His voice seems to Marlow stronger than he himself, serving to hide in its folds the evil, the barren darkness within him. His talk is haunted by shadowy images of wealth and fame. Kurtz had gone into the jungle with the illusion that endless good was possible. He retains his sense of omnipotence and thinks of kings coming to meet him at railway stations on his return. As Marlow looks down at Kurtz, he seems to him like a man lying at the bottom of a precipice where the sun never shines. It was a civilized European Kurtz that went to the Congo, but now Marlow is not hopeful about him.

Marlow is rewarded for his tenacity at the moment of Kurtz's death. This is the culmination point of Marlow's experience, the heart of the darkness, and a sign of darkness within himself. One evening, Marlow stands in nearby attendance to Kurtz, awaiting death. During this climactic confrontation with Kurtz, Marlow notices a change come over Kurtz's features. Fascinated, he gazes at Kurtz's expression, compounded "of sombre pride, of ruthless power, of craven terror—of an intense and hopeless despair." (141) At this moment, Kurtz's face becomes the very portrait of the possibility of human depravity. And then, as at some vision, Kurtz cries out: "The horror! The horror!" (141)

This is Kurtz's supreme moment of complete knowledge.[10] His words of truth rend the veil of illusions—the illusions that had brought him out to the jungle. These words are uttered in recognition of the depths of depravity into which his ideals have led him. That Kurtz is aware of his actions is supported by this statement. Marlow considers it to be Kurtz's pronunciation of a judgment upon the adventures of his soul. Kurtz has not only perceived the truth of his existence but also judged it.

The meaning of Kurtz and his expression of horror are central to the theme of inward journey, perhaps the most significant aspect of Marlow's tale. What Kurtz attains at the point of his death is transmitted through Marlow's extended narrative. Kurtz's instantaneous vision makes him aware of the illusion of man's institutions, the vainness of his knowledge. What Kurtz perceives within himself is not so much evil but a void—a world much like the jungle he sees without. In a letter to Cunninghame Graham, Conrad used the image of a vast knitting machine to convey his vision of the unreasoning universe, a machine "which knits us in and knits us out. It has knitted time, space, pain, death, corruption, despair and all the illusions,—and nothing matters."[11]

Marlow feels that Kurtz is vindicated by a full emotional realization of his experience just before he dies. Even if it is too late for redemption in this life, the realization itself is a victory of some sort. It lends dignity to the terrible destiny of Kurtz's ideal. Kurtz mouths his last words as a message to himself and, through Marlow, to the world. He has not really explained himself to Marlow before his final exclamation. Through Marlow's summary and moral reactions, we come to a sense of possibilities of meaning rather than definite meaning. Marlow himself has glimpsed the "horror" and acts as a surrogate for his listeners. The message is more Marlow's than it is Kurtz's.

With his final words, Kurtz regains in part the moral universe from which he had fallen. To Marlow, Kurtz's final words are an affirmation because Kurtz has perceived not only what has happened to him, but also what he has become. Kurtz's last cry is described by the impressed Marlow as possessing "a vibrating note of revolt in its whisper" and as an "expression of some sort of belief . . . an affirmation, a moral victory paid for by innumerable defeats, by abominable terrors, by abominable satisfactions." (151)[12] Marlow discovers that human spirit is indeed stronger than the powers of darkness.

Through this existential encounter with Kurtz, Marlow gains valuable knowledge about himself, the nature of evil and the world. This knowledge is accompanied by a sense of isolation and also brings about a change in his character and behaviour. However he accepts the world as it is, in spite of his disillusionment with it.

The severe ordeal in which Kurtz fails enlightens Marlow finally as to the evil in human nature. When ill and fighting his battle with death, Marlow realizes that Kurtz's moral triumph is peculiarly his own. It is not his own experience but that of Kurtz which affords this insight. Marlow shares the test undergone by Kurtz whose tragic fall becomes Marlow's ordeal: "It is his extremity that I seem to have lived through." (151) Marlow himself does not die but is spared to show his loyalty to Kurtz once more.

In philosophizing about life, Marlow spells out the meaninglessness of existence: "Droll thing life is—that mysterious arrangement of merciless logic for a futile purpose." (150) It is a definition of Conrad's almost existential pessimism. Feeling frustrated with life and the human condition, Marlow experiences the anguish of being and comments: "The most you can hope from it (life) is some knowledge of yourself—

that comes too late—a crop of inextinguishable regrets." (150) It seems that here Marlow has given us a clue to Kurtz's cry. Though Kurtz has achieved self-knowledge, it is too late and he dies amid "inextinguishable regrets."

Marlow's struggle with death takes place "in an impalpable grayness, with nothing underfoot, with nothing around, without spectators, without clamour, without glory, without the great desire of victory, without the great fear of defeat, in a sickly atmosphere of tepid scepticism, without much belief in your own right, and still less in that of your adversary." (150) Though Marlow does not die, he remembers "a passage through some inconceivable world that had no hope in it and no desire." (152) Across the very brink of the grave, Marlow finds that he has nothing to say: "I was within a hair's-breadth of the last opportunity for pronouncement, and I found with humiliation that probably I would have nothing to say. This is the reason why I affirm that Kurtz was a remarkable man. He had something to say. He said it." (151) More than his own struggle with death, Marlow seems to have lived through Kurtz's extremity, except that Kurtz stepped over the edge whereas Marlow has been permitted to draw back his hesitating foot. He realizes that perhaps it was the reality of death that enabled Kurtz make the pronouncement: "perhaps all the wisdom, and all truth, and all sincerity, are just compressed into that inappreciable moment of time in which we step over the threshold of the invisible." (151) A complete knowledge of truth comes only after death. In that short moment which divides life from death lies all the difference. It is this that makes Marlow's partial knowledge differ from Kurtz's supreme view. Through his heroic struggle of attaining self-knowledge, Kurtz has shown to Marlow a moral standard by which to live.

Kurtz dies but Marlow must return to Europe to face the Intended, to live with his knowledge, and to tell his tale to the director of companies, the lawyer, and the accountant.[13] He narrates his disorientation upon return to Europe. Back in Brussels, he resents the sight of people hurrying through the streets. A significant change in his world-view has taken place. His Congo experience has given him such tremendous insight that he cannot communicate with the bulk of mankind. They do not understand, *cannot* understand, as they have not faced the darkness. They have not looked over the edge as Marlow has. Their knowledge of life is superficial, an irritating pretence. Indeed, most of them are unaware that the darkness exists. As Marlow comments: "I felt so sure they could not possibly know the things I knew." (152) He knows so much more than those he sees in the Brussels streets; he is possessed of knowledge.

Marlow goes to meet Kurtz's radiant and deluded Intended to hand over to her, Kurtz's slim packet of letters and the girl's portrait. He finds it difficult to analyze the reason of his personal visit: "Perhaps it was an impulse of unconscious loyalty, or the fulfilment of one of these ironic necessities that lurk in the facts of human existence." (155)

The Intended's house creates an atmosphere of waste and sterile futility. Very significantly, the house is situated on a street as still and decorous as a well-kept alley in a cemetery. Struck by the deathlike-quality of the place, Marlow experiences a sudden recollection of Kurtz, a vision of him on the stretcher, his mouth wide open "voraciously, as if to devour all the earth with all its mankind." (155) Part of the vision seems to enter the house, as if Marlow himself were bringing darkness into the house. Kurtz's life and death become simultaneous to Marlow.

The Intended, a figure of unblemished purity and devotion, enters the room all in black. She has been mourning since Kurtz's death more than a year ago. The grief-stricken girl has a mature capacity for fidelity, for belief, for suffering. Her glance is open and trustful. She bemoans Kurtz's loss to the world, to her personally. The intensity of her grief reminds Marlow of Kurtz's death: "I saw her and him in the same instant of time—his death and her sorrow—I saw her sorrow in the very moment of his death. . . . I saw them together—I heard them together." (157) Kurtz's death, for her, seems to have happened only yesterday, so deep is her grief. Unable to understand the logic of existence, Marlow experiences a moment of panic and wishes he had not come there: "I asked myself what I was doing there, with a sensation of panic in my heart as though I had blundered into a place of cruel and absurd mysteries not fit for a human being to behold." (157)

The Intended is an idealist who asserts during the conversation that it was impossible for anyone to know Kurtz and not to admire him. She is sure that Kurtz drew men towards him by what was best in them. Her forehead illumined by unextinguishable light of belief and love, the Intended talks easing her pain in the certitude of Marlow's sympathy. With despair in his heart, Marlow is forced to bow his head "before the faith that was in her, before that great and saving illusion that shone with an unearthly glow in the darkness, in the triumphant darkness from which I could not have defended her—from which I could not even defend myself." (159) The situation robs Marlow of his keen sense of the possibility of moral triumph.

The Intended pleads with Marlow to relay Kurtz's last words, for she needs something to live with. Under pressure from forces within and without which seek to control him, Marlow is confronted with a choice: he can tell the truth to preserve his commitment and honour, or he can tell a lie and save the young woman's illusions. Under this extraordinary pressure, he restrains himself and says slowly that Kurtz had died speaking her name. He sustains her illusion by feeding it with a lie.

The reality of existence is too menacing, too dangerous. Marlow saves the woman the agony of knowing what Kurtz really said, and thus saves probably her very existence. His answer satisfies her need and, uttering an exulting and terrible cry of inconceivable triumph and of unspeakable pain, the Intended exclaims: "I knew it—I was sure!" (162) The lie makes Marlow feel so guilty that it seems to him that the heavens are about to fall upon his head. On the face of it, it seems an act of moral failure. In telling a lie, Marlow participates in death. Emphasizing the significance of truth, he had said earlier: "There is a taint of death, a flavour of mortality in lies—which is exactly what I hate and detest in the world." (82) But Marlow could not have told her the truth for that "would have been too dark—too dark altogether." (162) The Intended could not have faced the reality of life.

Marlow takes cover in a lie, in an illusion, so that the Intended's fantasy world is not shaken—he tells a lie for her sake. To protect the Intended, he forsakes his own idealistic commitment to truth, honour and justice. The springs of his action are loyalty to Kurtz, pity for the Intended, despair for himself. At this moment, he proclaims his own values and acts according to them.[14] It may be noted that although in lying he acts deliberately, Marlow does not act freely, because the need of lying is dictated to him by the circumstances. He does what the situation demands. If he does not tell a lie, his Congo experience and Kurtz's life will lose all their value. Marlow's lie thus is a heroic action. He fulfils his responsibility towards Kurtz by telling this lie. Through this authentic decision, Marlow becomes his unique self.

It is difficult to accept F.R. Leavis's view that the last scene weakens the novel. The final episode was important not only to the structure and meaning of *Heart of Darkness* but also to the novelist himself. In a letter to William Blackwood three years after he had penned the last pages, Conrad stresses this aspect of his method:

> . . . in the light of the final incident the whole story in all its descriptive detail shall fall into its place—acquire its value and its significance. This is my method based on deliberate conviction . .

. the last pages of Heart of Darkness where the interview of the man and the girl locks in as it were—the whole 30,000 words of narrative description into one suggestive view of a whole phase of life, and makes of that story something quite on another plane than an anecdote of a man who went mad in the Centre of Africa.[15]

The phrase "locks in" is important. By the device of the last scene, Conrad shows us the interdependence of all values which makes the predicament relevant to us.

Marlow's lie has been treated as an enigma by various critics.[16] It presumably reflects the change in Marlow's state of mind after the experience with Kurtz. His loyalty to Kurtz is the most significant choice that Marlow makes during the course of the story. He feels that this contains the forbidden, secret knowledge that lies hidden beneath the surface appearance of existence. Kurtz's realization of the forces of evil in his own being makes Marlow discover a potential hell in the hearts of all men. Marlow finally accounts for Kurtz when he tells a lie to the Intended. He chooses the human over that which would destroy the human. He does not want to shatter the Intended's faith. In telling a lie, Marlow affirms those very few simple ideas which give significance to human existence. The epigraph which Conrad chose for the *Youth* volume confirms this:

. . . but the Dwarf answered:
"No—something human is dearer
to me than the wealth of all the world." (1)

As Marlow sits apart, after finishing the tale, we know that something has ended. Not only Marlow's narration, but something of life. Kurtz will live on, in Marlow and in many others.

III

Lord Jim brings out existential truths about the nature of man and of moral behaviour. The existential truths are not easily stated; they must be groped for by the reader; in this novel, they are groped for by the questioning protagonists—Jim and Marlow. Throughout, Jim is engaged in the deeper quest of why he acted as he did. He does not fully understand the complex reasons for his act, although he senses some of the truth. The rest he may search out with the help of Marlow, and this search constitutes the major action.

The main concern of the novel is Jim's attempt to be authentic, "to lounge safely through existence." (viii) Marlow voices an existential concern soon after he is introduced into the story as a narrator-observer: "Of course there are men here and there to whom the whole of life is like an after-dinner hour with a cigar; easy, pleasant, empty, perhaps enlivened by some fable of strife to be forgotten before the end is told—before the end is told—even if there happens to be any end to it." (35) Jim's life is not unauthentic like this, nor of Marlow's for that matter.

The main incident which Conrad uses as his plot kernel for *Lord Jim* is the case of the pilgrim ship *Jeddah* which set out from Singapore in 1880 and experienced much the same fate as the *Patna*. Her officers deserted her in much the same manner and the scandal of the *Jeddah* affair was the talk of eastern seaports. Conrad must have heard the story when he first touched at Singapore in 1883 and utilizes it in *Lord Jim* fifteen years later when William Blackwood asked for a long story. He realized that the pilgrim ship episode was an event "which could conceivably colour the whole 'sentiment of existence' in a simple and sensitive character." (35)

The novel opens with a description of Jim dressed in immaculate white from shoes to hat. His existence at this point in time is unauthentic. Jim earns his living as a ship-outfitter's water-clerk in various eastern seaports. The peculiarity about Jim is that although he is very efficient and very much in demand, he never sticks to any job. He seems to be running away from some incident in his past and a reference to it makes him leave the seaport where he is working and move onward, generally further East. His consciousness of guilt makes him go from one place to another. In his flight from one place to another, he has lost his identity and is reluctant to reveal his last name.

Unable to take decisions in life, Jim drifts away from life and becomes a detached person. His inner life becomes a dream world: "They (the dreams) were the best parts of life, its secret truth, its hidden reality." (21) His fondness for the light holiday literature about the sea has contributed to the imaginative frame of his mind. During his sea journeys, Jim spends much of his time day-dreaming about imaginary feats of heroism. He wishes to experience the romance and adventure of "saving people from sinking ships, cutting away masts in the hurricane, swimming through a surf with a line . . . always an example of devotion to duty, and as unflinching as a hero in a book." (6)[17]

Conrad focuses attention on a moment in Jim's past when he

showed a curious lack of decision and action. On board the training ship, Jim met his first test of courage. During a storm, the trainees were called on to launch a boat to pick up survivors of a collision. The indecisive Jim hesitated to jump into the boat and was left behind on deck. He was paralyzed when a call to real action came. Lost in his reveries, he found it difficult to make the transition from the world of fancy to the world of fact.

Jim's predilection for dreams of heroism dulled his ability to participate in the world of action."He stood still"—Conrad twice repeats the phrase. Jim felt like leaping overboard but the restraining hand of the captain stopped him. Subsequently, he justified to himself his own inaction and came to the conclusion that he was not really afraid or fearful, but was capable of heroic actions. He put the blame on Nature for taking advantage of him: "He felt angry with the brutal tumult of earth and sky for taking him unawares and checking unfairly a generous readiness for narrow escapes." (9) Jim does not learn anything about his character from this incident.[18] Rather than criticise himself, he rationalizes his behaviour by consoling himself that in a greater crisis he would be prepared: "When all men flinched, then—he felt sure—he alone would know how to deal with the spurious menace of wind and seas." (9) He exults in a sense of many-sided courage. Alienated from the community, Jim takes refuge in dreams.

Jim has the central experience of his life on the *Patna*, an old iron ship, engaged in transporting eight hundred pilgrims to their holy land. He has no understanding of the hardships of life on the sea, its dangers, hard work and struggle. He has become "chief mate of a fine ship without ever having been tested by those events of the sea that show in the light of day the inner worth of a man, the edge of his temper and the fibre of his stuff; that reveal the quality of his resistance and the secret truth of his pretences, not only to others, but also to himself." (10)

The *Patna*'s steady journey across the placid sea allows Jim to live quite isolated. Nature seems to be in perfect harmony with man. Conrad shows the stillness and peace of the eastern seas. Jim's thoughts are full of valorous deeds and heroic adventures and produce a marvellous sense of confidence in him. He sighs with contentment and feels "the great certitude of unbounded safety and peace." (17) There is nothing he cannot face.

Jim remains sublimely unaware that the manifest incompetence of his fellow officers saddles him with an added burden of responsibility. He exists under the delusion that he is superior to them and waits for an opportunity of heroic action. He listens in languid indifference as the skipper and the second engineer quarrel and freely hurl abuses at each other. He does nothing to stop the macabre row and despises them as they do not belong to his world of heroic adventure. He remains aloof, calmed by the assurance that "the quality of these men did not matter; he rubbed shoulders with them, but they could not touch him; he shared the air they breathed, but he was different." (24-25) The sea, which was 'without a ripple, without a wrinkle—viscous, stagnant, dead' before the collision, threatens to disrupt the calm surface of their orderly existence. The ship quivers; the crewmen are thrown headlong. They hear a deep rumbling below, like remote thunder, as they look first at the undisturbed level of the sea and then upwards at the stars. The *Patna* has collided with a submerged derelict. The skipper feels that the ship has come to a standstill. The two Malays working at the wheels find that the wheels will not move. The engines have stopped.

Conrad's technique of time-shift keeps the existential act, one of the novel's most important elements, constantly before the reader's eyes. The scene shifts abruptly to the official hearing convened to investigate the incidents which occurred on the *Patna* after the collision. A month has passed since the accident and the Inquiry is under way in the police court of an eastern port. The three judges question Jim, the only white crew member of the *Patna* who faced the Inquiry. Before the court, he is guilty of desertion, of having violated the seaman's code of conduct. Jim feels humiliated and quite ill-at-ease and his answers shape themselves in pain and misery. He is a trapped and cornered man. He feels attentive eyes stabbing him. The court wants facts, the exact story of what happened, but Jim could not give facts.

Conrad was convinced of the meaninglessness of facts. In a letter to Sir Hugh Clifford, he wrote: "Moreover, you know my opinion—that criticism is a vain thing against a man's conception as to life, character, morality and whatever else goes to make up the only truth that matters. Criticism can only be applied usefully to facts—which don't matter."[19] An incident has to be approached through different angles to get at the truth. Jim feels that mere facts can never explain this affair and is exasperated at the misdirected Official Inquiry: "They wanted facts. Facts! They demanded facts from him, as if facts could explain anything!" (29) Jim tries to tell the truth but the judges, in their appetite for mere factual information, repeatedly interrupt him. To determine guilt, they demand only "facts." The absurdity of their demand completely eludes them. Later Marlow tells us that the important thing would have been to inquire into"the state of a man's soul," (57) since only the individual can be the ultimate judge of his actions. Jim feels trapped as no one realizes the true situation:

> His mind positively flew round and round the serried circle of facts that had surged up all about him to cut him off from the rest of his kind: it was like a creature that, finding itself imprisoned within an enclosure of high stakes, dashes round and round, distracted in the night, trying to find a weak spot, a crevice, a place to scale, some opening through which it may squeeze itself and escape. (31)

It is Jim's capacity for moral anguish that sets him apart. In the midst of his frustration, Jim sees a white man, sitting apart from others, who seems to be aware of his difficulty in explaining the incident. This man is Marlow who with quiet eyes glances straight, interested, and clear; his glance is not a "fascinated stare" but rather "an act of intelligent volition." (32-33) Marlow, a spectator at the trial, easily identifies with the young seaman since both he and Jim are Englishmen. Jim looks at him, then turns away resolutely, "as after a final parting." (33)

Jim is determined to expiate the failure which he feels has thrust itself upon him in some inexplicable way. Marlow admires him for voluntarily submitting himself to the trial: "I became positive in my mind that the inquiry was a severe punishment to Jim, and that his facing it—practically of his own free will—was a redeeming feature in his abominable case." (68) Jim shows extraordinary courage in owning up his conduct. Of the four who deserted the ship, Jim alone is left to face the court. The others disappear from the scene. The captain quits the port altogether. Both the engineers land up in the hospital where one develops *delirius tremens* and the other manages to sneak out of the city. By deciding to face the Inquiry, Jim dissociates himself from the group: "I couldn't clear out.... The skipper did... I couldn't, and I wouldn't. They all got out of it in one way or another, but it wouldn't do for me." (79) Jim protests that he is not one of them; he is altogether of another sort.

Marlow also does not include Jim in that group of men and women of "that good, stupid kind": "This has nothing to do with Jim, directly; only he was outwardly so typical of that good, stupid kind we like to feel marching right and left of us in life, of the kind that is not disturbed by the vagaries of intelligence and the perversions of—of nerves, let us say." (43-44) Marlow categorizes Jim into that type of young men whom Marlow the mentor has trained on numerous ships: "the kind of fellow you would, on the strength of his looks, leave in charge of the deck—figuratively and professionally speaking." (44)

Outwardly Jim seems to be the ideal representative of certain virtues that Marlow most admires. He appears trustworthy and reliable, but he has already shown his vulnerability. He has been guilty of the most shameful conduct in deserting the ship. He looks as genuine as a new sovereign, but Marlow knows that there is some infernal alloy in his metal. How much, that is what he wants to ascertain.

Marlow cannot explain his curiosity about this *Patna* business, but it seems to the reader that Marlow is searching for some extenuating circumstance, a redeeming motive, some merciful explanation of Jim's cowardly act. He is trying to discover why Jim has shown such weakness. Marlow feels an attraction that becomes a personal involvement:

> Perhaps, unconsciously, I hoped I would find that something, some profound and redeeming cause, some merciful explanation, some convincing shadow of an excuse. I see well enough now that I hoped for the impossible—for the laying of what is the most obstinate ghost of man's creation, of the uneasy doubt uprising like a mist, secret and gnawing like a worm, and more chilling than the certitude of death—the doubt of the sovereign power enthroned in a fixed standard of conduct. . . . I was . . . looking for a miracle. (450-51)

Marlow is unable to explain why he was going into the details of the affair and wonders at his obsession to prove Jim right: "Was it for my own sake that I wished to find some shadow of an excuse for that young fellow whom I had never seen before?" (51) He feels that the object of the Inquiry is to determine not the all important fundamental "why" but the superficial "how" of the affair.

Jim's process of self-discovery is aided by the experiences and actions of other characters. In keeping with this, before giving us the details about his conversation with Jim, Marlow brings up Brierly's suicide. Montague Brierly is one of the assessors on the Board of Inquiry. Already in command of the *Ossa* at the age of thirty-two, he seems the epitome of maritime success: "He had never in his life made a mistake, never had an accident, never a mishap, never a check in his steady rise, and he seemed to be one of those lucky fellows who know nothing of indecision, much less of self-mistrust." (57) But the same Brierly commits suicide by jumping from the deck of the *Ossa* within a week of the *Patna* Inquiry. His suicide is not an impulsive act, but a perfectly planned one.

Jim's behaviour of deserting the ship, contrary to the traditions of the merchant service, exposes Brierly to the doubt of his own infallibility in similar circumstances. The proceedings of the court make Brierly impatient. He asks Marlow: "What's the use of it? . . . Why are we tormenting that young chap?" (65-66) and subsequently offers two hundred rupees to furnish Jim with the means of escape. He is certainly disturbed by Jim's case. "Such an affair destroys one's confidence," (68) says Brierly. He sees an image of his own self in the accused. His identification with Jim provokes his suicide. Brierly has admitted to himself that in a test similar to Jim's, he too might have failed. The incident shatters his faith in the maritime code and he takes recourse to this desperate act. Brierly cannot live after such self-knowledge.

Brierly goes through a kind of agony during the hearing, feeling himself as much on trial as Jim.[20] Marlow is right when, speculating on Brierly's motives, he says that while listening to Jim's case "he was probably holding silent inquiry into his own case. The verdict must have been of unmitigated guilt, and he took the secret of the evidence with him in that leap into the sea." (58) Brierly is driven to suicide because Jim's predicament compels him to recognize that his own life has been empty of true honour.

Jim realizes that he has failed to execute his responsibility. His desertion of the *Patna* was an impulsive act. Having acted impulsively, he broods self-consciously over it. He is extremely intolerant of any reminder or insinuation of his guilt in the past. That Jim is painfully sensitive about his guilt is brought out in his very first meeting with Marlow. After a session of the Inquiry, Jim threatens Marlow and accuses him of having insulted him by referring to him as "a wretched cur." Marlow tries to assure Jim that the remark had no reference to him. But the incident has revealed to Marlow Jim's involuntary acknowledgement of guilt. Marlow reflects: "There had never been a man so mercilessly shown up by his own natural impulse. A single word had stripped him of his discretion—of that discretion which is more necessary to the decencies of our inner being than clothing is to the decorum of our body." (74)

Jim feels isolated and lonely during the course of the Inquiry. His act of cowardice has cut him off from the society. He is to endure the humiliation and embarrassment of realising that his jump was not necessary. He is to live in a society which condemns him for his act. He needs somebody in whom he can confide. In his epigraph to *Lord Jim*,

Conrad writes: "It is certain any conviction gains infinitely the moment another soul will believe in it." (1) Jim narrates the story of his abandonment of the *Patna* to Marlow because it is a relief to him to "make a clean breast of it to an elder man." (128) Jim is in search of a sympathetic soul; he wants to be understood: "I don't want to excuse myself; but I would like to explain—I would like somebody to understand—somebody—one person at least!" (81)

While narrating Jim's experiences, Marlow realizes that communication is a difficult task. He describes the solitariness experienced by men and women in their relationship:

> It is when we try to grapple with another man's intimate need that we perceive how incomprehensible, wavering, and misty are the beings that share with us the sight of the stars and the warmth of the sun. It is as if loneliness were a hard and absolute condition of existence; the envelope of flesh and blood on which our eyes are fixed melts before the outstretched hand, and there remains only the capricious, unconsolable, and elusive spirit that no eye can follow, no hand can grasp. (179-80)

Marlow acknowledges his uncertainties, his feeling that he sees only the surfaces, beyond which he occasionally glimpses, a reality he can never fully know. He realizes that what is not oneself is unknowable.

Like Sartre, Conrad believes that communication is a cumbersome and painful process. It is a problem that adds a great deal to the fact of man's tragic isolation from others. In *Chance*, Marlow challenges his listeners thus: "How many sympathetic souls can you reckon on in the world? One in ten, one in a hundred—in a thousand—in ten thousand? Ah! What a sell these confessions are! What a horrible sell! You seek sympathy, and all you get is the most evanescent sense of relief—if you get that much." (212) Jim is confined to the solitariness of self and feels hopelessly alone in the world. He reiterates how hard it is to express his true meaning and finds language itself to be an inadequate and imperfect medium to communicate. Words seem to fail Jim when he tries to express his gratitude for Marlow's sympathetic attention to his story. (128) Marlow makes it clear to the reader that even Jim cannot be trusted fully as a source of knowledge because he cannot explain in clear terms why he had jumped. Marlow maintains: "It is my belief no man ever understands quite his own artful dodges to escape from the grim shadow of self-knowledge." (80)

The reader sees Jim through Marlow's sympathetic eyes and emotions. Marlow does not claim to understand Jim because he catches only fragmentary glimpses of his inner self as through the shifting rents in a thick fog. He is puzzled by the young man's attitude but catches glimpses of his tormented soul. Marlow asks Jim how he felt to be in the witness stand. The response is shockingly immediate. Jim clutches at Marlow's hand, glares fixedly, and bursts out in a muffled voice: "It is—hell." (78) Marlow advises Jim to run away and thus avoid the rest of the trial. But Jim cannot even dream of such a thing. He is not a coward though he has seemingly committed a cowardly act.

Although Jim resents his jump from the *Patna*, yet it is an action that he himself has done. He had a choice before him: he could have remained on the boat and proved himself a hero. As he narrates his story to Marlow, his eager mind darts forward to what might have happened had he stayed by the ship: "Ah! what a chance missed!" (83) He feels sorry to have missed a chance to be heroic.

Like existentialists, Marlow will judge Jim according to the subjective and private values. He understands the threat of ideas and therefore is not going to judge Jim according to the fixed maritime code of conduct:

> Hang ideas! They are tramps, vagabonds, knocking at the backdoor of your mind, each taking a little of your substance, each carrying away some crumb of that belief in a few simple notions you must cling to if you want to live decently and would like to die easy. (43)

Conrad's belief in the autonomous conscience is best expressed in his words to Edward Noble: "Everyone must walk in the light of his own heart's gospel. No man's light is good to any of his fellows. That's my creed from beginning to end. That's my view of life,—a view that rejects all formulas, dogmas and principles of other people's making."[21]

During dinner at the Malabar House, Jim begins his story of the *Patna*'s last moments. He insists that he was not afraid of death, but was appalled by the hopelessness of the situation. Marlow realizes that Jim was scared not of a quiet, ordinary death, but of death in the midst of that panicked throng. Commanded by the captain to go below to assess the damage, Jim sees the iron bulkhead actually bulge and a flake of rust as big as the palm of his hand fall off the plate. He is convinced that the ship would immediately sink if the bulkhead were to collapse. Mesmerized by the spectre of death, Jim looks at the sleeping pilgrims all around him: "They *were* dead! Nothing could save them! There were boats enough for half of them perhaps, but there was no time. No time! No time!" (86)

Jim is overcome by the absurdity of the situation. Finding sea oppressively present on all sides, he registers the enormity of the situation. He is lost in the overwhelming scene of nature. His imagination magnifies the dangers of the situation and fills him with imaginary fears and terrors. His first thought is to cut loose the lifeboats so that they could pick up as many pilgrims as may be found swimming. He finds the captain and the mate trying to sneak out in a boat and refuses to help them. He realizes that the last moment has come and still he does not move. He sees the futility of making any attempts at saving the pilgrims and remains immobilized—a silent spectator of the whole scene. His dream-making lulls him into inaction. In fact, during the crisis, he is left doing nothing. He fails to rise to the exigencies of the situation.

Marlow sees that Jim is speaking, not to him, but before him "in a dispute with an invisible personality, an antagonistic and inseparable partner of his existence—another possessor of his soul." (93) He is talking to his own guilty conscience with which he pleads for justification. It is his attempt to find out the true essence of life. As Conrad writes in *Nostromo:* "A transgression, a crime, entering man's existence, eats it up like a malignant growth, consumes it like a fever." (523)

When Marlow sharply reminds Jim that the unexpected always happens, the latter mutters that everything has betrayed him—the water, the ship, the men. He insists that he was not ready for what happened; he was not prepared. He feels that the unexpected nature of the emergency put an unfair burden on his will and that he has been tricked by the mysterious forces of nature. We find that Jim is doing just as he did back on the training ship when his terror of the storm kept him back from his assigned place in the cutter.

Jim describes the circumstances in which, overwhelmed by the menace of nature, he had jumped from the *Patna*. The ship seems on the verge of sinking. While Jim stands apart, the other white officers are furiously active, trying for self-survival. At last they are successful in launching a lifeboat. They call for George, the third engineer, to jump not knowing that he has already collapsed. Jim stands at the railing directly above them. He cannot see anything; it is pitch dark. The first blast of the squall hits the *Patna* and she begins a low plunge. The continued calls of the men in the boat for George work on Jim's nerves and, in a moment of dazed confusion, he jumps over the railing.

Jim does not make a conscious decision to jump into the lifeboat but suddenly discovers that he has jumped. His jump is an instinctive reaction to the calls of the deserters and he is pained to realize this: " 'I had jumped. . . .' He checked himself, averted his gaze. . . . 'It seems,' he added." And Marlow mutters: "Looks like it." (111) Jim relates the jump as if it had been an involuntary act; he never admits that he decided to jump. His immediate thought is: "I wished I could die. . . . There was no going back. It was as if I had jumped into a well—into an everlasting deep hole." (111) For Jim, a moment's indiscretion entails a lifetime of regret. He has fallen from his exalted heights. His action has carved out his destiny.

It is significant to note here that the two Malay helmsmen represent that tradition of reliability, efficiency and trust which Jim has betrayed. Totally devoid of imagination, they remain undisturbed by all the activity on board. They keep on working at the wheel as if nothing has happened. They stick to their duty; they stay on board. During the Inquiry when they are asked what they thought at that crucial time, one of them is interpreted thus: "He says he thought nothing." (98) The helmsmen did not leave the helm as they were not ordered to. They cannot believe that the white men fled through fear of death.

Jim is brought down as much by internal weakness as by the force of circumstance. Conrad stresses the complete aloneness of Jim at that moment of terror, his helplessness before the unexpected forces of circumstance. During the crisis at the *Patna*, Jim stands proudly aloof, resolved to go down with the ship. He isolates himself from the rest of the crew and is contemptuous of other members's eagerness to save their own lives at the expense of the passengers. As Marlow comments: "It is more than probable he thought himself cut off from them by a space that could not be traversed, by an obstacle that could not be overcome, by a chasm without bottom. He was as far as he could get from them—the whole breadth of the ship." (103-4)

The four men abandon the pilgrims to their fate. The *Patna* and the small lifeboat are quickly driven apart in the squall. Jim is disturbed, for he has failed to live up to the expectation of himself and others. Marlow speculates: "I believe that, in this first moment, his heart was wrung with all the suffering, that his soul knew the accumulated savour of all the fear, all the horror, all the despair of eight hundred human beings pounced upon in the night by a sudden and violent death." (113) Marlow begins to see the enormity of Jim's burden, the unforgiven guilt on his conscience. He begins to understand the young man's capacity for compassion and cries out: "Wasn't he true to himself, wasn't he?" (114-15) Jim communicates his anguish over his failure in his query to Marlow: "Isn't it awful a man should be driven to do a thing like that—and be responsible?" (119) Marlow is swayed; Jim appears innocent. Marlow begins to feel that in some vague way life has let Jim down.

Marlow sympathizes with Jim because he has also experienced aloneness and futility in a hostile and indifferent universe. He not only sympathizes but also declares: "I was moved to make a solemn declaration of my readiness to believe implicitly anything he thought fit to tell me." (127) Throughout the narration, Jim is trying to bring Marlow to his side, to win from him a gesture of absolution. Marlow is moved by Jim's belief in his own words—his sincere attempt to be absolutely honest with himself; but he is also aware of the unsoundness of the man.

Marlow feels irritated at Jim's effort to minimize the enormity of what he has done. Having identified himself with Jim, Marlow feels cheated: "Don't you see what I mean by the solidarity of the craft? I was aggrieved against him, as though he had cheated me—me!—of a splendid opportunity to keep up the illusion of my beginnings, as though he had robbed our common life of the last spark of its glamour." (131)

While in the lifeboat, Jim's test continues. He sits precariously on the gunwale and contemplates suicide. In his shame and despair, he is almost ready to throw himself overboard to share the fate of drowned pilgrims. He yearns to return to the boat and act heroically. He has an impulse to swim back to the place of death as if the reality of it would be easier to bear than the imagined picture.

Marlow has another glimpse of Jim through a rent in the mist with the night at his back and a still greater darkness beyond. Jim admits that his jump was an act of will; he did not stumble or fall into the lifeboat. He corrects Marlow's comment, "And so you cleared out—at once," by saying "jumped—mind." (131) Yet he tries to justify his act: "There was not the thickness of a sheet of paper between the right and wrong of this affair. . . . Not the breadth of a hair between this and that." (130-31) The choice between right and wrong was so complex that he could not decide. Although Jim admits his responsibility for having jumped, yet he blames the other officers of the *Patna* for it: "It was their doing as plainly as if they had reached up with a boat-hook and pulled me over." (123) He feels that he abandoned the ship under the influence of the morally degraded ship's company.

The *Patna* episode brings a total change in Jim. He suffers from the feelings of guilt and death. Marlow is disturbed to know that Jim has been contemplating suicide: "And he had been deliberating upon death—confound him! He had found *that* to meditate about because he thought he had saved his life, while all its glamour had gone with the ship in the night." (129) Jim admits that he thought of suicide as he was sick of life, but decided against it because it would have "ended nothing." He wants to do something that would wipe out the disgrace of that incident. He hopefully resolves to "wait for another chance." (132)

Jim is a dreamer and his dreams fail to grapple adequately with the factuality of the world. When the four men in the lifeboat, picked up by the *Avondale*, reach an eastern port, they hear the news that the *Patna* did not sink after all. Jim confesses that he had heard screams of the helpless passengers during the night in the lifeboat and for days after—presumably a product of his guilty conscience. It seems hard for him to realize that there were no deaths as a result of the collision. His imagination has deceived him once again.

Marlow recalls his conversation with the French Lieutenant who was on board the ship that towed the *Patna* to port. Marlow met him quite by chance in Sydney, a long time after the incident. The two begin a discussion of courage. The Frenchman presents his philosophy of courage: "I have known brave men. . . . Each of them—I say each of them, if he were an honest man . . . would confess that . . . there is somewhere a point when you let go everything. And you have got to live with that truth." (146) The French Lieutenant protests that he does not understand the problem of lost honour. Men are weak; and are subject to fear. The true courage consists not in the absence of fear but in overcoming it. Fear is a permanent inhabitant of human heart but man does not die of it. Man has to make courage a habit. Fear, necessity, the eye of others—all these help men to control themselves. Unfortunately, Jim had none of these when he abandoned the *Patna*. The French Lieutenant passes the most adverse judgment on Jim: "But the honour—the honour, monsieur! . . . The honour . . . that is real—that is! And what life may be worth when . . . when the honour is gone." (148) The Frenchman's story shows, however, that even the French rescuers took a heartless view of the pilgrims trapped aboard the *Patna*. Jim was at least at heart more merciful.

Marlow sits "alone and discouraged—discouraged about Jim's case" (149) after the departure of the French officer. He has recently seen Jim in Samarang, working for a firm of ship-chandlers as a water-clerk: "I kept my eye on his shabby plodding with a sort of notion that it was a punishment for the heroics of his fancy . . . and now he was condemned to toil without honour like a costermonger's donkey." (151) A mention of the trade reminds Marlow of Bob Stanton, chief mate of the *Sephora*, who also was disgusted with the water-clerk's job. He had told his friends that his immortal soul was shrivelled down to the size of a parched pea after a week of that work. Bob Stanton's dissatisfaction with his job emphasizes the appalling loneliness of Jim and his alienation from his fellow men. Marlow digresses to narrate the heroic incident in which Bob Stanton lost his life in an effort to save a lady's maid from drowning. A more sensible type of fear would have saved the life of Stanton. His heroism is contrasted with the apparent cowardice of Jim and provides a positive counterpart to the negative story of Jim and the *Patna*.

Marlow returns back to the evening at Malabar House where he and Jim are having a long conversation. The night before the last day of the trial, Marlow suggests to Jim Brierly's plan of evasion. Jim turns down the offer straightaway and decides to fight it out. He gives a peremptory reply to Marlow: "Clear out! Couldn't think of it . . . I've got to get over this thing, and I mustn't shirk any of it or . . . I won't shirk any of it." (153-54) Marlow reminds him that better men than he have found it expedient to run away on occasions. Jim stands firm: "I may have jumped, but I don't run away. . . . I am not good enough. I can't afford it." (154) Jim is determined not to accept any version of reality other than the one he defines for himself by his own actions. This existential gesture of defiance is by no means unique in Jim.

The bond of intimacy between Jim and Marlow seems broken by the offer. There is some embarrassment over their leave-taking. Jim seems to feel that Marlow will not want to shake hands with him. Marlow wishes to spare Jim the torment of what he must face at the Inquiry. Jim has enlisted his sympathies—has reached the secret sensibility of his egoism. Marlow says: "I heard the quick crunch-crunch of the gravel under his boots. He was running. Absolutely running, with nowhere to go to. And he was not yet four-and-twenty." (155)

Jim's act of cowardice is abhorrent to the British Marine Service. The verdict is delivered the next day: "in utter disregard of their plain duty, . . . abandoning in the moment of danger the lives and property confided to their charge . . . James So-and-so . . . mate . . . certificates cancelled." (160) For Jim, the judgment is worse than death; he can no longer pursue the profession for which he has been trained. It means an end to his career as a seaman. The court's finding has the effect of banishing him from society. Outside the court, Jim turns away from Marlow as if he were the embodied evil of life. Marlow belongs to the society from which Jim is exiled. Jim walks slowly, seems to find it difficult to balance himself. The court's judgment literally staggers him.

Marlow now introduces into the story another of those important figures who shed some light on Jim's action. Chester, a man of many dubious exploits, having no morals and ideals, typifies the dark powers that lie in wait to swallow a discouraged and rejected man like Jim. Chester does not understand the importance of Jim's loss of his certificate and unfolds a plan to ship guano from an island in the Pacific. He offers to take Jim into his service. Jim is to act as an overseer for the forty coolies he intends to put on the guano island. Marlow, now solidly on Jim's side, protects him from such distasteful and destructive adventures. He straightaway refuses the offer realizing that Chester is too phantasmal to enter into the future of any man as substantial as Jim.

In the entire world, Jim has no place where he can withdraw and be alone with his grief. So Marlow takes him back to his room at the hotel and busies himself in writing letters. Jim is very much disturbed and feels the anguish of existence. He regards himself no better than a vagabond. He is faced with the problem of adjusting to his new status in society—that of an outsider. Jim thanks Marlow for giving him "a bit of shelter." (178)

Marlow makes himself unreservedly responsible for Jim, as he sees him standing "on the brink of a vast obscurity, like a lonely figure by the shore of a sombre and hopeless ocean." (173) Jim is tormented with such a hopeless agony that it seems to Marlow that "to bury him would have been such an easy kindness!" (174)

Marlow experiences a sense of responsibility towards Jim and flashes ahead to hint at the felicity Jim is eventually to know, the time when he will be "loved, trusted, admired, with a legend of strength and prowess, forming round his name as though he had been the stuff of a hero." (175) After assuring his listeners that Jim had captured much honour and respect at Patusan, Marlow expresses a belief in the individual's capacity to shape his life.

Jim's mind is fixed only on the glory he could have secured for himself; he is not scared by the sense of honour irrevocably lost: "He had no leisure to regret what he had lost, he was so wholly and naturally concerned for what he had failed to obtain." (83) Marlow feels that Jim is concerned not with the guilt of his treacherous act, but with its shameful consequences: "The idea obtrudes itself that he made so much of his disgrace while it is the guilt alone that matters." (177) The end of the story, however, shows that this is not true. Jim never forgives himself.

Jim is a very fine, but a very unfortunate person. As Jim elaborates upon his situation, Marlow reflects that Jim was not able to explain himself fully: "He was not—if I may say so—clear to me. He was not clear. And there is a suspicion he was not clear to himself either." (177) In some inscrutable way, Marlow feels responsible for Jim and realizes that "should I let him slip away into the darkness I would never forgive myself." (180) Marlow wants to save Jim from the degradation, ruin, and despair that closes so swiftly upon a friendless, homeless man. He therefore does not relate Chester's offer to Jim as he finds him "too interesting or too unfortunate to be thrown to the dogs." (177)

Back in the Malabar Hotel, Jim insists that "some day one's bound to come upon some sort of chance to get it all back again. Must! . . . Jove! I feel as if nothing could ever touch me." (179) He cherishes the idea of starting with a "clean slate" and is sure that given a second chance, he can still redeem himself. Jim admits that he is responsible for his action. When Marlow seems to concede that in a similar emergency he too might have acted as Jim did, Jim owns up: "All the same, one is responsible." (180) Marlow is sceptical of Jim's idea that one can obliterate the past and begin with a clean slate: "A clean slate, did he say? As if the initial word of each our destiny were not graven in imperishable characters upon the face of a rock." (186) Marlow here expresses the fatalistic philosophy, the view that man's destiny is determined by forces outside him. The end however reveals that Jim was not controlled by forces beyond himself; he *chooses* his destiny.

Jim is aware that in terms of public morality, he is guilty. He accepts the judgment of society as he keeps flying from the society. He accepts job after job only to leave when the *Patna* affair comes up. He feels as though he is an object of scorn, scoffed at by other men who refuse him positions of responsibility where he could demonstrate his superiority. Jim conducts himself in a way that Marlow does not understand. Although he had asserted to Marlow that he would face the problem, he seems unable to do so. He is holding fast to some deep idea which Marlow cannot comprehend. He goes farther and farther eastwards in the search for a refuge where he can start with a clean slate and prove himself to be a respectable man.

Marlow needs advice about Jim's dilemma and hence resolves to confer with Stein, an old friend, one of the most trustworthy men he has ever known. Stein is the owner of a trading company with several branches in the Far East. Marlow considers him to be an eminently suitable person to receive his confidences about Jim's difficulties. Stein combines in himself the courage of a man of action with the thoughtfulness of a scholar. He is constantly obsessed with the complexities of existence: "Sometimes it seems to me that man is come where he is not wanted, where there is no place for him." (208)

Stein listens to Jim's story with sympathetic interest and diagnoses the case very well as he puts his finger on the sensitive nature of Jim: "I understand very well. He is a romantic." (212) The problem is not how to cure Jim of romanticism, but to discover how Jim can live with romanticism: "the question is not how to get cured, but how to live. . . . That is the question. . . . How to be! *Ach!* How to be." (212-13) Being a romantic, Jim wants to behave in an ideal fashion not only when things are fine, but also in the most unpromising conditions: "every time he shuts his eyes he sees himself as a very fine fellow—so fine as he can never be." (213) And there lies Jim's tragedy. He cannot live the role envisioned by his imagination. Jim's being a romantic, says Stein, "is very bad—very bad. . . . Very good, too." (216)

Stein feels that in life some opportunities we avail of and some we miss. The opportunities are bound to arise which will help us not only to discover the highest limit of heroism of which we are capable, but also to give us that sense of achievement or fulfilment which alone justifies human existence. One must prove himself a hero when the opportunity comes. Jim has failed to avail himself of his romantic opportunity. Stein is seized with the problem of how to live and his advice is: "to the destructive element submit yourself . . . In the destructive element immerse!" (214) He sums up the whole truth of life in these lines.[22] Like most existentialists, Stein is saying in essence that life may indeed be absurd and meaningless, but we must not try to escape from it, we must live it. Thus Jim must be given another chance to prove himself—to live up to his expectations of himself.

Stein does provide Jim a chance to rehabilitate himself in a different set-up. He maintains an unprofitable trading-post at Patusan, a settlement forty miles up a jungle river in a distant native state where three warring factions are contending for supremacy. There, Jim is to replace Cornelius, a Malacca Portuguese, as Stein's resident manager. This is no doubt a second chance for Jim—the chance he has been waiting for: "I'm ready for any confounded thing." (235) To send Jim to "a star of the fifth magnitude" could not have been a greater change of environment.

The offer delights Jim as he has an existential belief in starting his life anew. As Sartre says: "Man is nothing else but that which he makes of himself. That is the first principle of existentialism."[23] To existentialists and to Conrad, ultimately it is the individual who counts. Jim wishes for another occasion to redeem himself. He reaches Patusan in his quest for some purifying ordeal. Jim feels that he can bury his past completely and no one will ever find him out: "it would be for the outside world as if he had never existed." (218) He will be starting a new life, starting afresh as it were, with no past as known by others: "He left his earthly failings behind him and that sort of reputation he had, and there was a totally new set of conditions for his imaginative faculty to work upon."(218) He welcomes the opportunity to live apart from all other white men and exclaims: "Jove! I feel as if nothing could touch me. Why! this is luck from the word Go. I wouldn't spoil such a magnificent chance!" (241)

Jim wants to redeem himself in his own eyes and in the eyes of the world. So he proceeds to Patusan believing that "his opportunity sat veiled by his side like an Eastern bride waiting to be uncovered by the hand of the master." (243-44) He is a romantic, thinking in terms of a boy's adventure story. Hardly does he realize that the past will cast its shadow on the present--that his visit will prove fatal. Marlow feels disgusted at his elation over this venture: "Where was the sense of such exaltation in a man appointed to be a trading-clerk, and in a place where there was no trade—at that?" (236) He makes it clear that it is Jim alone who cannot forget his past: "It is not I or the world who remember. . . . It is you—you, who remember." (236)

At Patusan, Jim is completely isolated. Cut off from his group, man is the most lamentable of all creatures. Marlow realizes that the solution to spiritual isolation is social commitment: "Woe to the stragglers! . . . We exist only in so far as we hang together." (223) Jim has straggled and is aware of it with an intensity that makes him touching.

For Marlow, Jim has become a symbol of hope, a necessary affirmation of the human potential to overcome the darkness of a meaningless universe. Marlow exchanges his last words with Jim in "a moment of real and profound intimacy, unexpected and short-lived like a glimpse of some everlasting, of some saving truth." (241) Jim makes his second jump into the unknown: his future is uncertain and dark. Patusan is so dangerous that the captain of the ship taking Jim there says that he regards him as already a dead man. Once again Jim seems to stand isolated in a circle of light, for Marlow tells that his "eyes were too dazzled by the glitter of the sea below his feet to see him clearly; I am fated never to see him clearly." (241)

Marlow finds Jim firmly established in his new environments. Jim has become heavily involved in the social and political life of Patusan and has found self-assurance and success. He feels that he has atoned for his earlier failure and looks at Patusan "with an owner's eye." (247) He is needed, trusted and revered by the natives. He is responsible for the peace and prosperity of the land. Jim has come "to love the land and the people with a sort of fierce egoism, with a contemptuous tenderness." (248) He acts authoritatively and exhibits personal pride: "He had regulated so many things in Patusan! Things that would have appeared as much beyond his control as the motions of the moon and the stars." (221) Marlow sees Jim at the height of his career and personal happiness. He has availed of the chance offered to him by Stein. He has found a new existence. Marlow affirms that Jim "had achieved greatness." (225)

While Jim and Marlow make a visit to the Rajah, Jim points out the stockade where he was held captive. In a dare-devil act, he had escaped from the place. Jim relates to Marlow how he conquered his enemies and earned the adoration of his people. He had decided to take aggressive action against Sherif Ali and made Dain Waris, the only son of Doramin, his partner. He reaches the natives through Dain:

> When he got his idea he had to drive it into reluctant minds, through the bulwarks of fear, of selfishness. He drove it in at last. . . . He had to inspire with his own confidence a lot of people who had hidden and absurd reasons to hang back. . . . Dain Waris, the distinguished youth, was the first to believe in him. . . . He not only trusted Jim, he understood him. (261-62)

Sherif Ali is routed in a bold attack. Jim's success in the venture makes him a hero in Patusan. People are highly excited at his success. Jim can look down to the village and see the wild seething rush of people in the streets. He can hear the din of gongs and shouts of crowd in faint bursts of roaring. Marlow comments: "Immense! No doubt it was immense; the seal of success upon his words, the conquered ground for the soles of his feet, the blind trust of men; the belief in himself snatched from the fire, the solitude of his achievement." (272) The people have begun to trust Jim: "Him alone! His bare word. . . ." (268) In conference with Dain Waris and Doramin, Jim appoints the headmen and thus becomes the virtual ruler of the land.

Marlow finds Jim "very near at last to mastering his fate." (278) However, there is a mood of foreboding sadness when Marlow describes his talk with Jim as they sit on the mountain top: "A brooding gloom lay over this vast and monotonous landscape; the light fell on it as if into an abyss. The land devoured the sunshine; only far off, along the coast, the empty ocean, smooth and polished within the faint haze, seemed to rise up to the sky in a wall of steel." (264-65)

Jim's act of decision in raiding Sherif Ali's camp is followed by a seeming indecision. He fails to take action against Old Tunku Allang and decides to live in peaceful co-existence with the forces of the Rajah. All the Malays trust Jim but his difficulty is that he can never make them know the real truth.

Cornelius deeply resents Jim's presence in Patusan but her daughter Jewel is another reason of Jim's sticking on to Patusan. Their mutual unhappiness in the household brings them together. She keeps a watch over Jim during the night and helps him in thwarting her father's plan to kill him. As Jim stands beside Jewel in the darkness, after overcoming the four men who have come to kill him, he realizes that Jewel loves him and so does he. He tells Marlow: "She was fond of me, don't you see. . . . I, too . . . didn't know, of course . . . never entered my head. . . . I—I love her dearly. More than I could tell. Of course one cannot tell. You take a different view of your actions when you come to understand, when you are *made* to understand every day that your existence is necessary—you see, absolutely necessary—to another person . . . Well, it is a trust, too." (304) Jim tells how much different his life has been since he understood that someone needed him. He feels equal to the responsibility of love.

Jim is self-exiled in Patusan. Pointing to the lights of the town's houses, he tells Marlow: "Look at these houses; there's not one where I am not trusted. Jove! I told you I would hang on. Ask any man, woman, or child." (246-47) He cannot conceive of leaving Patusan: "Leave! Why! . . . it would have been harder than dying . . . Leave! For where? What for? To get what?" (247) He has not quite forgotten his earlier shame and the very thought of outside world frightens him. Although Jim declares himself to be "satisfied . . . nearly," (306) this conversation reveals that Jim is not yet redeemed in his own eyes. He suffers from the anguish of existing.

Both Doramin and Jewel are anxious to know if Jim can be counted upon to remain with them for ever. Doramin is sure that Jim, like all the white men they had known, will leave them to go back to his own country. He is worried about the fate of Patusan after Jim's departure. Marlow assures him but is not able to explain properly why Jim would not leave.

Marlow reports that Jewel, like Doramin, lives in constant fear of losing Jim: "She wanted an assurance, a statement, a promise, an explanation—I don't know how to call it: the thing has no name." (307) The suspicion lingers in her mind that Jim would desert her. She thinks that Marlow has the power to cause Jim to depart. Marlow is moved by her pathetic pleading: "She feared the unknown as we all do, and her ignorance made the unknown infinitely vast." (309) She feels insecure for she cannot make herself believe that Jim will never leave her. She asks: "Why is he different? Is he better?" (314) Marlow assures her that Jim is different because he is more true than any other man. Jewel divulges that she knows Jim has a secret, something he can never forget. She begs Marlow to tell her what it is. Marlow attempts to dispel her fear by telling that there is no one in all the world who will ever need Jim. No one will ever call him. When Jewel insists on knowing the reason, Marlow answers in total exasperation: "Because he is not good enough." (318) Jewel turns to Marlow with scathing contempt, bitterness and despair: "This is the very thing he said. . . . You lie!" (318) She is so upset that Marlow tries to moderate his words by saying, "Nobody, nobody is good enough." (319)

Marlow's commitment to Jim becomes permanent as he shares his experience with Jewel. He tries to convince her that she has nothing to fear from his presence in Patusan. For some time, Marlow seems to be suspicious of man's ability to shape his own destiny: "It was as though I had been shown the working of the implacable destiny of which we are the victims—and the tools." (321) The future is unknown. Marlow says: "There came upon me, as though I had felt myself losing my feet in the midst of waters, a sudden dread, the dread of the unknown depths." (312) Yet when he talks to Cornelius, his confidence returns: "Nothing mattered, since I had made up my mind that Jim, for whom alone I cared, had at last mastered his fate." (324) Utterly repelled by the whining absurdities of the defeated old man, Marlow tells him clearly that Jim will never leave Patusan. Cornelius cannot face this fact and is furious: "Never go—ah! He—he—he comes here—devil knows from where—comes—devil knows why—to trample on me till I die . . . We shall see! We shall see! What! Steal from me? Steal from me everything! Everything! Everything." (324)

There is some awkwardness between the two friends as they part for the last time. Marlow reminds Jim that he has had his opportunity and Jim agrees that he has regained his confidence and his good name: "I must go on, go on for ever holding up my end, to feel sure that nothing can touch me. I must stick to their belief in me to feel safe. . . . I shall be faithful. . . . I shall be faithful." (328-29) He feels responsible towards Jewel also who is absolutely devoted to him: "And then there is Jewel." (335) Jim asks Marlow when they will meet next and himself answers: "Never—

unless you come out." (335) As Marlow is carried away in a small boat to his waiting schooner, Jim lifts his voice and calls: "Tell them . . . No—nothing." (335) Marlow has his last look at Jim:

> He was white from head to foot, and remained persistently visible with the stronghold of the night at his back, the sea at his feet, the opportunity by his side—still veiled. What do you say? Was it still veiled? I don't know. For me that white figure in the stillness of coast and sea seemed to stand at the heart of a vast enigma. The twilight was ebbing fast from the sky above his head, the strip of sand had sunk already under his feet, he himself appeared no bigger than a child—then only a speck, a tiny white speck, that seemed to catch all the light left in a darkened world. . . . And, suddenly, I lost him. . . . (336)[24]

After about three years of success, Jim is presented with a situation that he fails to decide definitively. He is vulnerable to external forces and powers. While he is loved and trusted in Patusan, the outside world enters his sanctuary in the person of Gentleman Brown and upsets his life. Driven by hunger, Brown, a piratical sea-captain, and his crew invade Patusan to find food and water. Once again Nature plays a destructive role in Jim's life—the Sea drives Brown and his crew to Patusan and this produces for Jim the final test of his heroic character.

The dependence of the people of Patusan on Jim is not illusory. They are unable to face danger without the leadership of Jim. When Brown reaches there, Jim is away in the interior. Dain Waris directs the repulse of the Brown party and wants to finish them off at once, but Doramin fears for his son's safety. Kassim, Rajah Allang's spokesman, opens communication with Brown, using Cornelius as his interpreter. Cornelius enlightens Brown about affairs in Patusan and tells him that he needs only to kill Jim. Brown is eager to meet Jim and find out what kind of a man he is to have won the confidence of the natives, and acquire such mastery over them. He asks Cornelius to arrange their meeting.

Jim and Brown confront each other in the wilderness with no checks of civilization. Jim comes unarmed, dressed in spotless white, and looking supremely unconcerned and self-confident. Brown hates Jim at first sight: this is not the man he had expected to see. He curses Jim's youth and assurance, his clear eyes and untroubled bearing. Even the neat whiteness of Jim's clothes annoys him and seems to his irritated eyes "to belong to those things he has in the very shaping of his life condemned and flouted." (380) Brown proves to be more dangerous to Jim than the crawling Cornelius. His question, what has made Jim come to Patusan, exposes Jim. Brown insists that Jim has come there out of fear; he has run away from something. His remark, "I am not a coward. Don't you be one," (382) cripples Jim. Through all his talk there runs an insinuation of something shady in Jim's past, an allusion to a common guilt: "Let us agree . . . that we are both dead men, and let us talk on that basis, as equals." (381) Referring to his own men, Brown says: "There are my men in the same boat—and, by God, I am not the sort to jump out of trouble and leave them in a d—d lurch." (382-83)

Brown's words sink deep into Jim's guilty conscience and rob him of the power to act decisively. His tainted past restricts him from passing strictures against even a criminal. He feels a kinship with Brown. There is in Jim's mind a common bond between himself and Brown: both of them are guilty.

Brown has a satanic gift for ferreting out the best and the weakest spots in his victims and Jim, with his guilty conscience, is pitifully vulnerable. Jim develops a fellow-feeling for Brown because he cannot forgive himself. This feeling warps his judgment and destroys him. Brown wants to play havoc with the village of Patusan because it has defied him. He wants to see it strewn over with corpses and enveloped in flames. He realizes that the village men outnumber his party two hundred to one. So he tries to strike terror by killing a man. Fearing that Jim and the natives might simply wait until Brown and his men are starved to death, Brown asks Jim to either give them a chance in open battle or to allow them to return to the sea. He asks Jim if he does not understand that when it comes to saving one's life in the dark, one doesn't care who else goes, "three, thirty, three hundred people." (386) Brown hits the mark "as if a demon had been whispering advice in his ear." (386-87) He pursues the point, asking Jim if he does not have something fishy in his life to remember: "And there ran through the rough talk a vein of subtle reference to their common blood, an assumption of common experience; a sickening suggestion of common guilt, of secret knowledge that was like a bond of their minds and of their hearts." (387) Clearly Brown has a psychological advantage in his parley with Jim. At last Jim promises him a clear road.

Jim commits an error of judgment in allowing Brown a safe passage out of Patusan. He pledges his own life as security, should any harm come as a result of letting the Brown party go free. Doramin agrees to this arrangement only because he is reluctant to have his son lead the attack.

Tamb'Itam, who relates this part of the story to Marlow, remembers that his master was sad that night and walked back and forth with bowed head and his hands behind his back.

Advised and guided by the sneaking Cornelius, Brown leaves as planned but treacherously fires on a party of Malays under Dain Waris. The chief's son and many of his soldiers are killed. Tamb'Itam stabs Cornelius and carries the news of the disaster to Jim.

At the extremity of life, there are three choices open to Jim: he can abscond from the scene in the interest of his future; he can fight; he can give himself up according to Malay custom. Jim's first reaction to the unexpected treachery of Brown is to prepare boats and pursue the murderers. But when Tamb'Itam reminds him that it is not safe for his servant to go out amongst people, Jim realizes that his world has fallen in ruins upon his head. Both Tamb'Itam and Jewel plead with him to either stand seige in the fortress or try to make good their escape, but Jim stands firm against their pleas. He has had enough experience of running away and knows how futile it would be. A fight would have entailed much bloodshed and loss of life. So he decides to "prove his power in another way and conquer the fatal destiny itself." (410) He takes it upon himself to die.[25]

Even while in a state of confusion about the objective validity of his motives, Jim realizes, almost with an outcry, that individual existence is impossible without individual choice and action. He places his egoism above his duty to others; to Jewel, to Stein, to the colony, to Marlow, to Doramin. Each of these duties has his claim on Jim. But he considers his duty to himself only, to the exclusion of all others. In an agony of despair, Jewel pleads with Jim to remember his promise that he will not leave her. Becoming hysterical, she demands that he defend himself but Jim does not listen to her. He considers the event to be his supreme test and goes to Doramin. On an earlier occasion, he had explained to Marlow: "It is all in being ready. I wasn't; not—not then." (81) He wants time to prepare himself because he feels that true courage is a product of will rather than impulse. So now when he has time to think over, he decides to face Doramin.

Bent on living up to his responsibilities, Jim does not try to escape and faces the angry crowd. The town is chaotic with sorrow, lamentation and horrible doubts. Jim comes up slowly and lifts the sheet to look at Dain Waris, his dead friend. Then, alone and unarmed, he faces Doramin. As the latter struggles to get to his feet, the ring rolls to Jim's feet. He glances at the "talisman that had opened for him the door of fame, love, and success." (415) While Jim stands stiffly with bare head, looking Doramin straight in the face, Doramin shoots him through the chest. Jim flashes "his last proud and unflinching glance" (416) on all the assembled Malays and falls at Doramin's feet, a hero in death. He goes to his death with cool determination. Marlow regards Jim's last defiant gesture as a great triumph, "an extraordinary success." (416) This is the chance, the opportunity he had been waiting for. He has conquered his fear and his shame. He sacrifices his life to prove his capacity for genuine faithfulness and courage. His dreams of a special destiny have come true.

Jim's violent death at the end has confused the critics. Is it suicide or an act of heroism and martyrdom? Conrad's novels do not yield to a univocal interpretation that can satisfy all readers. As Marlow puts it, Jim remained an insoluble mystery to the end. Full knowledge can never be achieved. Marlow's hesitations and questionings reveal his uncertainty about the meaning of the whole story: "I ask myself whether his rush had really carried him out of that mist in which he loomed interesting if not very big, with floating outlines." (224) Marlow points out the elusiveness of human nature. Jim "passes away under a cloud, inscrutable at heart, forgotten, unforgiven and excessively romantic." (416) In the letter written to the privileged man, Marlow comments:

> The point, however, is that of all mankind Jim had no dealings but with himself, and the question is whether at the last he had not confessed to a faith mightier than the laws of order and progress.
>
> I affirm nothing. Perhaps you may pronounce—after you've read. (339)

However, at the end Marlow believes that Jim has subscribed to a higher faith. Jim has acted according to his own private ideal of conduct, as a Sartrean hero would act. He believes that his sacrifice will atone for the death of Dain Waris. He eventually martyrs himself for the sake of his shadowy ideal of conduct. His death is his final acceptance of responsibility, a courageous gesture of atonement.[26] Marlow does not explicitly subscribe to Jim's ideal of conduct as a personal choice, chiefly because such an ideal is unique to the person who shapes it; nevertheless, Marlow explicitly identifies Jim's egoism with his own.

We should not forget that man has responsibility not only towards himself but towards the whole society. In *Existentialism and Humanism,* Sartre argues that "when we say that man is responsible for himself, we do not mean that he is responsible only for his own individuality, but that he is responsible for all men. . . . Our responsibility is thus much greater than we had supposed, for it concerns mankind as a whole."[27] When Jim deserted the *Patna*, he shirked his responsibility towards both himself and the pilgrims. Now when he chooses death at Patusan, he proves true to himself but not to the society. Jim's ultimate test involves not only his responsibility to himself and to the civilized manly values of the society in which he was raised, but also to those more primeval, womanly values that may be symbolized by Jewel. Jim is responsible not only to himself, but also to the woman who loves him. If Jim had only his own life to consider, it would be easy enough for him to act solely in terms of those masculine ideals of duty, pride, and bravery which were part of his early training. Jim is tested in such a way that in order to remain true to himself, he has to be untrue to Jewel. Jewel holds Jim accountable in love, declaring that in leaving her, he failed to live up to his commitment to her. Stein tries to convince her that Jim was true but she does not understand. He urges upon Marlow to talk to her: "We can't leave it like this. Tell her to forgive him. It was very frightful." (347) Marlow tries to console Jewel but she is frozen with unforgiving anger. Talking to Marlow, Jewel reflects bitterly upon the solitariness which invaded her relationship with Jim:

> When I used to sit at his feet, with my cheek against his knee and his hand on my head, the curse of cruelty and madness was already within him, waiting for the day. The day came! (349)

Jim might have fought for his life; he might have fled. He did neither. He chose, deliberately chose, to leave her. She feels that in going to Doramin, Jim has betrayed her. He has abandoned her to her fate: "He shall have no tears from me. Never, never. Not one tear. I will not! He went away from me as if I had been worse than death. He fled as if driven by some accursed thing he had heard or seen in his sleep. . . ." (349-50) Marlow feels Jewel's suffering and grief about the loss of Jim: "He is gone, inscrutable at heart, and the poor girl is leading a sort of soundless, inert life in Stein's house." (416-17)

Conrad gives a positive touch to Jim's death when, on the last page of the novel, Marlow approves of it: "It may very well be that in the short moment of his proud and unflinching glance, he had beheld the face of that opportunity which, like an Eastern bride, had come veiled to his side." (416) It is a path, however destructive, to discover truth and meaning in life. "To be hopeful," says Conrad, "it is not necessary to think that the world is good. It is enough to believe that there is no impossibility of its being made so."[28]

IV

In *Nostromo*, published in 1904, Conrad shifts his emphasis from the spiritual history of a solitary individual to a world in turmoil. He creates the impression that life is being lived all at once by a number of very different people. Unlike the novels and short stories which precede it, *Nostromo* does not have a single protagonist. It has a centre or core around which the major characters revolve. And that core is the city of Costaguana. Individual personalities are subordinated to the evolution of the state—the emergence of the Occidental Republic, an epoch in the destiny of Costaguana. At the end, society appears resurgent and confident.

Sulaco is isolated from the rest of the country by a high range of mountains. The islands called "the Isabels" form a kind of barrier against the open sea. The mercantile adventurers are kept away by the prevailing calm of the gulf and the mountains around preserve a quasi-independence for Sulaco. Sir John's comment emphasizes the isolation of Sulaco: "I had no notion that a place on a sea-coast could remain so isolated from the world." (36)[29] Through the mountain ranges, Conrad explores the vision of man lost in the colossal jungle. The towering mountain ranges offer a contrast to the midgety mankind and convey a sense of the loneliness of the characters. Intensely painful decisions and confrontations appear to take place in a void as real as the placid and impenetrably dark gulf.

The introductory description of the geography and history of Sulaco impresses upon us the frightening, sinister reputation of the San Tome Silver Mine. We learn that Charles Gould wants to reopen the mine in spite of the warnings of his father who had died hating this concession forced upon him by a corrupt political regime. Gould has studied in England to become a mining engineer and is completely under the spell of the mine by the time he is twenty.

Charles Gould consciously chooses to open the mine. With the establishment of the mine, argues Royal Roussel, Gould "is allowed to exist for a time with the freedom which comes when the self achieves an independent being."[30] Gould's youthful idealism convinces him that silver can be extracted from the mine and can be used to bring law, order, stability, peace and prosperity to a land of poverty. For him, the mine is a matter of life and death. He is aware of the precarious nature of its existence and the penalty of its failure—his father had died directly as a result of the burden of the thing. He wants to turn the "absurd moral disaster" of the mine into "a serious and moral success." (66) To Gould, the mine presents itself as a means to achieve a moral end. He feels "morally bound" (74) to dedicate himself to the rehabilitation of the mine.

Gould's decision to reopen the mine was to put it on a rational and stable footing. Morally bound to make a success of the mine, Gould is haunted by his *idee fixe* to the point of insanity: "A man haunted by a fixed idea is insane. He is dangerous even if that idea is an idea of justice." (379) With the help of Holroyd, the millionaire from San Francisco, the mine flourishes abundantly. But Gould's ideal—the search for justice and security—ends in a dangerous obsession. Having become his unswerving passion, the mine corrupts him gradually. He becomes a slave to the mine and the mine itself becomes anything but his ideal conception of it. Instead of being a means, it becomes his end and withers all that is fine and generous and human in his nature. Gould becomes a figure of inhuman coldness. The mine alienates him from his wife, his workers and himself.

The poison of the silver drains into the already tainted whirlpool of political life in Costaguana. Gould's idealism has to compromise with things as they are. He uses whatever means he deems necessary. Since the government is corrupt, he bribes the officials. The degradation of his ideal lies in the growing disgust he feels at methods which he nevertheless goes on using. He knows that he must continue in his course; there can be no going back. The mine brings a certain prosperity to the country but soon it develops into a tyrant. It becomes Gould's evil genius and brings evil upon himself as well as the rest of the major characters.

Material interests bring with them peculiarly cold forms of inhumanity in which the individual loses his authentic self. Gould's experience with the mine makes him aware of the insufficiency of the individual to attain his goal. The spell of the silver possesses and overpowers Gould. It brings to light the lack of integrity of his inner being. The obsession with silver weakens his capacity for love; he gains a lot of wealth but loses his peace of mind. His idealism gives way to fanaticism.

Idealistically attached to the mine and possessing a high sense of duty and rare abilities, Gould lacks imaginative insight that is necessary to make him a good husband to Emilia. The consuming passion for an idea leads to the sacrifice of love; the mine alienates him from his wife. At the time of his courtship, he had resolved—in a romantic way—to make the mine flourish. When Mrs. Gould lays "her unmercenary hands . . . upon the first silver ingot turned out still warm from the mould," (107) silver is not just a piece of metal for her; it is a symbol of her aspirations and her love for her husband. But this feeling soon disappears. From a romantic enterprise, the mine becomes an obsession which Mrs. Gould can no more share. She realizes that her husband lives for the mine rather than for her. This realization creates a barrier between the two and their marital bliss is destroyed. Their marriage bears no fruit: Mrs. Gould remains childless.

Gould's regular overnight stays at the mine suggest his physical remoteness from his wife. This physical separation magnifies the distance between the Goulds as man and wife. When Mrs. Gould tries to talk to him about her loneliness, Gould says: "I thought you had understood me perfectly from the first, . . . I thought we had said all there was to say a long time ago. There is nothing to say now." (207) The fact that they have nothing to share stresses the hollowness of their married life. Mrs. Gould regrets that her husband's whole life was swallowed up by his job. She sees herself irremediably separated from her husband by a wall of silver bricks.

The mine also brings to the fore the inhuman aspect of the human society. Mrs. Gould knows the barbaric history of the mine: "Worked in the early days mostly by means of lashes on the backs of slaves, its yield had been paid for in its own weight of human bones." (52) The excessive cruelty being perpetrated by "the rulers of the country with its story of oppression, inefficiency, fatuous methods, treachery and savage brutality" appalls Mrs. Gould and exasperates her "almost to the verge of despair." (109) Aware of man's inhumanity to man, she also knows that the situation in Sulaco is not peculiar to one place or one country: "In all these households she could hear stories of political outrage; . . . And on all the lips she found a weary desire for peace, the dread of officialdom with its nightmarish parody of administration without law, without security, and without justice." (88) Material interests perpetuate victimization, corruption, disappointment and frustration.

Gould's belief in the ideal value of the mine kills him spiritually. From an ideal conception of political order to be implemented through the mine, his vision gradually contrasts to an obsession with the security of the mine itself. At the time of the revolution, Gould openly supports the dictatorship of Riberia. His only interest is to save the mine and he makes elaborate arrangements to protect it. The corruption of political institutions dominates his imagination so much that he decides to blow up the mine than surrender. He entrusts Nostromo and Decoud with the responsibility of taking away by sea a vast quantity of the silver, the six-month output of the mine. His absorption in the mine is such that he would prefer the silver to go to sea than to the revolutionaries: "If it must be lost, it is a million times better that it should go to the bottom of the sea." (260) Thus the mine—a means to achieve an end—becomes the end itself.

The trip of Decoud and Nostromo out into the gulf with the lighter loaded with silver on an intense black night is a significant event. Both Decoud and Nostromo are conscious of the enormity of the dangers involved and the fact that they might not come back. Before leaving, Decoud leaves his pocket-book with Mrs. Gould with the request to send it to his sister: "Perhaps my last words to her." (260) And Nostromo tells Dr. Monygham: "It is as if I were taking up a curse upon me." (259) But at the same time, Nostromo views the trip strictly as an opportunity for doing great deeds and becoming a hero.

However, a little before he leaves, Nostromo commits, in Sartrean terms, an act of bad faith. He refuses to fetch a priest for the dying Teresa and tries to convince himself that he has not done anything wrong. He considers the various reasons for his refusal. First, he deludes himself into thinking that she may not die so soon and that Gould will get her a priest later. Secondly, he says he does not like priests. Thirdly, he is in a hurry to go in for saving the lighter full of silver. In this, Nostromo is motivated by his egoism—his desire to be more famous than he already is in Sulaco.

Later, however, he is haunted by his failure to get a priest for Teresa and wonders whether his refusal would not bring retribution upon his head. He also gives a thought to the idea that his troubles are directly traceable to that act of impiety.

Once out into the gulf, Decoud starts on the train of feeling and thought that leads to his suicide. Very tired and unaccustomed to rowing, he suffers cruelly. His scepticism is immediately touched by the isolation of the gulf. The time spent in the complete obscurity of the gulf separates him from life in Sulaco. He feels that his earlier life has been superficial. All life appears meaningless and futile, destined to end in a darkness such as this:

> Like a man lost in slumber, he heard nothing, he saw nothing. Even his hand held before his face did not exist for his eyes. The change from the agitation, the passions and the dangers, from the sights and

> sounds of the shore, was so complete that it would have resembled death had it not been for the survival of his thoughts. (262)

Decoud feels the overpowering weight of silence around him: "The solitude could almost be felt." (262-63) The blackness seems to weigh upon him like a stone.

The impenetrable darkness of the gulf destroys space and time for the human occupants of the lighter. When Decoud asks Nostromo if they are moving at all, the latter replies: "Not so fast as a crawling beetle tangled in the grass." (263) Nostromo's remark adds to the sense of frustration they are experiencing. It seems that they have been caught in a nightmare where their human powers are reduced to those of an insect, trapped by nature. In such a weird situation, all human emotions seem powerless—like those of a beetle tangled in the grass.

Nostromo feels helpless in this situation and grumbles about the responsibility he has undertaken. He tells Decoud the deadly curse that the silver is: "This thing (the silver) has been given to me like a deadly disease." (264) Decoud's thoughts are somewhat similar: it seems to him that he has been abandoned by all. Lacking the support of the world which he scorned, Decoud soon loses the control of his thoughts: "All his active sensations and feelings as far back as he could remember seemed to him the maddest of dreams. Even his passionate devotion to Antonia . . . had lost all appearance of reality." (267) The lines anticipate the cause of Decoud's suicide later when he is alone, with only himself to rely upon.

Decoud also reflects upon Hirsch's fear of death and his attempt to escape from Sulaco. The anguish that Hirsch experiences unsettles Decoud: "Nature, who had made him what he was, seemed to have calculated cruelly how much he could bear in the way of atrocious anguish without actually expiring." (274)

When Nostromo puts out the feeble light of the candle, complete darkness envelops the entire lighter. Decoud has a feeling as if the world of affairs, of loves, of revolutions is completely annihilated. He is unable to see even Nostromo and only the sound of Nostromo's voice makes him certain of his own existence. This human confirmation gives Decoud self-confidence; he needs Nostromo for survival. Without Nostromo, he possesses no resources of self to keep alive his convictions of reality. This uncertainty prefigures Decoud's later abandonment to suicide in the face of utter solitude. Separated from Nostromo, he loses the precarious hold upon himself.

Nostromo's being is defined entirely by his social context—his public image. "A man for whom the value of life seems to consist in personal prestige," (248) he is an egoist with a passion for reputation. He is presented as a man of impetuous activity and vanity who is resolute, courageous, vigorous, and honest in his own way. An Italian sailor, he is employed in the port of Sulaco as overseer in charge of the handling of cargo. Because of his efficiency, powers of leadership and general usefulness, he becomes a respected local figure.

The experience of the gulf alters Nostromo radically. After the lighter is run down by Sotillo's steamer, he hides the silver on an uninhabited island outside the port of Sulaco and leaves Decoud there to guard it. He swims back to the shore of Sulaco and falls asleep in the ruins of the old fort. When he wakes up after fourteen hours, he emerges "with the lost air of a man just born into the world." (411) His old identity is lost. He awakens with the strange sense that he has somehow "gone out of existence." (419) It seems to be "the end of things. . . . Everything that had gone before for years appeared vain and foolish, like a flattering dream come suddenly to an end." (414) He realizes that his livelihood is gone and with it the acclamations of the multitude. In the darkness of the gulf, his vanity is without an adoring public and he fails to withstand the test of isolation. Once his vanity is shattered, Nostromo ceases to exist. The shattering of his own ideal image of himself changes the course of his life and he emerges as a new man indeed.

Nostromo suffers from the discovery of his human condition. "His awakening in solitude, except for the watchful vulture, amongst the ruins of the fort" (414) is in a sense his moral awakening.[31] His external perceptions which direct his thoughts reveal his internal state of mind. The vulture suggests death and Signora Teresa; the empty fort brings to his mind the barrenness of his own position. The darkness of the sky makes him feel the pinch of poverty for the first time in his life: "since it was no longer possible for him to parade the streets of the town, and be hailed with respect in the usual haunts of his leisure, the sailor felt himself destitute indeed." (415) The lamentable shriek of the owl portends calamity and death.

Nostromo's whole vision of his life is shattered by the conditions of his mission. Angry at the rich people for having exploited him, Nostromo mutters a curse upon their selfishness and laughs with self-derision as he spits with disgust, straight out before him into the night. He has returned to Sulaco in spite of danger and the presence of revolutionary troops. But no one is bothered about him. He feels that something has gone out of his life. He has the disillusioning realization that he has been used by the rich and the aristocrats. "No one waited for him; no one thought of him; no one expected or wished his return. 'Betrayed! Betrayed!' he muttered to himself. No one cared." (422) The two lighted windows of the custom house frighten him; the house itself evokes his alienated and isolated life: "The solitude could almost be felt." (422) In this existential solitariness, his ideal conception of himself is shattered; he feels victimized, betrayed into a scheme.

The long exchange between Nostromo and Dr. Monygham in the custom house shows Nostromo's awakening to the insubstantiality of his former existence. Shaken by the events of his own isolation, Nostromo craves understanding but gets none. He is anxious that Dr. Monygham should ask him about the silver and is resentful when he does not ask. His vanity and pride are hurt. He tells Dr. Monygham that no one cared about what happened to him. A word from Monygham would have saved Nostromo from bitterness, would have changed the course of his life. But Monygham does not understand his need. Instead, he asks Nostromo to escape and summon help for the Sulaco Ribierists.

Dr. Monygham has his reasons for persuading Nostromo to ride to Cayta. He decides to help Nostromo so that it can ultimately help Mrs. Gould. He wants to save the city so that Mrs. Gould and her husband are saved. He acts neither from patriotic motives nor from material interests but from love. His haunting memories of the torture by the sadistic Father Beron, and his sense of shame at his betrayal of friends make him bitter about all humanity except Mrs. Gould—the one person to whom he has given his absolute devotion. He feels that "his devotion was the only thing that stood between an admirable woman and a frightening disaster." (431)

Dr. Monygham admires Nostromo for having swum to safety. He is also aware of "the human littleness which is what really defeats a man struggling with natural forces, alone, far from the eyes of his fellows." (433) But his sole obsession at this moment is the safety of Mrs. Gould.

Dr. Monygham is fully aware of his motive and of the risk he is running. When Nostromo accuses him for his responsibility in the horrible death of Hirsch, he accepts the guilt as part of the price he must pay for making his "sacrifice in a spirit of abasement." (439) To atone for his confession, he involves himself in an action which means almost certain torture and death.

Hirsch, the hide exporter, is a memorable case of Conrad's studies in fear. Sotillo, the leader of the insurgents, tortures Hirsch to know the whereabouts of the silver. The scene of torture is significant because in it Hirsch changes from an abject coward to a man brave enough to spit in his torturer's face. In death, the alien Jew attains a new dignity. His tortured body, left hanging from the roof, evokes compassion and indignation in Nostromo. It is a cruel reminder to Dr. Monygham of his own fears.

Dr. Monygham is given sudden prominence in the last section of the novel when he is revealed as the one man who stands against the evil forces until they are destroyed. In the beginning, he had been presented as "a bitter, eccentric character... whose short, hopeless laugh expressed somehow an immense mistrust of mankind." (44) His conviction is that "the last thing a man ought to be sure of" (310) is himself. He doubts humanity because he doubts himself. But through his mistrust and scepticism, he finally arrives at love and devotion. His cynicism is gradually overcome by a romantic feeling for Mrs. Gould whose humanizing influence brings a transformation in him.

Dr. Monygham suffers from existence malaise. His reaction when he wonders if Nostromo knows anything about his past life in prison, is a "simple dread." (453) He does have a profound self-distrust, but he has not lost his beliefs. And that is why he is tormented by his failure to live up to those principles in which he most deeply believed. Despite all his self-contempt and cynicism, Monygham holds on to an exacting ideal of conduct. It goes to his credit that he perceives the truth about the Goulds. After spending years in self-destructive isolation and remorse, he finds redemption at last when he offers to sacrifice his own life for the sake of Mrs. Gould.

The account of Dr. Monygham's degradation is given at just the moment when by his present action he is trying to regain his mastery of self. Conrad alludes briefly to the abortive conspiracy a long time ago in which Monygham had been subdued in the torture-chambers of Guzman Bento, the former dictator. Monygham had foolishly believed that he was strong enough to withstand any torture. But his experiences made him aware of his limited endurance power. His illusions were shattered along with his body when he was tortured by Father Beron, an army chaplain.

Dr. Monygham had confessed whatever the commission wanted and sat in prison waiting for death. He is not afraid of death thereafter, and during the latter part of his imprisonment even longs for it. He experiences "a pain which makes truth, honour, self-respect, and life itself matters of little moment." (373)

Dr. Monygham is set free when Guzman Bento dies of a stroke of apoplexy. But for the rest of his life, Monygham could not feel absolved of the disgrace of that hour of torture. He attaches an ideal value to his disgrace and becomes cynical of human nature. No doubt he has failed but the conditions were such that nobody except he himself would blame him. He scorns humanity because he did not fulfil his ideal in that particular circumstance and feels guilty of having betrayed his integrity.

Dr. Monygham's experiences during Bento's regime leave him with the worst possible view of human motives. His idealism is complicated by an awareness of fallibility almost to cynicism. His experiences have proved to him that there is no limit to the humiliation which a man can be made to endure and out of this comes his inveterate opposition to reform and his distrust of political idealists like Gould.

Dr. Monygham lives in the permanent consciousness of having betrayed his colleagues. His shame at his inability in the past to stand up to torture never leaves him. Though Father Beron, his tormentor, is dead now, Monygham experiences excruciating anguish to think that in the event of his meeting Beron in the street, he would quail before him. This feeling prevents him from "looking anybody in the face." (374)

On his own initiative, Dr. Monygham decides to delay Sotillo's entry into Sulaco by misleading him with false stories about the silver. To give Nostromo time to reach General Barrios in Sta Marta so that he can bring back his troops and retake the town of Sulaco, Monygham employs a ruse. He puts Sotillo on a wrong scent by giving him the impression that the silver is sunk in the harbour. Sotillo is thus kept occupied with dredging of the bottom of the sea.

Dr. Monygham knows that if his trick is discovered by Sotillo, he will be killed. But he voluntarily faces this danger. In his respectful love for Mrs. Gould, he chooses a kind of action which involves a risk to his life. But at the same time, his decision marks a step in his inner progress towards gaining self-respect. Through this selfless act, Monygham wins back his self-esteem and re-enters the human communion.

Decoud is the most important example of Nature's indifference to man's needs. As in the case of Jim, natural phenomena combine with temperament to bring about the tragedy. In his consideration of nature, Conrad often distinguishes between the external and internal realities of existence. There is a difference between the physical world that an individual perceives, and the psychological reaction he experiences in his relation to it. Man tries to find meaning in the world and is pained to see the vast indifference of nature. He finds that for centuries men live, suffer and die while the earth remains apparently unaffected. To protest against the seeming unconcern of matter and the elements which survive him, man sometimes puts an end to his life. That is what happens in the case of Martin Decoud, the young apostle of Separation.

Conrad isolates his character from society and the larger world of men so that he can put him *in extremis* and can make him act as the agent of his self-confrontation. Alone on a lonely island, man must depend on individual virtue. As long as Decoud is busy, he keeps absurdity away. But when he is alone, he cannot sustain his individuality in an uncaring universe. He is one of those who are demoralized by absurdity and find it difficult to live without the human orbit.

Decoud is defeated by an indifferent nature whose cruel relentlessness rejects man's persistent efforts to conquer it. His mental processes begin to merge into the physical realities of sea, sky and island. It seems to him that there is nothing alive in the world except himself. The island is barren of everything: there are no sounds, no birds. He realizes his ultimate loneliness and the indifference of natural forces to his plight. The vastness and the emptiness of the sea, the loneliness of the Isabels, the remote chances of his survival in view of the fact that only Nostromo knew of his presence on the island and he may never come back, and the working of the solitude on his mind lead to his collapse.

Decoud's existential solitariness makes him realize the futility of his existence; ten days of physical isolation lead to his death. His solitary vigil undermines his desire to go on living and his scepticism destroys his self-confidence. The first night he does not have even a wink of sleep. As the days pass, the silence and loneliness become more oppressive. After three days of waiting for the sight of some human face, he starts doubting his own existence: "Decoud caught himself entertaining a doubt of his own individuality." (497) He loses faith in the reality of his actions and is no longer able to distinguish between himself and the outer world.

Decoud does not have the resources to grapple with loneliness—he is not fit to be alone. Faced with himself, his inner resources fail him utterly. He feels that he has ceased to exist: "Both his intelligence and his passion were swallowed up easily in this great unbroken solitude of waiting without faith." (498) Cut off from the world and left to himself, his vaunted intelligence breaks down. He wants the universe to be coherent and rationally organized but finds it "a succession of incomprehensible images." (498) The sudden awareness of the non-meaning of the universe upsets him. All hopes of imposing order and justice on the world seem useless. The weight of the mystery of the universe seems unbearable and suicide appears the only sensible course of action. Decoud loses all illusions with which he had been wrapped so far. His consciousness fashions the mirage of silence: "He believed in nothing . . . and in this glory of merciless solitude the silence appeared again before him, stretched taut like a dark, thin string." (500)

Bereft of all reason for living, Decoud dies "from solitude and want of faith in himself and others." (496) Driven by his solitude and the sense of inadequacy, Decoud fills his pockets with the silver ingots, shoves off from shore and drifts far enough out into the gulf, shoots himself and drowns. His is the death of a man, driven mad on an island by his solitary confrontation with nature—a man who "disappeared without a trace, swallowed up in the immense indifference of things." (501) Finding himself unequal to life, Decoud ends at the bottom of the placid gulf.

Decoud is the intellectually isolated man. Unlike Nostromo, he has deliberately and knowingly uprooted himself, thereby becoming the intellectual expatriate. He has revived the idea of separating Sulaco from the rest of Costaguana. But he does not have the power to carry out his ideas. As Conrad says: "In our activity alone do we find the sustaining illusion of an independent existence as against the whole scheme of things of which we form a helpless part. Decoud lost all belief in the reality of his action past and to come." (497) Conrad believes that man needs illusions to bolster up his sense of personal significance. Earlier in the novel, he has asserted: "Only in the conduct of our action can we find the sense of mastery over the Fates." (66) In his sceptical bias, Decoud feels that the love of Antonia and patriotism are irrational desires. "The man with no faith in anything except the truth of his own sensations," (229) Decoud commits suicide because he has no ideology to enable him to endure his isolation. He is a man who suffers. He has no ideals, no inner reserve to sustain him in the lonely days of the Great Isabel. In his letter to his sister—his last communication with the world—Decoud rightly describes himself as "the man with a passion, but without a mission." (246) His suicide is a recognition that the world and the self are no longer tolerable. He is an admirable man wrecked by absurdity.

Like an existentialist hero, Decoud exercises his choice of suicide. He decides to do so when he experiences the absurd in the world. He believes that his suicide might have some value or meaning in a meaningless existence. Although unexpected, the turn of events has an air of inevitability. Needless as his death is, more so in view of Nostromo's later return to the island, the reader feels that Decoud could have taken no other course. His death demonstrates the author's great psychological powers in presenting the debilitating effect of silence and insomnia.

Like Decoud, Pedrito Montero also experiences a feeling of uncertainty. He has absurd visions which cause him to attach himself to strangers and to move restlessly from town to town. He has a feeling of uncertainty even after he has won a military victory and destroyed a town. As he confronts Gould in the Intendencia of Sulaco and demands access to the silver mine, Montero is somehow uncertain of his newly-won power and influence: "Pedrito's imagination was subdued by a feeling of insecurity and impermanence. That feeling and the firm attitude of Charles Gould who had not once, so far, pronounced the word 'Excellency,' diminished him in his own eyes." (404)

Like that of Almayer, Willems, and Kurtz, the character of Nostromo deteriorates through environment. Loneliness, remorse, superstition and poverty help to induce the change in him. Separated from human solidarity, he cannot escape himself and becomes an outcast. After finding Decoud gone and four ingots missing, Nostromo spends a sleepless night. He feels betrayed by Decoud's theft and disappearance but also realizes that now he is the only person who knows the secret of the lost treasure. He decides not to report the safety of the silver because Gould and others will think that he has stolen the four ingots. He fears that his reputation will be damaged and his incorruptibility questioned. He is a man who lives for the image he presents to the others. Considering his outer appearance to be more important than his moral integrity, Nostromo gives in to the temptation of letting everyone believe that the silver treasure has been lost.

Another factor which aids Nostromo's moral disintegration is the lack of human ties. Like other Conradian heroes, Nostromo is essentially rootless. He is an orphan who has run away from an abusive uncle. Sulaco is not his home and he has no connections with its past. With no roots at all, Nostromo has a sense of honour centred entirely upon himself.

Nostromo is the most complete idealization of the existential concept of a man of responsibility. During the struggles in Sulaco, he undertakes various political assignments and holds himself responsible for the successful completion of each one of them. It is his consciousness of his responsibility to live up to his reputation which leads to his decision to keep the treasure. And this decision he makes of his own free choice. He survives the sinking of the lighter but his character crumbles into uncertainty and indecision. By turning to crime, Nostromo kills the self by which he has lived till this time. Lacking true sense of the purpose of life, he is corrupted by the insidious influence of the mine.

Mrs. Gould, a sympathetic person, tirelessly works for the poor, the sick, and the lonely. Devoted to making others comfortable and happy, she exists only on a human level and has no time for abstractions of any kind. She protects Giorgio Viola's home from the encroachment of the railway and shelters the outcast Monygham unless he is able to work his way back into the community. She tries to humanize the effects of the mine and counteract the materialistic interests of her husband.

Mrs. Gould's keeping herself busy in ideal philanthropic activity cannot preserve her from disillusion. She realizes the insignificance and futility of her altruistic attitude to life. It occurs to her that all her philanthropic concerns are ineffectual and all her sacrifices futile. Her warm affection, her care for the people are of no use to her now. Her desolation is particularly pathetic because her husband has betrayed the values of personal relations which are her own supreme achievement. She cannot communicate with her husband in a way she would like to. Her life loses all its vitality.

The disconnected time-sequence of the novel shows the absurdity of Costaguana where every rational thing fails. The Sartrean thesis that time is entirely relative proves true in Mrs. Gould's case when it occurs to her that "for life to be large and full, it must contain the care of the past and of the future in every passing moment of the present." (521) Thus she lives in past, present and future at the same time.

Mrs. Gould's love for her intrinsically noble but misguided husband is frustrated by his monomaniacal attachment to his mine. By the time of the riot, she realizes the enormity of their mistake of reopening the mine. She has her moments of the recognition of the utter futility and unhappiness in the pursuits of material interests. She sees her marriage ruined and her life slipping into futility. She has sacrificed herself for her husband and now she is alone with her broken ideals. She is as solitary as any human being had ever been, perhaps, on this earth. The lonely childless existence of Mrs. Gould exasperates Monygham: "Was it for this that her life had been robbed of all the intimate felicities of daily affection which her tenderness needed as the human body needs air to breathe?" (512)

The sense of isolation exists since problems of communication occur in various situations and relationships. Mrs. Gould finds that "love was only a short moment of forgetfulness, a short intoxication, whose delight one remembered with a sense of sadness, as if it had been a deep grief lived through." (521) She understands that her marriage has been insidiously destroyed by the mine and reflects upon her solitariness. She feels a great wave of loneliness sweep over her head and speculates that no one will ever ask her with solicitude what she is thinking about. Sitting alone in the shade of the big trees in the garden, her husband at the mine and the house closed to the street like an empty dwelling, Mrs. Gould appropriately symbolizes alienation: "An immense desolation, the dread of her own continued life, descended upon the first lady of Sulaco. With a prophetic vision she saw herself surviving alone the degradation of her young ideal of life, of love, of work—all alone in the Treasure House of the World." (522) The aging Mrs. Gould lacks the companionship of shared thoughts. She fails to escape from the isolation which is the normal and almost inevitable condition of humanity as Conrad saw it.

Nostromo, after his decision to keep the silver for himself, works out an ingenious method to grow rich slowly but steadily. To express their sense of gratitude to him, the citizens of Sulaco have awarded a ship to Nostromo. With the help of this ship, Nostromo engages in extensive travel and trading, and these are taken to be the sources of his wealth. But actually, in between his voyages along the coast, he returns stealthily to his hiding place and removes a couple of ingots at a time.

Nostromo's conflict over the silver becomes a fear of losing his fine reputation and of the subsequent shame and disgrace if his theft is discovered. He is proud of being considered the dashing hero of Sulaco, the fearless, charming, resourceful, and dependable man of many accomplishments. He finds that to "become the slave of a treasure with full self-knowledge is an occurrence rare and mentally disturbing." (523) Nostromo is humiliated by his dishonesty and by having to conduct his life cautiously and secretly: "To do things by stealth humiliated him." (523) He suffers through his fear of being discovered as much as through his prudence in disposing of the silver a little at a time.

The secret knowledge about the buried treasure haunts Nostromo like a curse. He staggers under the weight of his secret and the loneliness which is its price. The tyranny of his treasure weighs upon "his mind, his actions, his very sleep." (529) He loses his peace of mind and feels morally isolated. The silver has him in his clutches and Nostromo feels that he will never be able to escape from it. Having made a conscious choice "to grow rich slowly," (503) Nostromo is aware that he must confront the consequences of his act:

> A transgression, a crime, entering a man's existence, eats it up like a malignant growth, consumes it like a fever. . . . His courage, his magnificence, his leisure, his work, everything was as before, only everything was a sham. (523-24)

By his decision, Nostromo has forfeited his integrity in his own eyes. When he handles the ingots, he imagines that they leave a stain on his fingers. He lives in constant apprehension and anxiety that someone will see him disposing of the silver or will discover that he has hidden it.

One day returning from the longest of his voyages, Nostromo finds a lighthouse being erected on the Great Isabel. His despair and dread know no bounds "at this turn of chance, that would kindle a far-reaching light upon the only secret spot of his life." (525) Suspecting that his treasure might be discovered, Nostromo contemplates committing suicide. He imagines "the disgrace, the shame going on" (525) even after death and chooses, instead, the risk of removing the treasure from that location. Though his corruption is not discovered, his initial dread proves right because the lighthouse turns out to be the indirect cause of his death. And the dread he experiences is existential in nature.

The idea of saving the silver for himself takes possession of Nostromo. He solves the problem of the lighthouse by arranging the appointment of Giorgio Viola as its keeper. He becomes involved with Linda, Viola's older daughter, who is openly in love with him. However he prefers her younger sister Giselle, with whom he plans to run away. His affair with her continues while he remains officially engaged to be married to her elder sister.

Nostromo's enslavement to the silver and entanglement with Giselle lead to his death. Trapped by the twin forces of greed and love, Nostromo fails to make the right choice. He seals his fate by his inability to run away with Giselle: the treasure stands between them and freedom. Nostromo shows great prudence in using the treasure but loses control over his life. He dares not tell Viola of his secret passion for Giselle because he fears that Viola may forbid him to visit the island. He divides the time between the two girls and is accidentally shot by their oblivious and somewhat senile father at the end.

When Nostromo is dead, the disillusioned Mrs. Gould tells his sweetheart, Giselle: "Console yourself, child. Very soon he would have forgotten you for his treasure." (561) When Giselle protests that Nostromo loved her "as no one had ever been loved before," Mrs. Gould replies: "I have been loved, too." (561) The corrupting power of the mine has driven Mrs. Gould to cynicism. Her disillusionment with material interests, which have made her own married life unhappy, is genuine.

Dr. Monygham's horrid sufferings at the hands of the Bento regime had left him disillusioned and bitter. But these do not prevent him from turning his life from a negative awaiting of death into something positive. Through his misfortunes, he has understood the meaning of compassion. He has learnt that material interests know neither peace nor rest; they take man's life into their hands and destroy it. His final comment on the mine shows his humane temperament and disillusioned eye for facts:

> There is no peace and no rest in the development of material interests. They have their law, and their justice. But it is founded on expediency, and is inhuman; it is without rectitude, without the continuity and the force that can be found only in a moral principle. (511)

It is only humanistic and spiritual values that can bring about peace and order. These values in Monygham raise him above the inhuman. His love for Mrs. Gould manifests his belief that in sympathy alone can man expect help.[32] Monygham seems to have achieved the shaping of a new, positive life on the experiences won through moral failure. Though he does not believe in political reform, only his courageous action makes possible the independence of Sulaco.

The last three chapters of the novel also give us a hint of the future course of Costaguana. All through the book, Costaguana has been in a state of perpetual revolution, which signifies meaningless struggle. One government is almost as futile as another; therefore governmental changes bring no relief and are no real or permanent solution. At the end, Sulaco becomes independent of the rest of Costaguana but this independence is achieved through an entry into a larger subjection. Moreover new revolutions are brewing; the inimical forces are beginning to gather strength. No doubt, the revolution has brought financial prosperity to the state but this has been at a high cost of individual suffering. Don Jose Avellanos, who had devoted himself to right and justice, dies after the lifelong effort. The Gould's success is once more brought into question. Father Corbelan as newly-accepted Cardinal, Holroyd's Protestant invasion, Nostromo's involvement with the Italian radicals—all portend ominously for the future of the mine and the material interests. For Sulaco, progress has come out of chaos but it is likely to degenerate into chaos once again.

The future of Sulaco is not very hopeful. Absolute good has not been achieved. But as the engineer-in-chief says: "Things seem to be worth nothing by what they are in themselves. . . . the only solid thing about them is the spiritual value which everyone discovers in his own form of activity." (318) Don Jose Avellanos is an idealist who guides his nation out of a very barbaric, primitive stage in politics. His achievement leaves the reader with the feeling that the struggle with evil is not useless.

Man's unprincipled avarice for silver excludes love as a redeeming force. Linked with the spiritual distress of Gould and the ruin of Decoud and Nostromo are the grief-stricken figures of their women. At the end of the novel, all the women—Mrs. Gould, Antonia, Giselle and Linda—are left alone. The novel aptly ends with the image of the solitary Linda tending the light above the darkness in which lies the treasure of the mine.[33] Love is the only value which can transcend the egotism of the materialistic world. The kindness of Mrs. Gould brings hope and a certain form of fulfilment to Dr. Monygham.

Through an extreme situation occurring at a crucial time in his life, man is forced to confront the conditions of existence, to reflect upon himself and life, and contemplate the meaning of his freedom and responsibility. What he learns from his experience becomes the measure of his courage and dignity as a man. On his deathbed, Nostromo declares himself responsible for allowing the treasure to ruin his life. He confesses to Mrs. Gould that he has taken the treasure, and offers to tell her where it is: "The silver has killed me. It has held me. It holds me yet." (559) In a sense, he once again becomes the man of integrity. He meets death away from home, isolated, at night. Such a death comes as a fit climax to a career both mysterious and unusual. Nostromo dies attempting to choose an authentic action, so that while he loses the treasure, he will not forfeit completely his reputation. Thus Conrad implies that Nostromo's choice of action is consistent with his need to maintain appearances. Even in death the Captaz de Cargadores is the romantic, courageous hero of Sulaco.

There is a tragic nobility about Nostromo's end. We seem to hear Conrad saying: "Here at least was the real man." Since the final tragedy brings out his best human qualities, Nostromo's defeat is really his victory. Death is a determining element insofar as it renders final judgment on a person because it is an irreversible act. The novel ends with an affirmation of human sympathy and dignity. Linda's scream of grief as she learns of Nostromo's death, "I shall never forget thee. Never!" is aptly described by Conrad as "another of Nostromo's triumphs." (560)

NOTES

1. *Heart of Darkness* in *Youth: A Narrative and Two Other Stories.*
2. Douglas Hewitt, *Conrad: A Reassessment* (Cambridge: Bowes and Bowes, 1952), p. 18.
3. William Bysshe Stein, "The Lotus Posture and *The Heart of Darkness,*" *Modern Fiction Studies,* II (1956), p. 235.
4. Joseph Conrad, *Last Essays* (Garden City, New York: Doubleday, Page, 1925), p. 17.
5. John A. Gee and Paul J. Sturm, ed., *Letters of Joseph Conrad to Marguerite Poradowska,* pp. 45-46.
6. Wilfred S. Dowden, "The Light and the Dark: Imagery and Thematic Development in Conrad's *Heart of Darkness," Rice Institute Pamphlet,* XLIV (1957), p. 49.
7. Ted E. Boyle, *Symbol and Meaning in the Fiction of Joseph Conrad* (London: Mouton, 1965), p. 107.
8. According to Garrett Stewart too, the helmsman's death "solidifies the sense of human commonality. He dies without uttering a sound . . . awaiting completion in the articulate death of Kurtz." "Lying as Dying in *Heart of Darkness," PMLA,* XCV (1980), p. 322.
9. "In Marlow's progress towards an indissoluble association with Kurtz," asserts Jan Verleun, "the harlequin constitutes a linking and conditioning stimulus." "Marlow and the Harlequin," *Conradiana,* XII (1981), p. 196.
10. Bruce Harkness holds the opinion that "Kurtz sees the ultimate truth: it is not that man has an evil side. It is that in his essence Kurtz is evil. Marlow is evil. All men are evil. And finally that evil is the essence of the universe," "Conrad, Graham Greene, and Film," *Comparative Literature Symposium* (Lubbock: Texas Tech. Univ., 1974), p. 80.
11. Jean-Aubry, *Joseph Conrad: Life and Letters,* p. 216.
12. Bringing out similarities between the two protagonists, Kurtz in Conrad's *Heard of Darkness* and the Reverend Arthur Dimmesdale in Nathaniel Hawthorne's *The Scarlet Letter,* M.H. Goldwyn asserts: "Both characters appear, to a certain extent, to perish from moral exhaustion, but they manage at the end to achieve a kind of moral victory. *In extremis* they seem to experience a profound

epiphany which impels them to acknowledge absolutely the error of their ways, nobly judging and triumphing over themselves." "Nathaniel Hawthorne and Conrad's *Heart of Darkness,*" *Conradiana*, XVI (1984), p. 73.

13. As Janis P. Stout points out, the tone of Marlow's narrative may be largely gloomy, but the fact that he asserts his will against the brute matter of things in making the narration is itself an affirmation. "The Possibility of Affirmation in *Heart of Darkness* and *Henderson the Rain King,*" *Philological Quarterly,* LVII (1978), p. 121.

14. In Marlow's meeting with the Intended, S.D.V. Hoffman detects "something like another choice of nightmares. . . . In a dead city, it is another journey to another heart of darkness, a heart of darkness in a civilized setting." *Comedy and Form in the Fiction of Joseph Conrad* (The Hague: Mouton, 1969), p. 34.

15. William Meldrum, ed., *Joseph Conrad: Letters to William Blackwood and David S. Meldrum* (Durham, North Carolina: Duke University Press, 1958), p. 154.

16. Bruce R. Stark very interestingly argues that this apparently nameless woman actually has two symbolic names: "My Intended" and "The horror." As a result, he points out, when Marlow says to her that "the last word he pronounced was—your name," he is in fact telling a truth that his own illusions prevented him from saying. "Kurtz's Intended: The Heart of *Heart of Darkness,*" *Texas Studies in Literature and Language,* XVI (1974), pp. 535-55.

17. Paul L. Wiley fittingly characterizes Jim's dream world as "the imaginary realm, timeless and ordered, in which Jim dreams of himself as a hero and a savior." *Conrad's Measure of Man* (Madison: The University of Wisconsin Press, 1954), p. 55.

18. Tony Tanner points out that in this incident "we can see signs of his lack of self-knowledge, his habit of skirting personal guilt." *Lord Jim* (New York: Woodbury, 1963), p. 9. D.L. Mensforth also recognizes that "this is to become one of his principal failings, in that he sees the cause of his failures as external, whereas it is in fact within his own nature." *Lord Jim* (Oxford: Basil Blackwell, 1970), p. 12.

19. Jean-Aubry, *Joseph Conrad: Life and Letters,* I, p. 309.

20. Frederick R. Karl identifies Brierly's suicide with Jim's failure: "Brierly is a successful Jim who recognizes that failure is a

condition of life and who destroys himself while still in good fortune, with his ship on course and his log up to point." "Conrad's Stein: The Destructive Element," *Twentieth-Century Literature,* III (1958), p. 164.

21. Jean-Aubry, *Joseph Conrad: Life and Letters,* I, p. 184.
22. Robert W. Stallman feels that "Stein's famous metaphor in *Lord Jim* poses the enigma of life: to be or become." "Conrad and *The Great Gatsby,*" *Twentieth-Century Literature,* I (1955), p. 10.
23. Jean-Paul Sartre, *Existentialism and Humanism,* p. 28.
24. Martin Bock rightly feels this to be the Conradian "moment of vision." In this image, Conrad is able "to sum up the temperament of the romantic *Tuan* Jim, the ambience of Patusan, and the human condition as expressed by the outcast in an alien land." "The Sensationist Epistemelogy of Conrad's early fiction," *Conradiana,* XVI (1984), p. 14.
25. It is hard to agree with Arnold E. Davidson who argues that "Jim, even in dying, fails one more time to be the man whom he would die to be." "The Abdication of Lord Jim," *Conradiana,* XIII (1981), p. 19.
26. Likewise, Gerald M. Garmon comments: "Conrad recognizes full well the limits of ordinary mortals, but he also urges, through his characterization of Jim, that man can do heroic things. He can be brave, though once he was not." "*Lord Jim* as Tragedy," *Conradiana,* IV (1972), p. 38.
27. Jean-Paul Sartre, *Existentialism and Humanism,* p. 29.
28. *Notes on Life and Letters,* p. 9.
29. *Nostromo* (Garden City, New York: Doubleday, Page, 1925).
30. *The Metaphysics of Darkness* (Baltimore and London: Johns Hopkins Press, 1971), p. 117.
31. Royal Roussel holds a similar view when he says that Nostromo's failure "serves to drive a wedge between self and world, to effect that detachment which causes (him) to realize the instability of the surface of things." *Ibid.,* p. 124.
32. Bruce E. Johnson advances a similar reason for Monygham's existence: "Monygham, tortured like some Sartrean hero until he finds himself capable of anything, exists only in the light of Emilia Gould's regard." *Conrad's Models of Mind* (Minneapolis: University of Minnesota Press, 1971), p. 117.
33. Discussing how *Nostromo* will gradually emerge as one of the great

books of world literature, E.M.W. Tillyard writes: "It echoes and confirms the hopes of those who wish to have reasons for living vigorously in a world that threatens to baffle them at every turn. Thus *Nostromo* fulfils the choric task that belongs properly to the epic." "Conrad: Nostromo," *The Epic Strain in the English Novel* (London: Chatto and Windus, 1958, rep. 1967), p. 166.

The Final Phase: Existential Affirmation

Conrad's third and final phase brings the threads of his themes full circle. With *The Secret Agent, The Secret Sharer, Under Western Eyes* and *Victory*, Conrad brings in more and more of existential vision into developed artistic form. In these novels, he reiterates in unequivocal terms his commitment to the values of life despite the threats posed by human society and by an enigmatic universe. Indeed, all the major novels published after *Nostromo* are logical extensions of these commitments, exploring either their social implications or their broad philosophical assumptions.

The period between 1906 and 1915 represents Conrad's last effective work. With *The Secret Agent* and *Under Western Eyes,* published in 1907 and 1911 respectively, Conrad moves toward a more profound examination of man in relation to society and to the claims of his fellow men. *The Secret Sharer*, serialized in *Harper's Magazine* from August to September 1910, was later included in the volume *'Twixt Land and Sea* published in 1912. *Victory,* completed just before the First World War, was published in 1915. In *Victory,* his last major novel, Conrad finally resolves the moral and philosophical complexities that had motivated his fiction from the beginning. The novels of the last phase develop the metaphysical and epistemological beliefs that had always been implicit in his early fiction. The preoccupations central to Conrad's existential humanism culminate in these novels and demonstrate his existential affirmation.

II

The Secret Agent, an exciting story about anarchy and murder, expresses Conrad's existentialist attitude towards the universe and man's place in it. Here, Conrad is preoccupied with the cruelties and inanities that are enacted in the name of political ideologies and progress in society; his attitude of scorn towards the anarchists is also evident. The "Author's

Note" of 1920, written long after the novel's original publication in 1907, is highly revealing. In this, Conrad declares his concern with "the criminal futility of the whole thing, doctrine, action, mentality." (ix)[1]

The theme of the novel is man's attempt to live authentically in a meaningless and absurd world. The gory destruction of a feeble-minded boy in a bomb-outrage is the central incident of the novel and provides a commentary on man's existence in the world. Conrad terms the incident as an "absurd cruelty" (xii) and wonders why a boy should be "blown to bits for nothing even most remotely resembling an idea, anarchistic or other." (x) The novel's subtitle, "A Simple Tale," encloses the totality of the world's absurdity in it; the simplicity is only of the surface.

Conrad offers no hope for the anarchists: they are corrupt, selfish, morally bankrupt who can stoop to anything for the attainment of their ends. The novel explores the absurdities of espionage and "the poor expedients devised by a mediocre mankind for preserving an imperfect society from the dangers of moral and physical corruption." (258) The great brooding city of London, which forms the background for the story, is "a cruel devourer of the world's light" (xii) and gives rise to a picture of squalor, misery and the meaninglessness of life.

All the characters—the Verlocs, the anarchists, the police officers—are cut off from their pasts and have no opportunity to make their present lives significant. "The characters," says Joseph I. Fradin, "are possessed, to use the 'existential' word, by non-being, by the void which lies not only beyond their lives but everywhere within them as well, and what is most striking and original about Conrad's achievement comes from the way he makes that void so inescapable and so thickly felt a presence in the novel."[2]

The novel brings out the failure of modern science and technology to solve the problems of man's life in the world. The city fails to achieve the idea of a human community. Man's reason is unable to cope effectively with a confused world. Conrad seems to make us believe that the values which tend to make life capable of honour and dignity are illusory and that the life of the civilized man is constantly tinged by death.

The novel presents a grim picture of London—its disintegration, death and annihilation. Throughout the novel, the city threatens to stifle and suffocate. The scene is set in the squalid shop of Mr. Verloc. Outwardly Verloc is a bookseller, dealing in pornographic literature, but actually the bookshop is used by his anarchist friends for their secret meetings. Both the merchandise and the customers visiting the premises are shady. It is a world out of joint where Verloc's shop door is closed during the day and open at night.

Originally, Verloc was to be the title character of the story. But the emphasis shifted to Winnie as Conrad set himself to writing it. As it is, the central character of the novel is Winnie whose devotion to her mentally retarded brother Stevie has impelled her to marry Verloc. She has forsaken a handsome, vital young suitor, a butcher boy because he could not have provided a home for Stevie. She chooses Verloc and lets the butcher boy drift because her prime consideration is security for Stevie. In fact, she is thankful to Verloc for bringing her mother and Stevie to live with him at his shop in Soho and for assuming responsibility for them. She feels little love for Verloc and does not really understand him. The only thing that she knows about his mysterious job is that it is "in a way political." (7) Verloc often makes trips to the Continent and has round about ways of returning home. But Winnie asks no questions and works silently in the house. It seems that she has no independent existence apart from being Stevie's sister. Her only worry is Stevie who has a poor memory and sometimes forgets even his name and address. It is quite logical then that later on Winnie prints these on a tag inside his coat-collar.

The secrecy with which each character operates for his own motives reveals the isolation, the lack of communication in the society portrayed. When Winnie marries Verloc, she accepts the secret places in his life. Her habit of not looking into things symbolizes death itself. Winnie and Verloc do not let each other into the secret of their personal thoughts and this non-communication is responsible for their fatal illusions: Winnie's that Verloc is like a father to Stevie, and Verloc's that he is loved for his own sake. They do not go beneath the surface to examine the basis on which they have founded their most cherished expectations. Similarly, Winnie's mother is unable to understand her daughter's deliberate sacrifice of herself for her brother: "She had never really understood why Winnie had married Mr. Verloc. It was very sensible of her, and evidently had turned out for the best, but her girl might have naturally hoped to find somebody of a more suitable age." (40)

Apart from being a bookseller and an anarchist, Verloc has been working as an agent provocateur for a foreign embassy in London. Vladimir, the embassy representative, expresses his dissatisfaction with the kind of work that Verloc is doing for them. He berates Verloc's lack of activity and asks him to organize some anarchist activity which would shock the people and make the London police take more vigilant and repressive measures towards anarchistic movements. It would make them conscious of the danger to be apprehended from revolutionaries, and so be persuaded to stop offering sanctuary to anarchists from the Continent.

The whole discussion between Vladimir and Verloc is presented in existential terms of the absurd. Vladimir considers the country to be "absurd with its sentimental regard for individual liberty," (29) and decides to undermine public confidence. His plan is to stir the middle classes by perpetration of a series of outrageous acts of violence and destruction, not necessarily sanguinary, but effectively terrifying. His concept is to impress or shock the public: a bomb-outrage would serve the purpose. His philosophy of bomb-throwing is aimed at effecting a change in British society.

Vladimir, whom Fleishman terms as "Conrad's representative of the essential irrationalism,"[3] explains to Verloc that there is no point in throwing a bomb at the royal palace, church buildings, theatres, or art-galleries; the outrage must be such as to appear utterly senseless and meaningless. His sole ambition is to shatter the British public's faith in liberal institutions. He therefore proposes, as a political tactic, "an act of destructive ferocity so absurd as to be incomprehensible, inexplicable, almost unthinkable; in fact, mad." (33) His decision that Verloc should bomb Greenwich Observatory, that embodiment of pure science, stems from his intention to discredit the anarchists in England.

Verloc is given a month to prove his worth by arranging an explosion at the Observatory or be dismissed. Horrified at the demand, Verloc pleads the difficulties and incidentally makes a mention of his wife. The fact that Verloc is a married man, shocks Vladimir who comments sneeringly: "Married! And you a professed anarchist, too! What is this confounded nonsense?" (36) His considered opinion is that the anarchists should never marry.

The novelist presents here an irrational and disordered world. In the "Author's Note," Conrad emphasizes the seeming incongruities of Vladimir's argument in the form of inversion of logic and illogic: "It was impossible to fathom its origin by any reasonable or even unreasonable process of thought. For perverse unreason has its own logical processes." (x)

In existential terms, Verloc's response to Vladimir's ultimatum is man's reaction to the absurd. Verloc's harrowing interview with Vladimir leaves him totally frustrated. He returns home angry, bewildered and disturbed. All his efforts to convince Vladimir about his usefulness to the embassy have proved futile. He has been insulted and humiliated by Vladimir but feels quite helpless. Verloc's humanity is almost lost due to this depressing and demoralizing experience. He feels isolated and broods in silence about his horrible mission. Though nothing unusual in the household, his stony silence that evening seems thoughtful to Winnie and her mother. Actually the harassed agent is depressed at feeling his security threatened.

Verloc faces an existential choice of action; he has to make up his mind about Vladimir's ultimatum. His perfect accord with life is shattered by Vladimir's unexpected intrusion. Despite his isolation, he is dominated by the outside world. His actions are determined by conflicting forces which dominate him from without: he is a victim. He hates Vladimir and is consumed with a slow rage at his entrapment. For some time he lives in a state of unnatural tension, with his hidden life struggling to reach accord with the public life he is violating.

Conrad condemns anarchists because they live lives of illusion, unaware that their moral judgments are contaminated by self-interest. They have no capacity for loyalty and place no value on life itself. They are referred to not as men of character and ideals but as misguided creatures. The prominent anarchists who meet at Verloc's house are engaged in the various occupations of social revolution and propaganda. However, their views on methods of revolution vary. After long years of lonely cogitation in prison, the ticket-of-the-leave apostle Michaelis believes that economic pressures will in time change society. While talking, he remains indifferent to the reactions of his listeners. Living in the solitude of the four white-washed walls of his cell, Michaelis has acquired the habit of thinking aloud, of talking to himself. The mere fact of hearing another voice disconcerts him painfully and confuses his thoughts at once.

The terrorist Karl Yundt has never taken any violent action himself but dreams of a small band of ruthless men absolute in their resolve to destroy everything. He shares the Professor's faith in total destruction: "No pity for anything on earth . . . and death enlisted for good and all in the service of humanity—that's what I would have liked to see." (42) Comrade Alexander Ossipon is the theorist who writes revolutionary pamphlets intended to stir people's emotions.

These anarchist-associates have nothing in common except their dependence on women for their well-being. Their addiction to anarchy as a way of life is attributed to their extreme sloth. Verloc realizes that these anarchists with their fatuous ideals can be of no help in his arranging the outrage. They are all sham. There is hardly any relationship between what they say and what they do, between theory and action. In the light of Vladimir's philosophy of bomb-throwing, the group of anarchists appears "hopelessly futile." (42) The cruel dilemma with which Vladimir has confronted Verloc cannot be resolved by these anarchists. Consequently, Verloc becomes conscious of the loneliness of his responsibility.

It is of interest to note that Verloc himself is no real anarchist. He professes to be an anarchist but is constitutionally opposed to the disruption of society. He wants a safe and unruffled life with a minimum of effort. His purpose is to preserve the status quo as long as it guarantees him repose, security and respectability. That is why he is furious with Vladimir for threatening the stability of his existence. In existential terms, Verloc remains unauthentic in life because he does not define himself in his actions.

Yundt's talk of the gruesome details of his destructive ideas excites Stevie's heated imagination. Unlike his sister who put her trust in face values, Stevie wishes to reach the bottom of the matter. He feels agitated at the mention of words suggesting cruelty. So he keeps himself busy in drawing endless intersecting circles, "a rendering of cosmic chaos, the symbolism of a mad art attempting the inconceivable." (45) Drawing circles is one of the pastimes of Stevie's unproductive existence. Normally circles signify wholeness and completion. But as drawn by Stevie, these represent emptiness, chaos and disintegration. His circles are as irrational as the numbers of the houses in the street through which Verloc had walked earlier.

After the meeting of the anarchists, Verloc feels lonely and disconsolate at the plight of a secret agent being unwillingly forced into violence. Nature too seems quite hostile. Looking out of the cold windowpane of his bedroom, Verloc sees a rainy darkness overtake all London, creating a world of things "unlovely and unfriendly to man." (56) He feels the latent unfriendliness of all out of doors with a force approaching positive bodily anguish. It is a city immersed in futility.

Verloc experiences a sense of loneliness and desolation, since he has no one to turn to. He cannot share with Winnie the responsibility that has been thrust upon him. He sees her enter the room and get into bed in a calm, business-like manner which makes him feel hopelessly alone in the world. She scarcely notices the anxiety and sleeplessness of her husband and talks about Stevie. Verloc's anxieties however prevent him from making any sense out of what she is saying. It is as if her voice is coming from behind a thick wall. Wholly self-absorbed, neither listens to the other. Trying to fall asleep, Verloc is conscious of "the dreary conviction that there was no sleep for him" and this holds him "mute and hopelessly inert in his fear of darkness." (60)

Conrad emphasizes here the impenetrability and insensitivity of mankind. He dwells upon the solitariness of Verloc and Winnie who have spent together seven years of married life. Winnie could have been a source of comfort to Verloc only if she had shared his political responsibilities. But this does not happen. She neither offers nor invites confidences. In all her actions and relationships, she presents the idea of a person who lives deliberately on the surface of life and refuses all real communication with those around her. She has cultivated incuriosity. The Verlocs's failure to communicate is a kind of betrayal of the marriage relationship.

Verloc's glum mood forces Winnie's mother to take a decision. A woman capable of heroism and sacrifice, the mother decides to get herself admitted to an almshouse. She feels that the first sense of security following Winnie's marriage is wearing off. But she does not want Stevie's security to be threatened. Her departure, she thinks, would give Stevie a greater moral claim on Verloc. For Stevie's sake, she decides to leave a comfortable existence in her daughter's home and goes out to face a hostile and indifferent world. While going, she takes only the oldest pieces of furniture with her, leaving the rest for Winnie. She gives nothing to Stevie, thus making him totally dependent on the Verlocs. Her abandonment of Stevie is actually "an arrangement for settling her son permanently in life." (162)

Winnie is surprised from her usual calm self-sufficiency by her mother's decision. She had noticed the unusual activity on her mother's part and had drawn Verloc's attention to it. But Verloc is so immersed in his private meditation that the outside world hardly exists for him. The sacrifice of the heroic lady is not fully appreciated by the Verlocs. Winnie, with her philosophy of "not taking notice of the inside of facts," (154) assumes that the mother did what suited her best whereas Verloc has a tendency to intense meditation which, "like a sort of Chinese wall, isolated him from the phenomena of this world of vain effort and illusory appearances." (154)

The mother goes to the almshouse accompanied by Winnie and Stevie. They go off in a particularly dilapidated cab with a one-armed cab driver and a woefully infirm horse. Winnie's mother is repulsed to see the "hooked iron contrivance" (156) in place of the hand of the cab driver. Conrad comments on the absurdity of the world these people face: "The conveyance awaiting them would have illustrated the proverb that 'truth can be more cruel than caricature,' if such a proverb existed." (155) To top these physical facts, the cab driver keeps whipping the horse. In spite of his retardation, Stevie feels distressed at the cab driver's treatment of his horse.

In this scene, Stevie emerges as a humanitarian and idealist. Intensely responsive to pain, he sees the suffering beneath the calm surface of things but becomes speechless in his anguish and cannot explain his ideas. Conrad's symbolism is quite strong in this scene. The cab is the Cab of Death and the almshouse a grave. The cab-drive through the foggy, dark, damp, grimy maze of London, with its hints of a funeral procession, points forward to the three absurd deaths in the novel.

When the cabman, on reaching the almshouse, is paid decently, Conrad feels it to be a fit opportunity to comment on the general human condition. In this world, mankind does not receive appropriate reward for its toil. The money that the crippled cab driver earns is nothing compared to the labour he puts in: "The cabman looked at the pieces of silver, which, appearing very minute in his big, grimy palm, symbolised the insignificant results which reward the ambitious courage and toil of a mankind whose day is short on this earth of evil." (165)

Stevie looks at the miserable horse and converses with the cab driver. The latter is a poor man who finds it difficult to provide even the basic necessities of life to his wife and four children. He explains his poverty to Stevie by saying that world may be hard on horses but is a "dam' sight 'arder on poor chaps like me." (167) The cab driver whips the horse not because his soul is cruel and his heart evil, but because he has to earn his fare. Faced with this human and equine misery, Stevie bursts with compassion and helplessness. The disparities that exist in standards of living of different men makes him miserable. The word "shame" uttered in this connection contains "all his sense of indignation and horror at one sort of wretchedness having to feed upon the anguish of the other—at the poor cabman beating the poor horse in the name, as it were, of his poor kids at home. And Stevie knew what it was to be beaten. He knew it from experience. It was a bad world. Bad! Bad!" (171)

Stevie may not be able to remember his name and address but he does remember the beatings that he has received from his father. He knows what comfort he drew from the safety of his sister's bed. The same comfort he visualizes for the horse but soon realizes the incongruity of the whole thing: the horse cannot be taken to bed. The only solution to the problem of poverty that he can think of is police. The occasion is utilized by Conrad to comment on the condition of men: "Like the rest of mankind, perplexed by the mystery of the universe, he had his moments of trust in the organised powers of the earth." (172) But Stevie's solution is not fit to be applied to this irrational world.

Winnie deliberately refrains from trying to pierce beneath the surface of life. As long as Stevie is protected, she calmly accepts life. However, she reproaches her mother for going away. Her main anxiety is not for the mother but what the neighbours would think and how upset Stevie would feel without the mother. Not much interested in probing the mysteries of the universe, Winnie feels that "things do not stand much looking into." (177) She does not go into things like motivation and thinks it better not to know too much. She notices Stevie's excitement but does not go into its cause. Stevie tries to explain to Winnie the plight of the cab driver and his world: "'Poor! Poor!' he ejaculated appreciatively, 'Cabman poor, too. He told me himself.'" (170) From this experience, Stevie has come to the conclusion that it is "bad world for poor people." (171) There exists a wide gulf between things as they are and things as they ought to be. Winnie's incomprehension of Stevie's sympathy for the cab driver brings out man's inhumanity to man.

Verloc remains indifferent to the news which evokes in him a vision of rats leaving a sinking ship. He sits brooding, sunk in silent gloom. Pursued by other thoughts, he goes out silently. Consumed by anxiety and indecision, he wanders aimlessly. At night, he feels like confessing it all to Winnie but finds communication very difficult. Winnie dislikes any controversy that will disturb the equable manner with which she conducts life. Verloc, on the other hand, feels quite lazy in attempting something difficult and this prevents him from revealing his worries to her until it is too late.

Verloc is quite considerate to his wife and does not want to intrude on the peace of her mind. When he announces that he is going abroad, Winnie remains unperturbed. After all, Verloc did this quite often and without explanation. The novelist comments that by a mystic accord of temperament and necessity, Verloc has been set apart to be a secret agent all his life. Winnie's temperament of not looking beneath the surface of meaning, a result of her irresponsibility, makes her shy away from investigating Verloc's cryptic remark about her mother's departure being for the best. Winnie misses another chance of winning her husband's confidence. Once again, she turns off the lights in the room: the light of truth is not available to her.

Verloc's concern with the financial and marital problems forces him to plan the explosion. He is sullenly bewildered at Vladimir's order and looks around for an agent. Forced with the need to act, Verloc visits the Continent to find an agent to carry out the plan but fails to get one. He returns home gloomy and taciturn.

Anxious to increase the good relations between Verloc and Stevie, Winnie forces Stevie upon Verloc's attention. She calls notice to his usefulness: "You could do anything with that boy, Adolf. . . . He would go through fire for you." (184) In the beginning, Verloc remains indifferent to Stevie but soon notices Stevie's devotion to him, his loyalty and reliability. The idea to use Stevie grows in his mind. He suggests that Stevie be sent on a holiday to Michaelis's cottage in Kent. Winnie is agreeable and, with her inflexible assurance, comments that her husband is growing fond of Stevie.

On the day of the bomb-outrage, Winnie is alone in the house. The weather is so foul that she spends the day in the shop and hears no news. Verloc returns in the evening and his behaviour disturbs her. He is feeling miserable because things have gone wrong. He proposes a foreign sojourn but Winnie argues against any such plan.

We know by now that Verloc has attempted to damage Greenwich Observatory and has failed. A man has blown himself up in the premature explosion in Greenwich Park. The Professor, a "frail, insignificant, shabby, miserable," (311) and dingy little man, has supplied the bomb used in this outrage.

The Professor is the fanatical anarchist who believes that his job is to incite the world to annihilate all authority, to persuade the people to break down and smash all legal movements. He has a singleness of purpose—to make a perfect detonator—and this governs all his acts. Single-minded and confident, he has a great scorn for other revolutionaries and for their contemptible futility. His zeal to destroy society urges him to criticize Ossipon bluntly:

> You revolutionists . . . are the slaves of the social convention, which is afraid of you; slaves of it as much as the very police that stands up in the defence of that convention. Clearly you are, since you want to revolutionize it. It governs your thought, of course, and your action, too, and thus neither your thought nor your action can ever be conclusive. (69)

In spite of his holding such an opinion of the anarchists, he readily supplies them with the explosives.

For his success, the Professor depends on "death, which knows no restraint and cannot be attacked." (68) He is a fearless man who carries in his pocket a flask of explosives which he can detonate at a second's notice. He intends to blow up both himself and the arresting officer with his pocket detonator if any attempt is made to nab him. Thus he attains a feeling of superiority over police interference, but it is only a sinister freedom that he gains. His defiant and destructive philosophy makes him distrust mankind itself. The idea that haunts the Professor is that mankind is indestructible "mighty in its numbers . . . numerous like locusts, industrious like ants, thoughtless like a natural force, pushing on blind and orderly and absorbed, impervious to sentiment, to logic, to terror, too, perhaps." (82) He is happy only when alone among his illusions. He remains indifferent even "to rain or sun in a sinister detachment from the aspects of sky and earth." (96)

The anarchist Ossipon's reaction to the explosion is one of fear. In the presence of the Professor, he suffers from a sense of moral insignificance. In an underground room of the Silenus Restaurant, he informs the Professor about the explosion in Greenwich Park, resulting in the disintegration of the body of the man concerned. In a perfectly detached manner, the Professor informs Ossipon that he had supplied a bomb to Verloc. From this fact, Ossipon concludes that Verloc has been blown up. He is anxious because this business may adversely affect the position of the revolutionaries in the country. He makes some of his remarks half-audibly and to himself "after the manner of a man reflecting in perfect solitude." (78) Though he has no clear idea of what to do, he knows that he must take some action. The Professor advises him to fasten himself to Mrs. Verloc for all she is worth. He is anguished that "the even tenor of his revolutionary life" is "menaced by no fault of his." (78)

Chief Inspector Heat feels annoyed at the news of the bomb-outrage since it has belied his assurance to a high dignitary that no outbreak of any anarchist activity was to be apprehended. The inspector has not acted wisely in giving this assurance. Conrad points out that in this world of contradictions, true wisdom consists in not being certain of anything. Even time and space, which frame all human existence and give it form and structure, are shot through with holes of uncertainty and sheer horror.

The grisly scene where Chief Inspector Heat views the gruesome fragmented remains of the thin, fair young man who has blown himself up shows man's dehumanization. He is pained and horrified at this random and total destruction. Stevie's death is the result of senseless anarchist activities. Stevie had died instantaneously but it seems impossible to Heat that a human body could have reached that state of disintegration without passing through the pangs of inconceivable agony: "The inexplicable mysteries of conscious existence beset Chief Inspector Heat till he evolved a horrible notion that ages of atrocious pain and mental torture could be contained between two successive winks of an eye." (88)

During the inspection, Heat discovers the velvet collar of a coat bearing a label on which is written Verloc's address. This, he feels, is a sure clue to the identity of the body. He reflects that indiscreet Fate has favoured him with this clue. Feeling that it would be better for his department not to discover the identity of this blown-up man, he decides to conceal the fact.

In a deserted dark lane, Heat meets the Professor in his state of empty nausea. Confronted with this unwholesome little figure, Heat remembers the qualities he has in common with the burglars. Heat understands all about thieves and burglars, but not the working of the mind of an anarchist. He therefore dislikes having to deal with anarchists whose morbid ideals he distrusts. He believes that the thieves have a sort of sincerity in their lives. They do not pretend to be anything other than what they are and express themselves in action. He, therefore, admires the decorum of the ordinary burglar, but is exasperated by "the general idea of the absurdity of things human." (91) He does not understand any act which is not committed for material reasons.

The Professor exults over his determination to blow up himself and those surrounding him if his arrest is attempted. This sinister freedom of the fanatical anarchist is guaranteed by the bomb in his pocket. His diminutive and weak physique is quite in contrast to his far-reaching plans and determined character. He is proud of the fact that he can look the police officer boldly in the face without flinching and talks of sudden death to Heat: "I've no doubt the papers would give you an obituary notice then. You know best what that would be worth to you. I should think you can imagine easily the sort of stuff that would be printed. But you may be exposed to the unpleasantness of being buried together with me, though I suppose your friends would make an effort to sort us out as much as possible." (93) Heat's sense of his own individuality is threatened: "Life had such a strong hold upon him that a fresh wave of nausea broke out in slight perspiration upon his brow." (94)

Chief Inspector Heat, however, stands up manfully to the Professor's threats of explosion and succeeds in shaking his self-confidence. He warns the Professor to desist from destructive activities. It is "a sad-faced, miserable little man" (96) who emerges from the narrow passage: the failure of his detonator has disappointed him. The unwholesome-looking moral agent of destruction has lost faith in mankind. Heat, on the other hand, walks with the consciousness of an authorised mission on this earth, having the moral support of mankind.

Chief Inspector Heat's feeling of self-confidence is soon dissipated. Under pressure, Heat reveals the crucial information about the address on the scrap of cloth which points to the Verloc household. Heat's immediate boss, the Assistant Commissioner for the Special Crime Department, also gets to know that Verloc has been working as a spy in the pay of a foreign embassy as well as giving Heat useful information about the anarchists's movements and plans. Heat distrusts the Assistant Commissioner who in turn hates him. The tone of the Assistant Commissioner's remarks is disparaging and Heat feels quite upset about it.

In the chaos of human relations, the Chief Inspector and the Assistant Commissioner act on selfish impulses. Both are considering a situation in which they must take action. Both try to head the inquiry away from the persons they wish to protect for private reasons. The Assistant Commissioner is shocked into activity by the news that the evidence points to the perpetrator of the outrage having come from the same district as Michaelis—the protege of the influential woman. He is worried because "if the fellow is laid hold of again . . . she will never forgive me." (112) To the Assistant Commissioner, Michaelis's safety takes precedence over the "truth" of the matter. His aim is certitude in both the public and the private realms. Heat, on the other hand, wants to implicate Michaelis because this will satisfy the public. He does not want to endanger Verloc in the interest of his own career: secret agents are after all indispensable to policemen.

In the apparently chaotic world of the novel, the moral values are so upset that an anarchist and a police officer hold similar opinions about the policemen. In the course of his discussion, the Professor equates the revolutionaries with the policemen: "The terrorist and the policeman both come from the same basket. Revolution, legality—counter moves in the same game; forms of idleness at bottom identical." (69) A little later, Chief Inspector Heat equates the thieves and burglars with police officers: "the mind and the instincts of a burglar are of the same kind as the mind and the instincts of a police officer." (92)

Similarly, both Vladimir, the embassy representative, and the Professor, an anarchist, recognize that it is the English conception of legality against which they are working. They want to provoke the forces of government control into anarchy. Vladimir tells Verloc that a bomb-outrage "must be purely destructive" and "make a clean sweep of the whole social creation." (32) The Professor also brings out man's potential for violence: "To break up the superstition and worship of legality should be our aim. Nothing would please me more than to see Inspector Heat and his likes take to shooting us down in broad daylight with the approval of the public. Half our battle would be won then; the disintegration of the old morality would have set in its very temple." (73)

Conrad tries to squeeze some sort of order out of chaos through his presentation of the facts of the police investigation. The ineffective anarchists can very well be set against the apparently effective policemen and their reasoned theories. The Assistant Commissioner reports of the anarchist outrage to the Secretary of State, Sir Ethelred, and takes his permission to take personal charge of the case. He voices the opinion that secret agents, especially double agents, are dangerous because they have no sense of responsibility. Their occupation is free from all restraint.

After lightly disguising himself by the simple method of assuming lower class clothes, the Assistant Commissioner plunges into the decadence of London which looks like a moral inferno in the darkness: "an immensity of greasy slime and damp plaster interspersed with lamps, and enveloped, oppressed, penetrated, choked, and suffocated by the blackness of a wet London night." (150) The Assistant Commissioner is not aware that his visit would perpetrate an appalling family crisis. His descent into the street is likened to "the descent into a slimy aquarium from which the water had been run off." (147) The image of drained aquarium suggests emptiness and vacancy. The Italian restaurant at which the Assistant Commissioner dines has an artificial atmosphere. He experiences "a sense of loneliness, of evil freedom." (148) He looks out at Brett Street which seems to represent human life itself: a short existence in this world and eternity beyond: "Only a fruiterer's stall at the corner made a violent blaze of light and colour. Beyond all was black, and the few people passing in that direction vanished at one stride beyond the glowing heaps of oranges and lemons." (150) In the harsh, garing light of pub and fruitstall, Verloc's shop looks "sullen, brooding and sinister." (151)

The Assistant Commissioner's visit to the shop greatly agitates Verloc. Winnie asks her husband if this is one of those embassy people of whom he has been talking in sleep. Verloc is horrified at the mention of the embassy people.

Soon after, Chief Inspector Heat visits the shop to see if he can find any incriminating evidence against Michaelis. He is vexed to know of the Assistant Commissioner's visit. He shows the address tag to Winnie. From her reactions, he realizes that Stevie was the victim of the bomb-outrage and Verloc the other man.

Winnie eavesdrops to Verloc's narration to Heat of the appalling story of her brother's death and her husband's part in it. Verloc's attempt seems totally irrational to Heat who questions: "He may've been half-witted, but you must have been crazy. What drove you off your head like this?" (212) Heat unofficially advises Verloc to clear out of the land while there is still time.

The revelation of her husband's true nature leaves Winnie intensely and devastatingly shocked and stupefied. The incurious girl is confronted with a shattering knowledge. In an instant, her whole world collapses. Her personality seems to have been "torn into two pieces." (254) She sits immobile, her hands covering her face as though under a spell. She becomes statuesque, her quietness being the calm before the storm: "The perfect immobility of her pose expressed the agitation of rage and despair, all the potential violence of tragic passions, better than any shallow display of shrieks, with the beating of a distracted head against the walls, could have done." (212)

The squalid, dehumanizing London that Conrad portrays in the novel inhabits a decaying society. This society is threatened by the forces of human selfishness, lack of self-discipline and indolence. Beneath a veneer of civilized life lurks irrationality. The moral anarchy of the modern world consists in people exploiting others for personal gain. Conrad discloses at this point that Winnie's only consideration in marrying Verloc was to give security and certainty to herself and her family. Her marriage thus is nothing less than a calculating deception and exploitation of Verloc.

Conrad consciously emphasizes the awareness both of the role of chance in human affairs and of the general unreliability of theories based on temporal cause and effect. Man has to deal with the unpredictable in this world and this causes anxiety and uncertainty. He has no established notions that will make his task a success. Verloc had not foreseen that Stevie will not be able to do a simple work like planting a bomb. Nor did he know that Winnie had sewn a label with his address on it in the collar of Stevie's coat as insurance against his being utterly lost. All Verloc's calculations come to naught due to the unpredictable simple act of love of Winnie. Verloc's intention was to use Stevie as a carrier only and Conrad emphasizes that Verloc "never meant Stevie to perish with such abrupt violence." (187)

It is strange that Verloc, unable to appreciate the depths of his stricken wife's emotions, thinks that the tragedy will make no difference to his relations with his wife. He is unable to see that Stevie's death will upset his domestic bliss. He realizes with relief that his wife knows all about Stevie's death and that the only thing that remains is to calm her grief. He lacks the moral judgment to feel as deeply as he should over Stevie's death. He is sorry about the tragedy but does not blame himself; he feels that Destiny has conspired against him. His moral depravity is evident from the fact that he has sacrificed Stevie so that his indolent mode of life can continue. Ironically, Stevie's death results in the total collapse of Verloc's well-regulated life.

Verloc's attempts to communicate with his wife's silences prove futile. Unconscious of the horror of his crime in his wife's eyes, Verloc expresses his desire to discuss with her his plans for the renewal of their life after his term of imprisonment. He tries to explain to Winnie that nothing could be helped now. He expresses his concern at the fact that in his absence she would be alone in the house and shop. For the first time, he takes Winnie into his confidence but she hardly listens to him. He does the talking while she broods in tortured silence like the one he had maintained in the earlier scenes. The wall of non-communication between them is now too strong to be broken. In fact, throughout the novel, the two remain unapproachable to each other.

Winnie considers Verloc responsible for the death of the loving, innocent, harmless Stevie. This, according to Paul Dolan, is "the tragic mystery of human motivation."[4] By marrying Verloc, Winnie had made him responsible for Stevie's life. She had not realized, however, that her noble intentions could lead to Stevie's death. In fact, it is only inadvertently that the vain conspiracy of the anarchists has achieved disaster. She thinks of Stevie's reliance on her and of his death. The thought recurs in her mind: "This man took the boy away to murder him. He took the boy from his home to murder him. He took the boy away from me to murder him!" (246) In the face of her despair, Verloc can only request her to pull herself together. But his efforts to pacify Winnie only increase the feeling of revulsion in her. Failing to understand the strength of her devotion to Stevie and her consequent utter estrangement to him, Verloc pleads to her to at least look at him. Her reaction to the pleading, however, is quite strong: "I don't want to look at you as long as I live." (233) This immobile taciturnity makes Verloc impatient. He wants sympathy but her passionate silence disappoints him. Holding on to the belief that he is loved for himself, Verloc appeals to her to be reasonable: "Do be reasonable, Winnie. What would it have been if you had lost me?" (234)

Slowly the knowledge grows in Winnie's stunned mind that she no longer need depend on Verloc. She becomes conscious of the great fallacy of her marriage. The reality of Stevie's death breaks up her illusions. It brings in its wake the realization that Verloc was never the man she took him for. Her contract with existence, as represented by Verloc, having come to an end, Winnie feels herself to be a free woman. Stevie's death has removed all need for her to live in that house with that man. She begins "to look upon herself as released from all earthly ties." (251) Verloc's plans of future hold no comfort for her. With Stevie gone, her life has lost its rationale: Stevie was her motive and her end. All meaning is gone from life. She wonders why she should continue to live on, what there is "to keep her in the world at all." (251) The shock she receives is of such great intensity that comparatively "the most violent earthquake of history could only be a faint and languid rendering." (255) The concern for Stevie turns her into a murderess.

The uncertainty and absurdity of human experience can be met by man's owning up his responsibility for his action. Verloc fails in this when he blames Vladimir and Winnie for Stevie's death. To defend himself, he starts a diatribe against Vladimir who, he says, has betrayed him. Irritated at Winnie's silence and lack of understanding, Verloc goes so far as to say that she was partly responsible for thrusting Stevie at him: "Don't you make any mistake about it: if you will have it that I killed the boy, then you've killed him as much as I." (258) By accusing her thus, Verloc completely alienates his wife from him.

Verloc feels more miserable at this moment than he did before the bomb-outrage. Flinging himself on the sofa, he calls Winnie who walks over to him with one definite purpose: to be free of this man. It is a moment of decision for her. Stevie's death serves as a catalyst which brings Winnie face to face with an existential choice: either to continue to tolerate this man or to sever all links. No longer passive, pessimistic or resigned to her fate, Winnie chooses the latter alternative. In fact, once outside the moral universe, once her contract with Verloc is broken by his murder of Stevie, Winnie is freed from all attachments to the world and becomes capable of committing murder. Stevie's death cuts her sole tie to the world. Verloc seems to her a monster from whom she must be free at any price. With the vision of Stevie's explosive death etched in her mind, Winnie picks up the carving knife and stabs Verloc. Thus she puts an end to "an existence foreign to all grace and charm, without beauty and almost without decency." (244) The long, nightmarish sequence of tension and misunderstanding comes to an end: Stevie's death has been avenged." (244)

Winnie's tragic realization leads to her revolt against the inevitable. Conrad portrays the power of the terrible absurd urge to destroy and be destroyed into utter, total blackness. The abortive bomb attack on Greenwich Observatory had occurred offstage in the obscurity of a foggy morning. But Verloc's murder is enacted in the full garish light of Verloc's parlour. Winnie hears the sound of blood dripping and then trickling. She dashes from the room, pushing aside the table and leaving Verloc's hat rocking slightly in the centre of the room. The killing of Verloc has left her completely free but this terrifying freedom is the freedom of a living corpse:

> She had become a free woman with a perfection of freedom which left her nothing to desire and absolutely nothing to do, since Stevie's urgent claim on her devotion no longer existed. Mrs. Verloc, who thought in images, was not troubled now by visions, because she did not think at all. And she did not move. She was a woman enjoying her complete irresponsibility and endless leisure, almost in the manner of a corpse. She did not move, she did not think. (263)[5]

Winnie's irrevocable act of murder leads to her defining her being. Turning away from the dead body of her husband, she is overwhelmed by nothingness of man:

> Mrs. Verloc entertained no vain delusions on the subject of the dead. Nothing brings them back, neither love nor hate. They can do nothing to you, they are as nothing. Her mental state was tinged by a sort of austere contempt for that man who had let himself be killed so easily. He had been the master of a house, the husband of a woman, and the murderer of her Stevie. And now he was of no account in every respect. He was of less practical account than the clothing on his body, than his overcoat, than his boots—than that hat lying on the floor. He was nothing. (266-67)

Winnie has acted freely but now she needs some support. The guilt of her action haunts her. Life appears to be terrible, crazy and incomprehensible. Dreading to be hung for the murder, she decides to drown herself in the river Thames. She perceives the utter impossibility of walking as far as the nearest bridge, and thinks of a flight abroad. But in her extremity, she is too ignorant to know how to do this. She has no friends or relations to turn to. She realizes that she has nobody to whom she could relate her feelings. She is passing through such a tremendous state of solitariness that Conrad remarks: "She was the most lonely of murderers that ever struck a mortal blow." (270) She plunges into the darkness of a London sunk "at the bottom of a black abyss from which no unaided woman could hope to scramble out." (271) Dressed in black from head to foot. Winnie becomes a part of this darkness. Her suicide at the end is a literal merging with darkness.

Once again Conrad brings to forefront the difficulty human beings experience in communicating with one another in their hours of stress and need. The encounter on the street convinces Ossipon that Winnie loves him. It is only when he sees the dead body of Verloc that the truth dawns upon him. After knowing the truth of murder, Ossipon switches from wooing her to getting her money. Winnie on the other hand believes that he will protect her since he has already figured out Verloc's death. Her inability to face the truth of her situation and her refusal to look deeply into the character of Ossipon lead ultimately to her despair and suicide.

Overwhelmed by her fear of death and by her sense of being hopelessly alone, Winnie is haunted by the refrain: "The drop given was fourteen feet." (268, 270) Her action is followed by terror and desperation. The instinct of self-preservation makes her turn to Ossipon who, believing that the man blown up in the bomb-outrage was Verloc, decides to act upon the Professor's advice: "Fasten yourself upon the woman for all she's worth." (78) Ossipon, who has been cheating money out of women who succumb to his manly charms, agrees to flee to the Continent with her on learning that she has all Verloc's money with her. But before that, they return to the shop where he learns the truth of Verloc's death. Ossipon had believed Verloc to be the victim of the Greenwich explosion and is stupefied at the sight of his body lying on the sofa. He finds Verloc's hat empty, with its rim upward, and experiences a feeling of nausea at the sight of knife in Verloc's chest: "he turned away . . . and retched violently." (285) Terrified to see Verloc murdered, he recoils from the dead body as well as Winnie.

Throughout her life, Winnie refrains from looking deep into things and prefers to remain in the dark. But as she confronts the consequences of her act of murder, she is "compelled to look into the very bottom of this thing." (267) Out of desperation, the gallows-haunted Winnie pleads to Ossipon to save her: "Don't let them hang me, Tom! Take me out of the country. I'll work for you. I'll slave for you. I'll love you. I've no one in the world. . . . Who would look at me if you don't!" (289) However, the feelings of "abiding dread" and "sickening impatience" (297) experienced by Ossipon make him leave the frightened Winnie to her fate. He is prepared to succeed to Verloc's bank account but is terrified when the truth about Winnie being a murderess dawns upon him.

In killing Verloc, Winnie has lashed out against the intolerable system. As Camus writes in *The Rebel:* "Rebellion arises from the spectacle of the irrational coupled with an unjust and incomprehensible condition."[6] Winnie's existential revolt is against the monstrous society of the city. Talking to Ossipon, she condemns herself for fearing death: "Oh, Tom! How could I fear to die after he was taken away from me so cruelly! How could I! How could I be such a coward!" (298) At the end, she vanquishes even this fear of death. In Winnie's suicide and grief for Stevie, exists "as often happens in the lament of poor humanity rich in suffering but indigent in words, the truth—the very cry of truth . . . in a worn and artificial shape picked up somewhere among the phrases of sham sentiment." (298) Although Winnie herself perishes, there is a triumphant quality in her struggle. Of all the characters in the novel, she is the only one who overcomes the fear of death. Through her act of suicide, Winnie defines herself and grows authentic.

Conrad is sceptical of the motives of the anarchists who plead for all kinds of creulty and sorrow because they feel that these will lead to a better state of affairs. Though they act with admirable motives, their actions are wrong when seen from the moral standpoint. The so-called anarchists in the novel want to improve the world and dream of social change and progress. The Professor explains to Ossipon his theory of the extermination of the weak—the theory of the survival of the fittest:

> Exterminate, exterminate! That is the only way of progress. It is! Follow me, Ossipon. First the great multitude of the weak must go, then the only relatively strong. You see? First the blind, then the deaf and the dumb, then the halt and the lame—and so on. Every taint, every vice, every prejudice, every convention must meet its doom. (303)

He pleads for "the destruction of what is" (306) and views with contempt Michaelis's humane hopes for a new world "like a beautiful and cheery hospital" (305) in which the strong take care of the weak. But the last glimpse that we have of the anarchists's world is quite nihilistic. The Professor is sorry to realize that his bombs are not powerful enough to annihilate mankind which is "as numerous as the sands of the seashore, as indestructible, as difficult to handle." (306) He tells Ossipon: "All passion is lost now. The world is mediocre, limp, without force." (309) The last scene shows the wholly dissociated Professor strolling the streets of society with a suicidal detonator in his hand—his terrible aim being the regeneration of the world by destruction.

The chain of disasters which wipes out three members of the family discloses a world of private horror. The three die needlessly: nothing is achieved from their deaths. The indifferent society, which had earlier remained unendangered by the activities of the revolutionaries, now does not even notice the disaster. It is a world which has no place for simple love, loyalty and true family feeling. The whole Greenwich Park business is absurd. The characters, drawn from a full spectrum of society, are selfishly irresponsible. As stated in the "Author's Note," Conrad brings the story "to its anarchistic end of utter desolation, madness, and despair," (xv) and shows in the world "the contemptible aspect of the half-crazy pose as of a brazen cheat exploiting the poignant miseries and passionate credulities of a mankind always so tragically eager for self-destruction." (ix)

Conrad's existential humanism becomes apparent from the fact that he concludes the "Author's Note" to the novel with a strong rebuttal to the critics who charged him with deep cynicism and moral baseness: "There was no perverse intention, no secret scorn for the natural sensibilities of mankind at the bottom of my impulses." (viii) The world of moral nihilism is indeed portrayed to shock the readers. Conrad does affirm positive values: the moral optimism of the novel resides in personal values of the individual characters.[7] Winnie's suicide, for example, is not "an act of madness or despair." (307) It is an act through which Winnie defines her being and grows authentic. Again, Ossipon survives Winnie's death but must live on with the terrible knowledge of her suicide. Haunted by this dreadful knowledge, he fears insanity. His overwhelming guilt has left him unable to "think, work, sleep . . . eat." (310) His roaming around the dark streets of London is a kind of poetic justice meted out to him. In the moral universe, Ossipon bears responsibility for Winnie's suicide. His sense of guilt embodies his humanity. Winnie's suicide is her victory over the fear of death.

III

The Secret Sharer, written in an extremely short span of time, is perhaps the most commented-on tale of Joseph Conrad. This novelette, a simple and straightforward narrative of a murder episode, is, as a matter of fact, so complex and rich in texture that it has been subjected to most curious interpretations. The much-discussed tale most skilfully dramatizes Conrad's concern with the existential need of making authentic choice.

The theme of isolation is introduced by Conrad in the very first sentence of the story: "there was no sign of human habitation as far as the eye could reach." (91)[8] The narrative starts with the description of a young captain standing alone on the deck of his ship and staring out across the horizon. The only sign of human life the anonymous captain sees around him is the slowly departing tugboat that has guided the ship to its present position. His gaze follows the light cloud of tugboat's smoke until it disappears behind the large and lofty mass of the great Paknam Pagoda. The sense of loneliness is deepened as the captain finds himself all alone on the deck. Even nature is conducive to the captain's sense of solitude. There is no sound in the atmosphere and the captain finds nothing that moves or stirs—not a canoe on the water, not a bird in the air, not a cloud in the sky. While the captain waits for a favourable breeze for his ship to move, he speculates on the long journey ahead. He feels that he and his ship are "measuring our fitness for a long and arduous enterprise, the appointed task of both our existences to be carried out, far from all human eyes, with only sky and sea for spectators and for judges." (92)

At the outset of his initiatory journey, the captain is unprepared to make an authentic choice. He considers the successful discharge of his responsibility a test of his moral fibre. On board the sailing ship, he struggles with the problems of first command. However, he is apprehensive of his ability to meet the appointed task courageously. The situation is further aggravated by the fact that the captain feels alienated from his surroundings. He summarizes his situation on board the ship when he says: "But what I felt most was my being a stranger to the ship; and if all the truth must be told, I was somewhat of a stranger to myself." (93) It is really very hard upon a man to find one's own self a stranger. The captain feels so because he is new to the ship, its officers and the crew. He has received his appointment only a fortnight ago, but all others aboard have already worked together for eighteen months. Under the circumstances, he feels a stranger even to himself. Further, he is the youngest man on board (barring the second mate), and as yet untried by a position of the fullest responsibility. He does not doubt the adequacy of others but wonders about his own ability to live up to "that ideal conception of one's own personality every man sets up for himself secretly." (94) We find the captain feel insecure in the face of a new command.

The feeling of strangeness prompts the captain to an unconventional arrangement. Concerned about the overworked and tired crew, he decides to take the responsibility of a five hours's anchor-watch on himself and hopes that in these solitary hours of the night he will be able to get on terms with the ship. His decision, an unheard-of caprice, astonishes the officers; the captain appears incomprehensible to his crew.

Through his generous and unthinking gesture, the young captain sets in motion a series of events involving the harbouring of a fugitive who has killed a fellow-seaman. It is evening and everything is quiet. All alone on the deck, the captain at first exults "in the great security of the sea as compared with the unrest of the land, in my choice of that untempted life presenting no disquieting problems, invested with an elementary moral beauty by the absolute straightforwardness of its appeal and by the singleness of its purpose." (96) The captain's choice of an "untempted life" at sea is based on his belief that this life is one of moral beauty and simplicity; he seems to be outrightly rejecting the "unrest of the land" for it offers only the disquieting problems. The land symbolizes the condition of human existence, and the mysterious communication that the captain seeks to establish with the mute sea transports him to a self-deluding romantic world of blissful quietude.

The captain's unaccountable behaviour of keeping the watch himself is responsible for leaving the rope-ladder dangling over the ship's side. The captain feels uncertain when he notices this; it is his conviction that exactitude in small matters is the very soul of discipline. He wonders if it was wise for him to interfere with the established routine of duties even from the kindest of motives. He fears that the action has made him appear eccentric to the crew. He is vexed with himself and takes on himself the blame for the lapse. It is this deviation from the accepted routine that opens the way for the appearance of Leggatt.

The captain is startled to find a corpse, apparently headless, clinging to the bottom of the ladder. The cigar drops out of his gaping mouth and strikes the water with a slight hiss. The commotion alarms the man below and he quietly raises his head, without making any attempt to come on board. On interrogation, the man below identifies himself as Leggatt, formerly chief mate of the *Sephora*, the Liverpool ship identified earlier by the second mate. Leggatt's voice is calm and resolute, and a strong self-possession characterizes his personality. He does not lose his balance of mind even after the strenuous two-mile swim.

Holding on to the ladder, Leggatt wonders whether he should go on swimming till he sinks from exhaustion or climb aboard. The captain surmises that the man must be young, for it is only the young who are ever confronted by such clear issues. He feels that youth is a common factor between him and the stranger. During their brief conversation, the captain feels that a mysterious communication has already been established between them. In fact, the captain has felt a need for a secret sharer from the very beginning and when Leggatt appears, his response is one of recognition and spontaneous sympathy: "The self-possession of that man had somehow induced a corresponding state in myself." (99) As the stranger climbs up the ladder, the captain feels that his secret sharer, his own ideal conception of himself, has arrived on the scene. He so completely identifies himself with Leggatt that he commits himself to protecting the stranger.

The captain is struck by the strong personality of the stranger—a young fellow of a well-proportioned body, with regular features. The grey-striped sleeping suit that he offers to Leggatt is of the same pattern as the captain is wearing and is just the right size for the stranger. At this point, the captain becomes so conscious of Leggatt as his reflector that he mentions him as "my double." Leggatt confides that he is a mate of the *Sephora,* the ship anchored inside the islands. He confesses having killed a man in a fit of temper several weeks ago. The captain soon discovers that the stranger, like him, is a *Conway* boy; they have taken training for the Merchant Navy from the same institute.

During this chance meeting with Leggatt at the dead of night, the captain feels as if he is faced by his own reflection in the depths of a sombre and immense mirror. No wonder, the captain does not feel shocked at Leggatt's revelation of murder. Further, he has learnt that his "double" is not a "homicidal ruffian." (102) He extends full sympathy to Leggatt and shares his point of view: "He appealed to me as if our experiences had been as identical as our clothes." (102) As Leggatt narrates the events, the captain cannot meet the stranger's gaze: "he stood by the door looking at me as if I had the halter round my neck already." (106)

Leggatt relates that when Archbold, the captain of the *Sephora,* came to know of his crime, he declared him morally unfit to retain the position as an officer aboard the ship: "Mr. Leggatt, you have killed a man. You can act no longer as chief mate of this ship." (103) He wanted Leggatt to face the consequences of his act. It is an irony that the members of the crew, whom Leggatt saves by a great resolution and a strong sense of individual responsibility, interpret his action as really criminal. Their response, like their captain's, is based on their adherence to a sense of conformity and an utter lack of involvement in life.

Leggatt finds his six-week captivity on the *Sephora* incomprehensible: "God only knows why they locked me in every night. To see some of their faces you'd have thought they were afraid I'd go about at night strangling people." (106) He breathlessly poses a question: "Am I a murdering brute? Do I look it?" (106) He admits that he had the opportunity to kill the captain of the *Sephora* in his room, and that his crime might have gone unnoticed in the cover of darkness. But he did not want to kill anyone without justification. For the same reason, he did not smash the door; for he knew that the crew would have been alerted, and in an effort to stop him somebody might have got killed. He would resort to violence only if it culminates to a vigorous meaningful action; his act of killing the intruding sailor is tantamount to saving twenty-four precious lives on board.

The idea of standing trial is repugnant to Leggatt. He apprehends an adverse judgment from the jury. The law, he knows, will judge him on the traditional society ethics. Leggatt, having acted on his own moral judgment, is unwilling to abide by such a law. He refuses to accept the dictates of law because he feels that innocence and guilt are private matters. He tells the captain that he does not fear the gallows or prison, but hates to face "an old fellow in a wig and twelve respectable tradesmen,... what can they know whether I am guilty or not—or of *what* I am guilty, either?" (131-32, Italics Conard's)

Leggatt has two alternatives before him: either to commit suicide by drowning or to swim until he sinks. His leap overboard is the consequence of a sudden impulse for survival. He has decided to swim until he sinks. Though all alone in the wide sea, he sustains a hope of lingering on as long as he can help it. Finally when his gaze picks up the riding light of the young captain's ship with its rope-ladder dangling over a side, he is too exhausted to go any further: "I wasn't capable of swimming round as far as your rudder-chains. And, lo and behold! there was a ladder to get hold of." (110)

A great deal depends on the interpretation of Leggatt's action in killing the rebellious sailor. Guerard, for example, opines that for Conrad, a crime on shipboard was simply and irrevocably a crime: "It is entirely wrong to suppose, as some readers do, that Conrad unequivocally *approves* the captain's decision to harbour Leggatt."[9] To the critic, Leggatt appears rather a questionable man, with a shady past. He labels Leggatt as one who is criminally impulsive. This indeed is the most uncharitable interpretation of his crime. There is no textual evidence to prove this charge; nor does the novelist lend any support to it. We have the testimony of Conrad who strongly resented Leggatt's being termed "a murderous ruffian" by a contemporary critic. In a letter to Galsworthy, he wrote:

> I cann't tell you what pleasure you have given me by what you say of the 'Secret Sharer,'—and especially the swimmer. I haven't seen many notices,—three or four in all; but in one of them he is called a murderous ruffian,—or something of the sort. Who are those fellows who write in the Press? Where do they come from? I was simply knocked over,—for indeed I meant him to be what you have at once seen he was.[10]

Evidently, the *Sephora* mate is not meant to be presented by the novelist as an embodiment of evil or a Kurtz-like figure. Conrad is careful enough in delineating the character of Leggatt. Leggatt has a noble heredity and has had best education. Even Captain Archbold, who expresses his open aversion to the man, testifies that Leggatt "looked very smart, very gentlemanly." (119) Indeed there is no indication, direct or implied, that Leggatt is meant to be presented as a criminal in the story. His action has saved the ship in a crisis. Leggatt's crime reminds us of Jim's desertion of the *Patna.* Both the heroes are highly conscientious, yet they commit some action on the spur of the moment that violates the legal laws and the maritime tradition. Interestingly, Leggatt has certain other affinities with Jim; he too is young, handsome, impetuous and the son of a parson.

Leggatt is a competent young officer whose crime is merely a part of his instinctive action to save his ship in a crisis. When the main topsail blows away, the ship's captain is highly frightened. Despite twenty years of immaculate command, he has lost his nerve. But Leggatt remains in full possession of his senses and exhibits no sign of panic. He must *either* assume command illegally and order the crew to help him set the sail, *or* give in and accept the impending disaster of the ship. Faced with a free choice, he acts on his own judgment and gives the necessary order to set the sail. An act of individual responsibility, it is expressive of his genuine concern for human life. "When we say that man chooses himself," says

Sartre, "we do not mean that every one of us must choose himself; but by that we also mean that in choosing for himself he chooses for all men."[11]

Leggatt is faced with an absurd situation when an insubordinate sailor hinders the setting of the sail. He must violate the traditional values and kill the man if he is to save the ship; he is left with no real alternatives. In the fight that ensues he holds the meddling sailor by the throat and goes on "shaking him like a rat" (102) until he crushes the "unworthy mutinous existence" (125) to death. The earnestness of his motive is obvious from his assertion: "It's clear that *I meant business*, because I was holding him by the throat still when they picked us up." (102, Italics mine) In any case, Leggatt has succeeded where his captain has failed. The qualities of self-possession, self-assurance, resolution, and ideal seamanship characterize his personality.

The narrator-captain must make a choice, and he decides to harbour the fugitive. In doing so he is abetting a criminal. His decision to protect Leggatt is based on his moral judgment. He finds Leggatt morally justified in his action in the face of the danger that threatened the ship during a terrible storm. He feels that Leggatt has acted precisely as he himself might have acted in a similar situation. In protecting Leggatt, the young captain asserts his individuality. If he were to follow the conventional morality, he would have handed the fugitive over to the law. But he is convinced that his double is not a compulsive criminal. Like Marlow in *Heart of Darkness*, the young captain chooses personal loyalty over conventional morality.

Captain Archbold's arrival on the scene is meant to strengthen the reader's sympathy for the captain and Leggatt. Archbold is a red-whiskered man with "a spiritless tenacity" (116) as his dominating trait. It is ironical that this gentleman, who professes to be the guardian of law, answers to the young captain "in the manner of a criminal making a reluctant and doleful confession." (116) The young captain behaves with a politeness which seems to disconcert Archbold. The captain takes him to his cabin and extends warm hospitality. Archbold is only mumbling and the captain feigns deafness so that Archbold talks in a loud and clear voice. This is a trick devised by the captain to make Leggatt hear all that is said.

Archbold is visibly distressed by Leggatt's crime. He has thought so much about it that it has muddled his senses. He expects sympathy from the young captain but the latter has become too involved with Leggatt to detach his mental vision from the unsuspected sharer of his cabin.

Archbold further alienates himself from the young captain for hypocritically concealing the purpose of his visit. Hiding his motive, he does not ask any direct question about Leggatt's presence on board. He has a hollow obsession with the legalistic aspect of the incident: "I have been at sea now, man and boy, for seven and thirty years, and I've never heard of such a thing happening in an English ship." (117) And his annoyance is greater, for the incident has occurred in none else's but his ship. He would like to adhere to the law for its own sake, and the law stipulates that Leggatt be tried for the sailor's death.

The captain is repelled by Archbold's hollow obsession with the letter of law: "His obscure tenacity on that point had in it something incomprehensible and a little awful." (118) There is a strong undercurrent of irony in the narrator's defence of Archbold's position: "Seven and thirty virtuous years at sea, of which over twenty of immaculate command, and the last fifteen in the *Sephora,* seemed to have laid him under some pitiless obligation." (118-19) Interestingly, the strong adjectives—virtuous years, immaculate command, pitiless obligation—convey the negative traits of Archbold's personality. Archbold is meant to be presented as a rigid and selfish figure who fails to distinguish between reality and appearance. Shamefacedly, Archbold even admits that he never liked Leggatt: "He looked very smart, very gentlemanly, and all that. But do you know—I never liked him, somehow. I am a plain man. You see, he wasn't exactly the sort for the chief mate of a ship like the *Sephora.*" (119) The young captain, who by now has completely identified himself with Leggatt, feels as if this judgment is being passed on him: "I had become so connected in thoughts and impressions with the secret sharer of my cabin that I felt . . . that I, too, was not the sort that would have done for the chief mate of a ship like the *Sephora.*" (119)

The narrator's response to Archbold lacks any curiosity or excitement, and this arouses the distrust of the visitor. Justifying his behaviour, the narrator says: "I had felt utterly incapable of playing the part of ignorance properly, . . . It is also certain that he had brought some ready-made suspicions with him, and that he viewed my politeness as a strange and unnatural phenomenon." (119-20)

We learn from Archbold that he actually did not command his ship: "I don't mind telling you that I hardly dared give the order." (118) Earlier, Leggatt had told the young captain: "He was afraid of the men, and also of that old second mate of his who had been sailing with him for years—a grey-headed old humbug; and his steward, too, had been with him devil knows how long—seventeen years or more—a dogmatic sort of loafer who hated me like poison, just because I was the chief mate." (107)

The captain's belief that Leggatt needs to be protected strengthens. He manipulates the situation in favour of the fugitive and is able to despatch Archbold empty-handed. But all is not over as yet. As soon as the *Sephora*'s boat pulls away, the first mate rushes to the captain to tell him that the *Sephora*'s crew suspects that Leggatt is hiding aboard. The crew is agitated at the accusation and wonders if it "would harbour a thing like that." (123) The captain senses that his apparently eccentric behaviour is producing a bad impression. It is a nerve-trying situation for he does not know if he should be on the deck with his crew or below with his "double." He feels anxious and uncertain: there is no one in the whole ship whom he dare take into his confidence. An accidental discovery of the fugitive is now dreaded more than ever before. While the steward is engaged in laying the table for dinner, the captain cannot talk but only see Leggatt.

Later, in the afternoon, the two cautiously talk in whispers. Leggatt denies Archbold's claim that he gave the order to set the sail: "He may think he did, but he never gave it." (124) Leggatt says that Archbold had whimpered but was too terror-stricken to give a command. It was actually Leggatt who had taken the situation in his hands and in reality saved the ship and its crew: "It was all very simple. The same strung-up force which had given twenty-four men a chance, at least, for their lives, had, in a sort of recoil, crushed an unworthy mutinous existence." (124-25) P.L. Brown rightly points out that Leggatt "acted in a way Sartre would approve—freely, individually, responsibly."[12]

The presence of Leggatt has, as it were, split the narrator's personality. While on one hand, he has to shield the fugitive, on the other, he has to discharge his duty as a skipper. When on deck he is not wholly in command; a part of his remains in his cabin. The task of keeping the fugitive concealed leads to such a terrible mental strain on the captain that he feels distracted almost to the point of insanity. The mental feeling of being in two places at one time affects him physically and he finds himself acting strangely. He senses that he is appearing an irresolute commander to the people who are watching him critically. This has resulted in strained relations with his officers.

The captain's efforts to keep Leggatt a secret from the crew becomes a supreme struggle. He suffers the agony of uncertainty about the whole thing. Every day he has to go through a horrible manoeuvering to keep the situation intact. So much so that he comes to hate the very sight of the steward and abhors listening his voice. He fears that this fellow might bring on the disaster of discovery. Leggatt, on the other hand, remains "perfectly self-controlled, more than calm-—almost invulnerable." (127) He shows the young captain how to stand up under pressure.

The captain's involvement is intensest at this moment. On the fourth day of the voyage, as he is having supper with his officers, the steward enters the room with a coat in his hand. Sitting stolidly at the head of the table, the captain is terrified to watch the steward go through his room. Shiver runs through his spine and he shouts out: "Steward!" (182) His nerves are so shaken that he cannot even govern his voice and conceal his agitation. But the captain's loud cry has achieved its object of warning Leggatt that someone is approaching. The captain suddenly hears the steward opening the bathroom door. He is so terror-stricken that his voice dies in his throat and he goes stony all over. He waits to hear a yell of surprise and terror. When nothing is heard, the captain wonders if his second self has taken the poor wretch by the throat. The captain has, as it were, eliminated his physical self and fused himself with his double.

The young captain has yet to acquire the self-assurance demonstrated by Leggatt in this scene. He becomes nervous as the steward opens the bathroom door. But Leggatt keeps his calm as the steward puts his arm to hang the coat. When the captain finds the steward coming out of his room, he lays his knife and fork down and leans back in his chair. All this while, the captain has held his breath in suspense, and the raised knife and fork indicate an unconscious preparedness to do whatever is necessary to protect his counterpart. The captain then, like Leggatt, has a capacity for violence. Leggatt after all is not a habitual offender and his act of killing the rebellious sailor was unpremeditated.

Another important decision that the captain has to take is to manipulate Leggatt's departure from his ship. Leggatt's flight is a step towards his freedom. Until he agrees with Leggatt that it is time for the secret sharer to depart, the captain cannot establish a rapport with the ship. Initially the captain protests at Leggatt's suggestion to maroon him on one of the islands that fringe the Gulf of Siam but agrees when the fugitive makes a strong plea for his flight. Leggatt agrees to accept the penalty of being driven off the face of the earth and decides to leave at night, just as he had come at night. At first, the captain demurs, but then he admits that his "hesitation in letting that man swim away from my ship's side had been a mere sham sentiment, a sort of cowardice." (132) Leggatt expresses a great satisfaction to have got somebody who can understand him.

The captain's decision to take the ship as close to the island of Koh-ring as possible has been a subject of divergent critical opinion. Why does the captain decide to take the ship so dangerously close to the shore when he is well aware of Leggatt's swimming ability and the fact that in covering the distance of two miles between the *Sephora* and the captain's ship, Leggatt swam the last spell of over a mile without rest. It seems incredible that he would risk his future when there is no absolute necessity for doing so. This is the captain's first command and in case of any mishap, his future will be ruined. His actions have already created apprehension among the crew. Failure now will completely destroy their faith in his ability and leadership.

We have a clue to this in the captain's statement: "It was now a matter of conscience to shave the land as close as possible." (139)[13] He feels that Leggatt must be put ashore: "Must! There could be no going back for him." (139) The extreme risk involved in helping the fugitive escape is not only a matter of conscience but also a test to ascertain whether he has been able to attain self-possession and confidence, qualities that he lacked at the outset of his voyage. The manoeuver provides the young captain with an opportunity of asserting his command. He acts boldly in this final, self-imposed test.

In Leggatt, the captain has identified many of his own traits. He has discovered that he is capable of doing what Leggatt has done. The escape operation will provide him with a crisis to test his capacity and judgment. His final resolve has been inspired by the strength and individuality of the fugitive's character whose decisive actions he had admired earlier. In this decision, he asserts his ability to go it alone. He achieves a new decisiveness in his captaincy.

As Leggatt is on the point of departure, the captain has a sudden image of himself: "I saw myself wandering barefooted, bareheaded, the sun beating on my dark poll." (138) He snatches off his floppy hat and rams it on Leggatt's head, as a protection against the tropical sun. As several thoughts intrude on the captain, his yearning stare distinguishes a white object in the water and he recognizes his own floppy hat: "It must have fallen off his head . . . and he didn't bother." (142) The floating hat symbolizes Leggatt's escape from the ship and his consequent role as "a fugitive and a vagabond on the earth, with no brand of the curse on his sane forehead." (142)

The Koh-ring venture is a test where all is at stake. The nearness of the land terrifies the second mate, and so alarms the captain that he closes his eyes. The black southern hill of Koh-ring seems to "hang right over the ship like a towering fragment of the everlasting night." (139) The situation is parallel to the *Sephora* incident. Both the ships are in extreme danger, and both protagonists act in a manner that baffles rest of the crew. Both the ships have rebellious mates, and in both instances a telling decision has to be made. The captain, like Leggatt, acts with resolution and confidence, and displays a far greater restraint. While Leggatt loses control and strangles his mate to death, the captain being in full possession of himself grabs his mate and shakes him, and manoeuvers the situation most skilfully.

In acting decisively to give effect to his decision, the captain proves to himself that he is fit to command.[14] He places the self before the crew. As the ship threatens to run aground, he is frightened like the rest of the crew. But he sees the hat, slipped from Leggatt's head, and orders the helm shifted. This move brings the ship around to safety; the captain has triumphed as he watches his ship drawing ahead. He has demonstrated the power of authority by taking the ship far too close to the rocky coast. He had started as a stranger to the ship but comes to full knowledge of it as a result of this encounter with Leggatt: "And I was alone with her. Nothing! no one in the world should stand now between us, throwing a shadow on the way of silent knowledge and mute affection; the perfect communion of a seaman with his first command." (143)

Starting with a feeling of insecurity, the captain ends on this note of extreme confidence. No longer does he feel alienated from the world around. He has resolved his problem of isolation, having measured his fitness during "a long and arduous enterprise." (92) By the end of the ordeal, he has achieved the self-knowledge essential for true maturity. By his responsible action, he has gained the confidence of both the crew and himself. The young captain's generous act of giving his floppy hat to Leggatt to save his head from the dangers of the sun ultimately saves the ship: "And now—behold—it was saving the ship, by serving me for a mark to help out the ignorance of my strangeness." (143) And like Leggatt, the captain is now a proud swimmer ready to strike out for a new destiny.

IV

Like *The Secret Sharer*, *Under Western Eyes* may be understood as a means of coping with the same central facts: crime and identity. The novel is concerned with the question of human freedom as it unfolds in Razumov's terrible ordeal, self-recognition and his expiation. It poses the existential queries regarding the ultimate purpose of human life. The novel deals with the accidental involvement of the young Razumov in the plot of violent young revolutionaries and shows how his betrayal works on his conscience and leads to his confession.

Razumov's carefully ordered life is thrown into turmoil when Haldin approaches him for refuge and help. He suddenly realizes that all his ambitions of life will come to naught as a consequence of Haldin's approaching him. He tries to extricate himself from this situation but finds himself entangled in another terrible situation. The conflict between personal and social values precipitates betrayal, death, intrigue and brutality. Razumov starts losing his grip on himself. The doubt, distress and confusion in his mind lead to his confession to Nathalie who subsequently becomes the agent of his conversion.

The theme of *Under Western Eyes*, like that of *Lord Jim*, is the exploration of the consequences of an act of betrayal. As Conrad wrote in the "Author's Note," the novel is "an attempt to render not so much the political state as the psychology of Russia itself." (vii) Its essential concern indeed is not political but the anguished discovery of an individual's self. Razumov becomes a victim of both the Czarist tyranny and the revolutionary brutality and faces an acute psychological conflict for the betrayal.

Razumov symbolizes Conrad's conviction about man's radical loneliness. The estrangement or isolation which he experiences is common to the Conradian and existentialist approach to man. Zabel draws a parallel between Razumov and other existential heroes of fiction:

> Razumov is what the Conradian hero invariably is: a solitary. He is the man designed by nature or circumstance to live not by the law of his kind but by self-law. Like Willems, Kurtz, Tuan Jim, Nostromo, Decoud, and Heyst, he is Conrad's version of the man—descendant of the self-willed heroes of Balzac, Stendhal, Turgenev, Dostoevsky, and Melville, and brother to those of Mann or Gide—who chooses or is compelled to live a life of egoistic self-regard or compulsive self-assertion: the existence *pour-soi* or the fate of estrangement and isolation.[15]

Loneliness is Razumov's most immediate characteristic and is described in an appropriate image: "He was as lonely in the world as a man swimming in the deep sea." (10) Throughout the narrative, the teacher of languages emphasizes Razumov's estrangement: "The word Razumov was the mere label of a solitary individuality. There were no Razumovs belonging to him anywhere." (10)

Razumov foreshadows the character of Axel Heyst, the protagonist in *Victory*, for he, like Heyst, is a social isolate and has no close emotional attachments or relationships at the start of the novel. His life centres around himself, his work, his studies, and his own future. The narrator informs us that Razumov attended the informal receptions given by university professors and goes on to add: "Apart from that Razumov was not known to have any social relations in the town." (6) The silent, unattached Razumov wants to avoid "taking definite sides" (11) and therefore tries to remain aloof from the warring political forces. He owes no allegiance to any of the parties.

Razumov tries his best to insulate himself from life by following a strict routine of lectures, work in the library, and intensive study in his room; he lives among books and papers. Security being his first concern, he keeps himself aloof from his fellow-students, maintains a superb disdain for them, and is ever reluctant to enter into conversation with them. He seems to have few acquaintances and no friends. He holds the view that fidelity to himself demands solitary and aloof dedication to his own goals.

Significantly Razumov is more isolated than any other protagonist of Conrad except perhaps Leggatt, that lonely swimmer in *The Secret Sharer*. His isolation underlines the misery of existence. He is portrayed as a solitary student without family or friends; he has "never known a home." (299) Life has stripped him of parental care and a family environment: "Officially and in fact without a family (for the daughter of the Archpriest had long been dead), no home influences had shaped his opinions or his feelings." (10)

The whole personality of Razumov revolves round the fact that he is the illegitimate son of a Russian prince. His illegitimacy determines the course of his whole life. Christopher Cooper traces Razumov's betrayal of Haldin to his unfitness to cope with conditions in which his birth has forced him to live: "Not just his birth, but the illegitimacy of it, combine to form his destiny. Every one of his choices of action can be referred back to the isolation of his situation, where family circumstances would have conditioned him to react quite differently."[16]

Razumov is acutely conscious of his illegitimacy. A distinct pressure of his aristocratic father's soft-white hand brings in a painful response: "The emotion of it was terrible. Razumov's heart seemed to leap into his throat." (12) When he learns of the scholastic success of a fellow-student, the quietly studious Razumov grimly responds that "his success would matter to *no one*." (11, Italics mine) Again, while talking to Haldin, he points out: "You are a son, a brother, a nephew, a cousin—I don't know what—to no end of people. I am just a man. . . . I have no domestic tradition." (61) Much later in the novel when Nathalie urges him to assist her in comforting a bereaved mother, Razumov tells her that he is unfit for the job:

> In order to speak fittingly to a mother of her lost son one must have had some experience of the filial relation. It is not the case with me—if you must know the whole truth. Your hopes have to deal here with "a breast unwarmed by any affection," as the poet says. (344)

Razumov has a genuine capacity for feeling but has not found many avenues for its expression. When Councillor Mikulin considers Razumov for an assignment in Geneva, he refers to him as "the obscure, unrelated young student Razumov, in the moment of great moral loneliness." (307) By not giving Razumov a personal history or family background, Conrad stresses his loneliness.

Placed in this unmoored, unanchored, alienated state, the rootless Razumov does his best to "keep an instinctive hold on normal, practical, everyday life." (10) The lack of family ties gives his studentship seriousness and intensity. Ambitious of intellectual distinction, Razumov consciously adopts a solitary life, a reserved manner and a neutral political position. The self-imposed isolation indicates Razumov's fundamental belief that he has power and freedom to define his own life. He wants to define his identity by becoming an eminent professor. The dream of a brilliant future in the university inspires him to attempt a prize-winning essay. He needs public recognition as an intellectual figure. He therefore rejects any life in the present for his projected life in the future.

The existentialists agree on the importance of freedom, the difficulty of achieving it, and its impact on integrity of conscience. Razumov is shocked when Haldin suddenly appears in his room after the assassination of Mr. de P—, an important figure in the Russian government. This shock propels him on a journey through all those boundary-situations which were first identified by Karl Jaspers and are now generally accepted by most existentialist writers.

According to Heidegger, the self that directs everyday life was never really chosen. What it calls choices are really adjustments to what seems either necessary or advisable. The sudden entry of Haldin, an irresponsible and irrational anarchist murderer, disturbs Razumov's precariously maintained existence and betrays him into a totally hostile and inimical situation. Razumov has a demand made out of him which is not altogether fair. He does not believe in what Haldin represents and yet is asked to make sacrifice for him. Involved in a situation which is of no real concern to him, Razumov is forced to surrender his personal freedom.

One may argue that Razumov has a freedom of choice: he could have stuck to his duty—his work as a student—if he had chosen to do so. His freedom, however, is not absolute; it is limited by his surroundings. Haldin's abrupt entry into his room destroys Razumov's belief that he can choose his identity.[17] It brings to him the dark and unhappy knowledge of the irrationality of the world. He feels "the safety of his lonely existence to be permanently endangered." (21)

The incident highlights man's predicament as an individual in society where he should fulfil his limited task. It is through a complete and absurd misunderstanding of Razumov's political and personal feelings that Haldin comes to Razumov for refuge. Razumov himself finds Haldin's choice to be inexplicable: "But pardon me, Victor Victorovitch. We know each other so little. . . . I don't see why you. . . ." (19) He finds it illogical and absurd that Haldin should have come to him. Razumov, a man of admirable intent, is wrecked by absurdity. He has the sense of being trapped by circumstances and curses fate for this.

However, Haldin has his own reasons for turning to Razumov which he describes as "a piece of luck." (15) He has approached Razumov because he has "confidence" (19) in him. The inwardness and circumspection characteristic of Razumov has given him the reputation of being a solid, dependable person. Haldin misinterprets Razumov's withdrawal as political silence, and assumes that Razumov is a lone anarchist. Secondly, he feels that Razumov has no one who would suffer from his being implicated in sheltering Haldin: "It occurred to me that you—you have no one belonging to you—no ties, no one to suffer for it if this came out by some means." (19) Razumov's loneliness and accessibility thus make him peculiarly vulnerable to unsolicited and incompatible claims on his allegiance and bring him face to face with a boundary-situation.

Razumov is a victim of chance and misfortune. Mistaking his reserved nature as a sign of strong character, Haldin confides in him. The moment Haldin expresses his confidence, Razumov is lost. He feels that involvement has been thrust upon him and feels anguished to realize that Haldin has not bothered for his safety. Haldin's fatuous assumption that Razumov would prove hospitable to a revolutionary terrorist offends Razumov who resents Haldin's implicating him in his folly. But towards the end, Razumov realizes that Haldin was right in reposing confidence in him, that he himself was wrong in this matter.

The disruptive presence of Haldin threatens Razumov's ambition to be a celebrated professor. Haldin's honorific appeal stifles external complaint but stimulates an unprecedented inward activity in Razumov. In his imagination, Razumov sees himself "shut up in a fortress, worried, badgered, perhaps ill-used." (21) Razumov's imagination, like Lord Jim's, proves to be his undoing. It conjures up graphic fantasies of terror. Razumov envisions his brilliant dream to be replaced by a nightmare: "He saw himself deported by an administrative order, his life broken, ruined, and robbed of all hope. He saw himself—at best—leading a miserable existence under police supervision, . . . He saw his youth pass away from him in misery and half starvation—his strength give way, his mind become an abject thing. He saw himself creeping, broken down and shabby, about the streets—dying unattended in some filthy hole of a room, or on the sordid bed of a Government hospital." (21)

Out of a calculated move to protect himself, Razumov agrees to take Haldin's message to the sledge-driver Ziemianitch. But chance intervenes again. He finds the man in a drunken stupor. All his efforts to rouse him, including a furious beating with a pitchfork, are of no avail. Fear gives way to rage, and rage to hate. In a fit of desperation, he even thinks of killing Haldin. The narrator introduces in the first person the thoughts which pass Razumov's mind as he experiences anguish:

> Razumov thought: "I am being crushed—and I can't even run away." Other men had somewhere a corner of the earth—some little house in the provinces where they had a right to take their troubles. A material refuge. He had nothing. (32)

Razumov meditates on his isolation. He has no one to turn to and feels cut off from the whole world: "To whom could he go with this tale—in all this great, great land?" (32) Razumov's musing at this moment is an apt definition of what Karl Jaspers calls a boundary-situation. It is a situation one can neither plan nor escape; one can just struggle with it and in the end be shattered by it. That is exactly what happens to Razumov.

Because of the circumstances, Razumov's attempt to arrange Haldin's escape through Ziemianitch proves futile. This increases his dilemma. He tramps the streets persuading himself to crystallize his decision to give Haldin up. The narrator records the moment-to-moment actions and thoughts of Razumov as he walks through the snow-covered streets. Razumov undergoes his travail in perfect isolation. His walk, which concludes with Haldin's betrayal, is a nightmarish experience. He angrily stamps his foot on the hard ground which, he finds, is "inanimate, cold, inert." (32-33) Nature is alienated too: "Under the sumptuous immensity of the sky, the snow covered the endless forests, the frozen rivers, the plains of an immense country, obliterating the landmarks, the accidents of the ground, levelling everything under its uniform whiteness, like a monstrous blank page awaiting the record of an inconceivable history." (33)

Failure occurs in this world of strife and anarchy, and threatens man's existence. Razumov encounters the dark powers while he debates whether to help Haldin or not. He experiences a feeling of fear which may be an anticipation of danger or an impending ill: "he felt a suspicious uneasiness, such as we may experience when we enter an unlighted strange place—the irrational feeling that something may jump upon us in the dark—the absurd dread of the unseen." (35)

After the failure of his mission with Ziemianitch, Razumov wavers between identifying himself with his situation and dissociating himself from it. His indecisiveness at this point is another example of what Sartre would call bad faith and Heidegger unauthentic behaviour. Razumov now sees Haldin as a "sanguinary fanatic" (34) and looks upon the beating of inanimate Ziemianitch as "a sign of intimate union, a pathetically severe necessity of brotherly love." (35) However, the argument does not satisfy him completely and he remarks: "Of course he was far from being a moss-grown reactionary. Everything was not for the best. Despotic bureaucracy . . . abuses . . . corruption . . . and so on." (35, Ellipses Conrad's) In an attempt to convince himself that his behaviour is inspired by his patriotism, he adds the revealing note: "I am not a coward." (36)

It is a testing moment for Razumov and choice is both unavoidable and dooming. John Hagan envisages only two alternatives: Razumov must either betray another or betray himself.[18] By denying responsibility for Haldin, Razumov infringes on the freedom of Haldin. He commits the unforgivable existential sin and he commits it freely, of his own choice. Though he attributes his impending betrayal of Haldin to a vague historical necessity: "Do I want his death? No! I would save him if I could—but no one can do that—he is the withered member which must be cut off," (36) we know that he could have saved Haldin if he really wanted to. The fact that he makes a trip to Ziemianitch shows his belief that such escape was indeed possible. Razumov's decision thus is intellectual, not impulsive.

In his solitary walk through the snow, confronted by the phantom of Haldin, Razumov attempts to cope with his decision to give Haldin up. We see him struggling with himself all the way from Ziemianitch to Prince K—. Guilt seeps into his consciousness as he tries to find public justification for the private morality of his decision; he is trying to find an excuse. His decision to report Haldin to the police is ostensibly a social duty, but the feeling of guilt forces him to probe his own values and those of the society in which he lives. Pulling his cap well forward over his eyes, he again debates the issue of betrayal and conscience:

> Betray. A great word. What is betrayal? They talk of a man betraying his country, his friends, his sweetheart. There must be a moral bond first. All a man can betray is his conscience. And how is my conscience engaged here; by what bond of common faith, of common conviction, am I obliged to let that fanatical idiot drag me down with him? On the contrary—every obligation of true courage is the other way. (37-38)

Although he does not seem conscious of it, there exists a bond between them—that of solidarity between fellow-beings. When Haldin appears in his room, Razumov rejects the proferred intimacy. From the first, he fears the consequences of their association. His unequivocal shriek to Haldin, "I am responsible for you," (60) reveals that a bond has been established between them. Razumov cannot tell Haldin to go away, cannot break this imposed alliance. However, the mind denies the fatal bond established instinctively and Razumov decides to break it.

Razumov calls his betrayal an act of "true courage." But as Sophia says later on, in an evil moment, a false courage may enter one's brain. (379) Razumov would indeed have needed a great deal of fortitude to shield Haldin. But he was incapable of this. The alternative that presented itself to him was his egotistical ideal versus compassion. And this lack of compassion is one of his chief faults. The picture of Razumov walking over the imaginary shadow of Haldin indicates lack of compassion, pity and charity in Razumov.

According to Sartre, the notion of voluntary deliberation is misleading. By the time a person deliberates, he has already conferred value on the cause and motive of that which he then deliberates about. Deliberation only makes his project clear to the person and this is what Razumov does. The narrator's description of Razumov's approach to his decision makes it quite evident: "He was firmly decided. Indeed, it could hardly be called a decision. He had simply discovered what he had meant to do all along." (38-39) Corruption had entered him a long time before, and the decision had been made as he first laid his eyes on Haldin. At the same time, his "need of some other mind's sanction" (39) indicates, in Sartrean terms, bad faith and an impersonal, unfree mode of action. To further his own aims, Razumov sacrifices the life of a man who has reposed complete trust in him.

Despite the inner feeling, Razumov tries hard to justify his apparently proper action. He feels terribly lonely and gives maximum importance to personal security. With his compulsive deep psychological need to tell his story to an audience of kindred souls, Razumov wishes deeply for the companionship he ordinarily rejects: "With something resembling anguish he said to himself— 'I want to be understood.'" (39) The universal aspiration for being understood with all its profound and melancholy meaning assails him terribly. He feels lonely and finds that amongst eighty millions of his kith and kin, he has no heart to which he could open himself. His need for a soul-mate accentuates his feelings of loneliness and betrayal.

All Razumov's actions spring from the ideal conception he has of himself: to become a famous personality of learning, to rise from his present low state in life. But his ideal is shattered through his contact with the criminal. The politics of oppressor and oppressed destroys him. He feels that Haldin is coming between him and his planned future. By choosing to betray Haldin, Razumov ignores the faith that Haldin has pinned on him. In order to keep his plans for the future intact, Razumov disregards his obligation towards a fellow-student. Thus although Razumov tries to preserve the social order and the government, his motives for handing Haldin over are wrong. He betrays Haldin for purely selfish reasons. He tries to keep his chances intact and when he sees them decline, his thoughts are bent on revenge on those responsible for it—the revolutionists. His unwillingness to be dragged down by someone else makes him fail Haldin.

Throughout this episode, Razumov sees only himself, his endangered prospects and plans for the future, but never the menaced life of his fellow. Therefore his first thought is: "There goes my silver medal!" (16) This egoistic thought in the presence of a mortally endangered being shows how preoccupied Razumov is with himself.

Having made the decision to betray Haldin, Razumov's initial response is self-righteous. He regards his act as "an act of conscience."

(38) Yet, the yearning for understanding and support also exists. A clear perception of his moral solitude drives Razumov to the verge of hysteria. The naked terror of utter loneliness seizes him and for a moment he considers rushing back to Haldin and embracing him and his cause, "to pour out a full confession in passionate words that would stir the whole being of that man to its innermost depths; that would end in embraces and tears; in an incredible fellowship of souls—such as the world had never seen." (40) The grey whiskers of a passer-by remind him of Prince K— and his handshake: "the man who once had pressed his hand as no other man had pressed it—a faint but lingering pressure like a secret sign." (40) Both incidents evoke "a strange softening emotion" in Razumov but he tries to repress it and dismisses "all that sentiment" as "pernicious nonsense." (40) The refusal to feel at this stage differentiates Razumov from Lord Jim. It is only when he is willing to yield to his feelings for Nathalie that Razumov has self-recovery and renewal.

There are critics who find no moral complexity in assessing Razumov's action of reporting Haldin to the Russian authorities. Fleishman subordinates the question of Razumov's guilt to the political drama which Conrad is exploring in this novel. He slights both the moral dimension and the issue of guilt, and sees Razumov searching for a true community.[19] Palmer also talks in a similar vein: "Razumov's tragedy is not that he breaks a moral bond, but that there exists in his society no proper and deserving object of political attachment, whether autocrat or revolutionary.[20] In fact, several critics have described the entire subject as a problem in the choice of political parties.

It is significant to note that Conrad presents neither the revolutionaries as the heroes nor the state officials as the villains. Razumov's resentment of revolutionary groups seems to be justified in view of the narrator's ridicule and scorn for the kind of work being done by Peter Ivanovitch and Madame de S—. The narrator also tells us that Councillor Mikulin, the faithful servant of the state, became, like Razumov, an innocent victim of persecution by a pitiless autocracy. When the teacher of languages asks Razumov if Haldin is a hero to him, Razumov's bitter reply reveals his hatred for the revolutionaries:

> Look here! I am a worker. I studied. Yes, I studied very hard. There is intelligence here.... Don't you think a Russian may have sane ambitions? Yes—I had even prospects. Certainly! I had. And now you see me here, abroad, everything gone, lost, sacrificed. (191)

He has no faith in revolutions. The thoughts which dart his mind as he faces Sophia are: "As if anything could be changed! In this world of men nothing can be changed—neither happiness nor misery. They can only be displaced at the cost of corrupted consciences and broken lives—a futile game for arrogant philosophers and sanguinary triflers." (261) He feels that both the tyrannical ruling party and the revolutionaries are characterized by irrationality. "The lawlessness of autocracy" is matched by "the lawlessness of revolution." (77)

Guerard is right in arguing the centrality of the moral issue and its impact on the development of the novel. He points out that the novel is "the story of a not uncommon man whom chance and suffering render extraordinary, who suddenly has to face a boundary-situation and most difficult choice; whose crime both makes and breaks him. The act of betrayal, carrying him out of one solitude and into another, lends him a somber magnitude and new moral awareness, and compels him to destroy himself at last."[21] Faced by a multiplicity of conflicting moral imperatives—loyalty to the autocratic state, commitment to the revolution, the right to self-preservation, and the dictates of human solidarity—Razumov makes the wrong choice. That his choice is wrong is made evident by Conrad by his repeated use of the unequivocally condemnatory word "betrayal."

Excessive loneliness leads to moral collapse in the case of Razumov. His alienation is not complete. He is aware of powerlessness, meaninglessness, isolation and self-alienation. But unlike Kierkegaard's individual who would wish neither to impose on others nor be imposed upon by them, he is unable to keep himself immune from the pervasive influence of the society. Society sustains him no doubt, but it also has the power to disintegrate. He is vulnerable to external forces and powers. When Haldin approaches him, he cannot keep himself aloof and realizes that the world outside is hostile. It seems bizarre to him that "secrecy should play such a large part in the comfort and safety of lives." (52) Razumov is aware that he has committed evil in terms of public morality but, like Jim, plays the game of evasion.

Razumov continues in his unauthentic manner of life even after the betrayal. As he returns home, he argues consolingly with himself. He believes that his situation has been solved, that nothing has changed: "The sense of life's continuity depended on trifling bodily impressions. The trivialities of daily existence were an armour for the soul. . . . To-morrow would be like yesterday." (53-54) As before, Razumov is ready and even eager to immerse himself in a depersonalized world of functions and things.

After his betrayal of Haldin, Razumov falls into a psychotic state. Apathetic and withdrawn, he remains in his room. As he tells Sophia later on: "Yes, I stayed at home. As my actions are remembered and written about, then perhaps you are aware that I was *not* seen at the lectures next day.... Well, I stopped at home—the live-long day." (260) He recognizes that he has forfeited his existence. He is no longer a participant in life, but the prisoner of his own consciousness. This intensifies his suffering. He drinks large quantities of tea, yawns frequently, sees spectres of Haldin, and attempts to justify his act. He envies a common thief and even a brute like Ziemianitch because "the consequences of their actions were always clear and their lives remained their own." (78) Razumov suffers a complete confrontation with his problem when Mikulin blackmails him into becoming a political spy. In moral loneliness and social isolation, he feels "at once, closely involved in the moral consequences of his act." (299)

When Razumov returns to his room after Haldin's arrest, his books seem to him "a mere litter of blackened paper—dead matter—without significance or interest." (68) In an attempt to convince himself that his actions have been in accordance with his beliefs, he draws up a list of ideas:

> History not Theory.
> Patriotism not Internationalism.
> Evolution not Revolution.
> Direction not Destruction.
> Unity not Disruption. (66)

Faced with the realities of power and death, he staggers. His growing guilt leads him into a world where he goes nervous and confused. His increasing uncertainty implies his future existence as a man totally isolated from everything external to himself.

Razumov consciously chooses to betray Haldin but he cannot escape his feelings of guilt and remorse. His betrayal, like Jim's jump from the *Patna,* is a betrayal of his innermost self. After Haldin's departure, Razumov's anxiety increases and he suffers from nausea. He is despaired to find that his watch has stopped. On the day after the crime, he finds himself deeply distressed. He tries but utterly fails to work. His capacity for rationalizing continues but affords him little peace. He experiences emotional and intellectual alienation from those around him.

In the morning he goes to lectures. But the work in the library is a mere dumb show of research. He sits with many volumes open before him, trying to make notes. But all this is of no avail and his sense of uneasiness returns: "His new tranquillity was like a flimsy garment, and seemed to float at the mercy of a casual word. Betrayal!" (71) The sense of uneasiness deepens as he experiences "a strange dread of the unexpected which he tries to shake off lest it should fasten itself upon his life for good and all." (71)

Haldin dooms Razumov to eternal political suspicion. Razumov becomes a suspect to the Russian police for no act of his own. He realizes the absurdity of his situation when his rooms are rifled by the police. He had acted through impulse without thinking of the consequences of his action. The moral implications of his act dawn on him now: "This disorder affected him profoundly, unreasonably. He sat down and stared. He had a distinct sensation of his very existence being undermined in some mysterious manner, of his moral supports falling away from him one by one." (76-77) The search at his house leads Razumov to wonder "if it were worth while to go on accomplishing the mental functions of that existence which seemed no longer his own." (77-78)

Razumov realizes that he is inextricably involved in the irrationality of others and that his self can be defined for him by those around him. With much vehemence, he denounces the unexpected intrusion in his life: "what security have I against something—some destructive horror—walking in upon me as I sit here?" (78) It is a pressure on his uncommitted soul. The sense of being turned into something other than himself is Razumov's torture. He feels it to be a "conspiracy of mistaken judgment taking him for what he was not." (82) His appearance forces him to perform a part which he does not like. He resents Haldin's erroneous impression about him:

> His solitary and laborious existence had been destroyed—the only thing he could call his own on this earth. By what right? he asked himself furiously. In what name?
>
> What infuriated him most was to feel that the "thinkers" of the University were evidently connecting him with Haldin—as a sort of confidant in the background apparently. A mysterious connexion! (82)

The sense of a lost freedom and a lost identity haunts Razumov. He feels that Haldin's revolutionary tyranny has taken his conduct out of his hands and that he has "lost all hope of saving his future, which depended on the free use of his intelligence." (83)

Razumov realizes that Haldin's misplaced trust has denied his whole life. It has given him a role over which he has no control. He feels disturbed for having been deprived of his heart's ambition. At last it occurs to him that he is under surveillance by the secret police, that he is a suspect: "He stared in dreary astonishment at the absurdity of his position . . . three years of good work gone, the course of forty more jeopardized—turned from hope to terror, because events started by human folly link themselves into a sequence which no sagacity can foresee and no courage can break through." (83) Razumov's words here give a fair description of the idea of absurdity.[22]

In the course of his painful interview with Mikulin, Razumov feels irritated, persecuted, and driven to a physical anguish. Life for him has become a grotesque pantomime, a hideous farce, a monstrous puppet show, a nightmare—anything but normal assuring reality. During the interview, he talks hysterically and accuses Mikulin: "You want in some way to shake my moral balance." (97) He complains that "the whole affair is becoming . . . a comedy of errors, phantoms, and suspicions. It's positively indecent." (99) However, his deepest desire, "the right to be done once for all with that man" (99) can never be granted; he is irrevocably linked to Haldin.

Mikulin's query "Where to?" (99) changes Razumov's whole view of life. His frightening query signifies Razumov's utter helplessness. Razumov knows that in the whole world, he has no place to retire to. In addition, he is forced to become a double agent. Mikulin threatens him with involvement and imprisonment for his association with Haldin and thus blackmails him. By reporting Haldin to the police, Razumov has lost his independence. Nothing can give him back his freedom. He realizes his cornered position with Mikulin as something "ugly, dangerous, and absurd." (297)

Shortly after his first experience with Mikulin, Razumov undergoes what existentialists call dread. It is an experience of meaninglessness, the feeling that nothing matters. Fear always has a specific cause, but dread is an emotion whose cause escapes the person enveloped in it. While waiting for Mikulin's second call, Razumov experiences something like dread: "Razumov for a moment felt an unnamed and despairing dread, mingled with an odious sense of humiliation." (301) For the moment, he ignores his real situation but the sight of his bed evokes Haldin's phantom and simultaneous images of General T— and Mikulin.

He reminds himself that youth and time can live down anything.

The feeling of dread returns as Razumov crosses the room: he intends to sit down on the sofa and compose his thoughts. He has a frightening sensation of losing hold over everything—hope, courage, belief in himself, trust in men: "His heart had, as it were, suddenly emptied itself. . . . Everything was gone." (303) A despair for his total existence permeates Razumov's sensibility: "His existence was a great cold blank, something like the enormous plain of the whole of Russia levelled with snow and fading gradually on all sides into shadows and mists." (303)

Razumov appears to be in the grip of Kierkegaardian dread. Such an experience is intolerable: Man either faces his dread or flees from it. In order to face this feeling or its variants, such as boredom, melancholy, and despair, man must try to open up his life all the way to death. This is an extremely difficult task. Nevertheless, it is the only path to authentic choice and genuine human freedom according to existentialists like Heidegger.

Razumov has no one in whom he can confide his feelings. Mikulin is the only person with whom he can experience the relief of speaking freely and that too because with him he can take for granted his experience with Haldin. Razumov brushes aside his confrontation with dread and sets out for his second meeting with Mikulin "with the eagerness of a pursued person welcoming any sort of shelter." (304) The meeting is however not of much help to Razumov because he has kept Mikulin in dark about his first impulse and action in trying to help Haldin.

Betrayal of Haldin is the turning point of Razumov's life. Razumov finds himself admired by his companions at the university and in the revolutionary circles as Haldin's close associate in the killing of the detested Mr. de P—. Mikulin, realizing the usefulness of this, asks Razumov to act as a government spy on Russian revolutionary exiles in Geneva. His decision to betray thus proves self-destructive. It dislocates his life and leads to his exile from the university where he had hoped to become an eminent professor. He therefore hates all those—whether autocrats or anarchists—who have deprived him of his place in the university. He realizes that he has become a pawn in the hands of both anarchists and the government and can be moved at will by either side. He is torn between the two forces, both utilising the individual in an indefensible manner.

Like Jim, Razumov is distanced from the community and this distance increases after the betrayal. He is haunted by his act of betrayal and his guilt produces a world which he inhabits alone. Haldin makes normal life forever impossible for his unhappy victim. The spiritual exile of Razumov from his fellows is symbolized by the physical exile he is forced into. Manipulated by Haldin and Mikulin, Razumov now tries to live in this world on its terms. He tries to know the thoughts of others while concealing his own. Shortly after his arrival in Geneva, Razumov meets a number of revolutionaries. His reserve creates the same impression with all of them: they see him as profound, enigmatical, an unconventional revolutionist and admire his reputed role in the assassination of Mr. de P—. His prestige is unassailable but his personality is puzzling.

Nathalie is a passive character and suffers through no fault of her own. She loses her brother and her lover; her lot is to suffer for the weaknesses and failures of her men. She is caught up in a chain of events leading to destruction for which she herself is not responsible. What brings the sensitive Nathalie and the intellectual Razumov together is also an irony of event. She believes Razumov to be Haldin's friend who has tried to help him escape. Actually, Razumov has been the betrayer of her brother. After Razumov's confession, she is whisked from the scene, never to appear again.

In her very first meeting with Razumov, Nathalie realizes how disturbed he is. When the teacher of languages asks her about her first impression of Razumov, she remarks: "He seems to be a man who has suffered more from his thoughts than from evil fortune." (168) Describing their encounter, she says: "You should have seen his face. He positively reeled. He leaned against the wall of the terrace. Their friendship must have been the very brotherhood of souls!" (172) it is interesting to note that here Nathalie echoes the words Razumov had used when he hesitated in betraying Haldin, "an incredible fellowship of souls." (40)

The scene between Razumov and the teacher of languages shows how much Razumov suffers the pangs of betrayal. After introducing the two men, Nathalie leaves them together. Razumov's suffering is apparent to the old man from the beginning of their meeting: "He (Razumov) made such a brusque movement that he even tottered a little. . . . He shrugged his shoulders so violently that he tottered again." (184) Convinced that Razumov is hardly able to stand, the teacher suggests that they sit on a vacant table. The old man does not realize that he himself is the cause of Razumov's uneasiness. To Razumov, he represents another threat to his tortured, suspicious existence as a police spy and as a betrayer of a fellow-student. The confrontation somewhat parallels the one in *Lord Jim* where

Jim faces Marlow across the table on the verandah of Malabar Hotel.

Unknowingly the old man touches on the secret gnawing at Razumov's whole being when he innocently inquires about the lack of details concerning Haldin's capture: "There was something peculiar in the circumstances of his arrest. You no doubt know the whole truth." (186) These details are needed to convince Mrs. Haldin that her son had planned to escape from Russia and had not allowed himself to be captured through despair. The teacher urges Razumov to visit Nathalie and her mother. Razumov dreads the suggestion. The narrator's query about Razumov's plans of leaving Geneva causes "positive anguish" (195) in Razumov. His exchange with the narrator is long and painful.

The old man is aware of Razumov's suffering but he does not have sufficient knowledge to understand the causes which have made Razumov what he appears to be. He has no basis for exploring the degree of Razumov's guilt as Marlow has in the case of Jim. Razumov therefore suffers in isolation. When the two men part, Razumov is leaning over the parapet of a bridge transfixed by the extremely swift current beneath, an image of the turbulence raging inside him.

Sophia Antonovna is undoubtedly one of Conrad's most intelligent women. She is a revolutionary and her influence on Razumov is startling. It is the careful planning of Sophia which ultimately leads him to join the camp of the revolutionaries. Of the declared anarchists, Sophia is the only one to show concern for the human condition. She has a clear vision of her life and herself: "In life, you see, there is not much choice. You have either to rot or to burn. And there is not one of us, painted or unpainted, that would not rather burn than rot." (250) She tells Razumov that death is "not a shameful thing like some kinds of life." (260) Her expansion of this view is similar to Camus's discussion of metaphysical revolt:

> The subservient, submissive life. Life? No! Vegetation on the filthy heap of iniquity which the world is. Life, Razumov, not to be vile must be a revolt—a pitiless protest—all the time. (260)

She admires Razumov for having "an immense force of revolt," for being "full of bitter revolt." (260-61) In *The Rebel,* Camus writes:

> Metaphysical rebellion is the justified claim of a desire for unity against the suffering of life and death—in that it protests against the incompleteness of human life, expressed by death, and its dispersion, expressed by evil.[23]

Razumov's attitude, however, is quite contrary to this. While he listens to Sophia unfold the details of her own life and tell him how she became a revolutionary, Razumov reflects that a revolutionist is seldom true to the settled type: all revolt is the expression of strong individualism.

Razumov hates all revolutionaries and Sophia accuses him of this: "the matter with you is that you don't like us." (243) She tries to get to the bottom of this hate and gives an indication of one of its possible reasons: "You are feeding on some bitterness of your own." (255) But despite his hate for all revolutionaries, Razumov cannot bring himself to hate Sophia: "he could not despise her as he despised all the others." (242)

The news of Ziemianitch's death brings with it a wholly illusory sense of freedom. Razumov realizes that he is at last free from suspicion on the part of the anarchists. He believes, erroneously though, that he is entirely his own man, that he is now "safe—absolutely safe." (317) This false identity protects him from guilt for the time being and he believes that "nothing could touch him now." (340) But this feeling soon gives way to the realization that in betraying Haldin "It's myself whom I have given up to destruction." (341) Like Winnie Verloc, Razumov realizes that his apparent freedom is an illusion and that atonement leads inevitably to self-destruction. That is why that he, instead of rejoicing in his freedom, decides in favour of confessing his crime.

The notion of remorse which makes its appearance with the news about Ziemianitch's death is another example of the absurdity of life: "Remorse indeed! It was a striking example of your true conspirator's blindness, of the stupid subtlety of people with one idea." (283) The revolutionary circles in St. Petersburg interpret Ziemianitch's suicide as a proof of his remorse for his part in Haldin's betrayal. But actually it is Razumov who experiences remorse. Before confessing, he asks Nathalie if she believes in remorse, "in the efficacy of remorse." (352)

Like Jim, Razumov is the guilt-ridden hero. The feeling of guilt which torments him throughout the novel suggests the burden of responsibility he suffers for betraying Haldin. Despite his attempts to rationalize and justify his act to himself and others, the feeling of guilt provokes in him the realization that in betraying Haldin, he has in effect betrayed himself and his conscience. Whatever he thinks or does reverts always to the day of betrayal. Time seems to stand still. Everything circles back to a point in the past when he betrayed. Musing over the reality of his secret mission, Razumov is overcome by a sense of futility: "He looked around despairingly, as if for some way to redeem his existence from that inconquerable feeling." (316) He seems to crumble under the strain of life beyond the possibility of redemption.

Again, while talking to Sophia, he has "a feeling of immense moral and mental remoteness." (249) The feelings of guilt make him acutely sensitive to any word or suggestion of his association with Haldin. He gasps guiltily during his discussion of Haldin's death with Sophia. He makes a gesture of despair and feels that the choking fumes of falsehood have taken him by the throat. The thought of being condemned to struggle in that tainted atmosphere terrifies him. Sophia tries to console him:"It is you, my dear soul, who are flinging yourself at something which does not exist. What is it? Self-reproach, or what? It's absurd. You couldn't have gone and given yourself up because your comrade was taken." (270) But such consolations do not lessen his feeling of guilt.

Razumov fails to get rid of Haldin's ghost which continues to haunt him throughout the novel. He compares his sleeplessness, his movements, his every act with that of Haldin. The image of Haldin overcomes him. In his meeting with Mikulin and with Mrs. Haldin, he loses control of himself: "It was impossible to get rid of him." (341) And Nathalie is the physical embodiment of this nightmare: "It was she who had been haunting him now. He had suffered that persecution ever since she had suddenly appeared before him in the garden of the Villa Borel with an extended hand and the name of her brother on her lips." (342)

The real tribulation is caused not by one's failure to move forward but by one's inability to retrace the steps once taken. In a letter to his aunt, Conrad wrote: "There is no expiation. Each act in life is final."[24] Each act carries its own inevitable consequences. Once he has acted, Razumov is unable to go back.[25] That, in essence, is his predicament: he is trapped and cornered. He goes round and round his prison under the delusion that he is moving forward. By his active assumption of the role of double agent, he has been drawn into the very movement he had deplored. As he encounters his potential enemy Peter Ivanovitch, Razumov has "a slight feeling of nausea." (215)

Razumov's developing feelings for Nathalie lead to his self-recovery. Until his feelings for her take root, one value Razumov seems authentically committed to is hard work. Detached from humanity, he is attached to the concept of the job at hand. Moreover, he has no illusions. When Peter Ivanovitch remonstrates him for casting aspersions on the revolutionaries, Razumov declares: "Indeed, I don't want to cast aspersions, but it's just as well to have no illusions." (207)

Razumov's admission of his feelings for Nathalie amount to a dramatic shift in his life-view. Till now he has had little opportunity of establishing personal relationships. He has consistently repressed all feelings, his own and those of others. He has never experienced that sense of belonging which grows out of living as a member of a family. The positive contact with Haldin's family makes him acutely conscious of the immorality of his action. When he meets Nathalie, a new weight of remorse mixed with bitter love penetrates his being. Gradually, through his effort to explore his suffering in writing and explaining himself to Haldin's family, the enormity of his guilt becomes clear to Razumov. He realizes that the love and security which his illegitimacy has always denied him can be had through love. He realizes that the way to end his secret life is to confess and accept the consequences.

Razumov probes his feelings and reactions to life in a journal. He suffers doubt about his role as a double agent when he sets down to write his report to Mikulin. He feels uncertain about "that incorrigible tendency to escape from the grip of the situation" (288) and tries to analyze his feelings: "Is it that I am shrinking? It can't be! It's impossible. To shrink now would be worse than moral suicide; it would be nothing less than a moral damnation, . . . Is it possible that I have a conventional conscience?" (288) From the beginning, Razumov has acted according to a "conventional conscience." It is this kind of conscience which existentialists call unfree and unauthentic.

Razumov's confession proves Sartre's belief that man is always free to choose his existence anew. His decision to affirm the primacy of love is a radically authentic decision; he has accepted his responsibility. His resolution to tell Nathalie that he has betrayed her brother is another step in achieving moral integrity. His confession to the revolutionaries in Peter Ivanovitch's suite is authentic and courageous. Finally, his willing acceptance of Tekla's devoted care shows a meekness in him, a quality hitherto missing from his temperament.

Nathalie drives Razumov to self-condemnation and confession, to the test of honour that at last breaks and redeems him. She has the essential virtues of compassion and faithfulness which bring mankind nearer to its goal of happiness—to the laws of humanitarianism. She represents the type of a good person who expects nothing evil from others. She accepts the dark side of life's ambiguity but stresses its hope and brightness. She has a resolute commitment to compassion and forgiveness. When the teacher of languages first meets Razumov, he tells him about Nathalie: "The girl is a frank and generous creature, having the noblest—well—illusions." (192) When they meet, Nathalie immediately notes that

Razumov suffers from "being alone in the world." (202) It may be noted however that Nathalie does not volunteer for her role; circumstances force her into it. But she can cope with whatever comes. She has the mental and physical strength of Conrad's men. Razumov is highly impressed by her and yields to her idealism.

Nathalie is repeatedly identified with her brother who has been killed for his revolutionary actions in Russia. As Peter Ivanovitch says: "The sister of Victor Haldin cannot be without importance." (131) When Razumov meets her, he is reminded of Haldin's description of his sister: "She has the most trustful eyes of any human being that ever walked this earth." (22) Razumov understands the impact of her eyes as he begins to write the final entry in his diary. He reflects upon the feelings which provoked his ostensible act of betrayal; he reviews the circumstances which led him to betray Haldin and to become a political spy; he agonizes over the feelings of guilt and remorse, and attempts to deal with his feelings of love for Nathalie. When he had arrived in Geneva, Razumov had hated the girl and had planned to steal her soul from her. He had decided to make use of the innocent girl to cover up his crimes. But this time he does not fail. Human goodness in Nathalie prevents the evil in Razumov from taking shape and he frees himself from his past.

Razumov's growing love for Nathalie becomes the source of keen torment. When this anguish becomes intolerable, Razumov confesses. The dread of moral isolation inspires love in him. In solitude of spirit, life has become untenable. He feels the need for love: "I've never known any kind of love. There is something in the mere word." (360) His written confession is a proof of his passion and of "the sudden power that Natalia Haldin had gained over him." (362) His love for Nathalie is so strong that he tells her: "I wish I could know the innermost depths of your thoughts, of your feelings." (352) It saves him from ultimate undoing just when he is through with life. Razumov's movement from detachment and isolation to passion for Nathalie signifies his involvement in life. Unfortunately, the moment of his confession of love for Nathalie also marks his inevitable separation from her.

Razumov discovers that the self remains somehow inaccessible, unpredictable, and incomplete. It needs, wants, lacks. He realizes that he must confess to Nathalie to expiate his guilt. And this he does when he realizes that there is a possibility of Nathalie loving him. His confession, the voluntary disclosure of a secret guilt, leads him to the role of spiritual regeneration. It gives him moral freedom. By confessing his guilt, Razumov prevents himself from destroying Nathalie and from going on living a lie. Razumov knows that *either* he confesses and thereby begins his moral amendment, *or* he does not confess and is safe in life but his soul perishes. Through his confession, Razumov wins life although he is crippled and doomed to an early death. His confession is life-preserving and regenerating because new life springs out of it.

Razumov's need to know himself is accomplished through action rather than through self-analysis. From the very start of his involvement with Haldin, Razumov is a conscious agent and not a passive victim. Nathalie's terrible murmur after Razumov's confession, "It is impossible to be more unhappy," (356) parallels Razumov's comment after Haldin's departure: "life without happiness is impossible." (69) As he walks home through the thunderstorm, Razumov feels that he is "washed clean," (357) absolutely purged by the cleansing rain.

On the night of his confession, Razumov sends to Nathalie his diary containing all the details of his life. The last four pages, addressed to Nathalie, explain the change in his thoughts about her. His suffering intensifies as he realizes that Nathalie's response to him is personal. Driven by love and lack of any moral support on which to rest, Razumov confesses to her his betrayal of her brother. He confesses—through his journal—to Nathalie, arguing "I was possessed! . . . The strength of falsehood seemed irresistible." (360) But now he finds that he cannot cope with the inner and outer duplicity of his life. He realizes that he will never be able to free himself from the toils of political complications.

The last words of Razumov's diary reveal a number of existentialist attitudes. Razumov feels a keen anguish as he confesses: "I am in the depths of anguish, . . . I suffer horribly, but I am not in despair." (361) For the first time since his betrayal, he finds that there is "air to breathe at last—air!" (361) At last, he has come to the true conclusion about his act and acknowledges that "in giving Victor Haldin up, it was myself, after all, whom I have betrayed most basely." (361) With these thoughts, he comes to the final confession. He asserts that he is not compelled to acknowledge his involvement with the revolutionists. He explicitly chooses independence, recovers his freedom, and becomes an authentic person. Razumov asserts his existence as himself: "I am not converted." (362) He acts according to his vision of himself. The closing lines of his diary, "have I then the soul of a slave? No, I am independent—and therefore perdition is my lot," (362) show that his tragedy has been brought about by his being too much an individual for the circumstances in which he found himself.

Razumov realizes the meaning of freedom only after experiencing responsibility for Haldin's death, after suffering remorse and guilt, and after revealing the truth about himself and his action. When he confesses to the revolutionaries, Razumov insists on his independence once more: "to-day I made myself free from falsehood, from remorse—independent of every single human being on this earth." (368) This remark is marked by the independence and pride peculiar to Razumov before he betrayed Haldin. A free spirit is most important to him. His remorse can no longer trouble him. His physical disabilities are nothing compared to the spiritual torture he has suffered since the betrayal of Haldin.

Finally, Razumov confesses to the assembled revolutionists who have held him in high regard because they thought that he had helped Haldin. Necator very expertly renders Razumov stone-deaf by shattering his eardrums. Razumov is subsequently crippled by a tramcar that he cannot hear approaching. His punishment is right because his deafness separates him finally from ordinary communication with his fellows. The punishment confirms the existence Razumov has led from the point of his betrayal. The moral chasm between himself and the world is given a physical counterpart.

Nathalie's words before she makes an exit from the novel are a sure indication of Conrad's belief in positive values of life: "But at last the anguish of hearts shall be extinguished in love." (377) Her observation puts forth the idea that a recognition and realization of the constructive values of life can work as a panacea for all the plague-spots of humanity. Her faith is pure and genuine. Her attitude towards the alleviation of an unhappy lot is a positive one. The novel ends on a very positive hopeful prospect expressed in Nathalie's "invincible belief in the advent of loving concord." (377)

Tekla, the good samaritan, is also devoted to the cause of love. She had joined the revolutionary movement to help the weak and suffering. She resumes her life's work and tends Razumov unweariedly with the pure joy of unselfish devotion. She intuitively understands Razumov's sensitive core and makes herself his fiercely protective companion. In nursing Razumov, she finds a meaning in life and has a sense of fulfilment. The self-effacing, suffering Tekla speaks not only for herself but on behalf of many others in Conrad's fictional world when she says: "To give one's life for the cause is nothing. But to have one's illusions destroyed—that is really almost more than one can bear." (148) Her illusion, that Razumov was Haldin's confidant in the bomb-throwing incident, is not shattered by Conrad. True knowledge of Razumov's conduct is not given to her to spoil her happiness.

The last word about Razumov discloses his failing health, his warm approval by Sophia, and a renewed spiritual life. His confession has truly redeemed him; he has achieved self-esteem. Sophia's account, two years later, of the whereabouts of all the characters also confirms Razumov's spiritual victory. As she explains it to the teacher of languages, she and the other revolutionaries visit Razumov often:"Some of *us* always go to see him when passing through. He is intelligent. He has ideas. . . . He talks well, too." (379) The visits of the revolutionaries show their appreciation of Razumov. They feel that Razumov has lived, made mistakes, suffered, but at the same time has discovered meaning in life. More so when we learn that Nikita was in reality a spy for the Czarist regime and that Peter Ivanovitch has married a peasant woman and is living in Russia. The lives of these revolutionaries serve as a contrast to Razumov's life. By complete truthfulness to both Nathalie and the revolutionaries, Razumov has been able to resolve his guilt. Whatever the physical loss, his spiritual redemption has been achieved. By breaking out of the "prison of lies" (363) built around him by the revolutionists and the servants of the autocracy, Razumov regains his authentic, individual self.

Sophia's comment on Razumov's confession is very significant. She sees his life in the right perspective. She explains to the teacher of languages the circumstances in which the betrayal occurred:

> There are evil moments in every life. A false suggestion enters one's brain, and then fear is born—fear of oneself, fear for oneself. Or else a false courage—who knows? Well, call it what you like; but tell me, how many of them would deliver themselves up deliberately to perdition . . . rather than go on living, secretly debased in their own eyes? How many? (379-80)

Razumov has confessed to those revolutionists who mistakenly admired his false role as Haldin's accomplice. And now they admire him for his confession. Sophia gives to the narrator the details of Razumov's conduct:

> And please mark this—he was safe when he did it. It was just when he believed himself safe and more—infinitely more—when the possibility of being loved by that admirable girl first dawned upon him, that he discovered that his bitterest railings, the worst wickedness, the devil work of his hate and pride, could never cover up the ignominy of the existence before him. There's character in

such a discovery. (380)

At the beginning of the third section of Part One, the narrator had remarked that "the object of every tale" should be "moral discovery." (67) And the moral discovery which Razumov makes is that in betraying Haldin, he has betrayed himself. Though defeated physically, Razumov wins a significant victory on the moral level. One may but concur with Sophia who remarks: "There's character in such a discovery." (380)

Razumov's confession, undertaken with the certainty of retribution, succeeds in making his character a unified entity. Razumov accepts his self-betrayal at the end and achieves wholeness. Existentialism gives priority to questions of freedom, conversion and transformation. It puts responsibility for values in man's hands. Razumov's conversion and transformation are the direct result of his taking the responsibility for his life into his own hands, thereby achieving freedom and authenticity. In choosing sincerity, courage and truth, not merely in the private realm but publicly, Razumov cuts away from the cynicism that had strangled the roots of his humanity. No doubt, the shattered and dying Razumov has paid a terrible price for his freedom. But his confession is some sort of moral triumph; he achieves a kind of peace. The willing surrender to feelings of trust and love rescues him. Ultimately he chooses those humanistic values—symbolized by Nathalie, Sophia and Tekla—which Conrad claimed were at the heart of his artistic vision.

V

Victory studies man's existence and his predicament in the universe. Lest the simple narrative be taken at its face value, Conrad's own pronouncement on this work is pertinent. In a letter to Henry Canby ten years after the publication of the novel, Conrad writes: "It is a book in which I have tried to grasp at more 'life-stuff' than perhaps in any other of my works."[26] Axel Heyst, the protagonist, struggles with problems of freedom and responsibility in deeply personal and individual issues of conscience and morality. He is a man "determined to remain free from absurdities of existence," (202)[27] but invariably finds himself involved with others. He admits responsibility for his actions and tries to live meaningfully in spite of the absurd or irrational conditions of existence.

Heyst is an isolated individual. His philosophy of detachment from the world results from his having spent his formative years with his father who was disillusioned, sceptical, and bitter in his observations of life. The elder Heyst was "an expatriated Swede who died in London, dissatisfied with his country and angry with all the world, which had instinctively rejected his wisdom." (91) Embittered, he had withdrawn from active participation in all the joys of the world. For more than sixty years, "he had dragged on this painful earth of ours the most weary, the most uneasy soul that civilization had ever fashioned to its ends of disillusion and regret." (91)

Tender at heart, Heyst wilfully subscribes to the nihilistic view of life advocated so strongly by his philosopher-father. The influence of the elder Heyst restrains him to take on full humanity. It also results in a desire for isolation. Heyst has learnt from his father that the world is a bad dog which bites, if given a chance. For three years, after leaving school, Heyst has lived with his father who was then writing his last book. Just before his death, the elder Heyst had admonished his son "to cultivate that form of contempt which is called pity," (174) and to look on without making a sound. Three years of such companionship at that plastic and impressionable age were bound to leave in the boy a profound mistrust of life. The young man learned to reflect, a destructive process that incapacitates one to do anything worthwhile. After his father's death, Heyst decides to detach himself from life, "to drift without ever catching on to anything," (92) and thereby establish his defence against life.

After fifteen years of wandering around the world, Heyst finally settles down on the island of Samburan in the Malay Archipelago. He is a loner by choice, and there seems no obvious reason for his presence on Samburan. Conrad's opening comment is significant: "There is, as every schoolboy knows in this scientific age, a very close chemical relation between coal and diamonds." (3) In Heyst, there are inherent qualities of both coal and diamonds. Coal is a practical commodity, whereas diamond is a mystical one. And these two considerations, the practical and the mystical, have prevented Heyst from leaving Samburan.

Conrad stresses the aloofness and indifference of the attitude of Heyst by comparing him to inert objects. He is seen in juxtaposition to an indolent volcano, his nearest neighbour, which smokes faintly during the day and at night emits "a dull red glow, expanding and collapsing spasmodically like the end of a gigantic cigar puffed at intermittently in the dark. Axel Heyst was also a smoker; . . . he made in the night the same sort of glow and of the same size as that other one so many miles away." (4) Within the body of Heyst, as in the depths of volcano which lies some miles north of Samburan, there is a fierce flame which cannot be extinguished. Outwardly disposed to inactivity, Heyst has a fervour and an indomitable spirit inside. In fact, it is this tension between nihilistic philosophy and practical action that lends interest to the character of Heyst throughout the story.

Heyst has been in the island for years, and because of the various stories which are afloat about him, he is thought to be a queer chap. Once, while playing billiards, Heyst had exclaimed to a bank manager: "I am enchanted with these islands!" (6) and some people started calling him "Enchanted Heyst." (7) His enchantment with Samburan is so strong that he remains within a circular area which has a radius of eight hundred miles drawn round a point in North Borneo, touching among other places, Manila and Saigon. Whenever Heyst tries to break out of this magic circle, he fails. During early years of his sojourn, Heyst gets the name of "Hard Facts," (8) when he tells Mr. Tesman that he is interested in hard facts. Years afterwards, when he playfully invites the drunken old McNab for a drink, the latter fastens upon him the epithet, "an utopist, a pursuer of chimaeras." (9)

Heyst yearns for a meaning in the ineluctable conditions of existence. When the novel begins, Heyst's Tropical Coal Company has just been dissolved. Conrad attributes Heyst's failure in coal business to the unnatural mysteries of the financial world that account for the evaporation of company's capital during the course of two years before it is forced to liquidate. Heyst, the manager in the tropics for this company, has located most of the coal deposits on the various islands during his aimless wanderings. Unlike Almayer, Heyst does not seem to have any visions of wealth for himself; his primary concern is the "stride forward" (6) in the general organisation of the universe.

The philosophy of detachment ingrained in Heyst during his impressionable youth has led him to withdraw from life. His aim is to avoid committal. As it is, he is free from all social contacts. He has an ability to exist without them, and to retain a sense of his own individuality despite the lack of external support. His personality is not dissipated into the immense indifference of things though he is acutely aware of an alien universe. Fifteen years pass after his father's death and nothing occurs to change Heyst's philosophy of nihilism. Then an unexpected event, his chance meeting with Captain Morrison, throws latent forces of his character in conflict. It is during his visit to Timor that Heyst meets Morrison and invites him for a drink. Morrison is in trouble with the Portuguese authorities who have levelled a certain amount of fine on him, failing which he would lose his ship. Heyst is moved by pity to perform a gratuitous act of kindness for a fellow human being.

Heyst is forced to choose between isolation and involvement, and he chooses the latter.[28] Faced with a concrete call upon his emotions, he is unable to remain detached. The tension between his philosophy and his action becomes intense at this point. He has been previously characterized by Conrad as an inert figure, aloof from the affairs of the world; but now his other side, that pulls him towards involvement with others, takes a stronger hold. He abandons his philosophy of scepticism and withdrawal to help mitigate Morrison's hardship. The reader is indeed bewildered in the face of his inexplicable act.

Morrison's intense gratitude deeply touches Heyst and results in their partnership in native trade. This involvement contradicts his previous pattern of life during which he remained isolated from humanity. The rumours which Schomberg, the innkeeper, spreads about Morrison and Heyst have no relation to reality. With malignant fury, he describes Morrison and Heyst as "the spider and the fly." (20) He advises his listeners to never go near Heyst, to never get caught in his web.

Heyst's attempt to meet the world on its own terms has apparently failed, and the dormant fear of the futility of human involvement strengthens. Morrison's natural but unexpected death in his native climate leaves Heyst stunned and grieved. He has tried to become involved with a fellow man and the result has been disastrous. He realizes the disparity between his inner conception of himself and the self he created by his actions. The episode warns him of the temptations of action and involvement, and leads to his further estrangement from the white-men of the sea. He is more convinced than ever that there is no place in the world for him, except on Samburan in solitude and exile. His statement to Davidson, "I am done with facts," (28) seems a clear renunciation of the world and its ways.

Heyst confides to Davidson that he has always had a taste for solitude. The enchanted Heyst suffers from remorse and thorough disenchantment at Morrison's death: "Heyst was disenchanted with life as a whole. His scornful temperament, beguiled into action, suffered from failure in a subtle way unknown to men accustomed to grapple with the realities of common human enterprise. . . . He deemed himself guilty of Morrison's death. A rather absurd feeling, since no one could possibly have foreseen the horrors of the cold, wet summer lying in wait for poor Morrison at home." (65)

Though Heyst decides to retreat from the world and live like a hermit, he is not a hermit by temperament. Davidson, the narrator, rightly comprehends Heyst's situation as he comments: "his detachment from the world was not complete. And incompleteness of any sort leads to trouble. . . . He had not the hermit's vocation! That was the trouble, it seems." (31) The events that follow confirm our suspicion that Heyst could never completely avoid involvement with other human beings and that he takes the initiative even after having firmly stated that all action is futile. Thus the running away of Heyst—a confirmed recluse—from Schomberg's hotel with a girl startles us.

After eighteen months of solitary existence since the collapse of Tropical Coal Company, Hèyst visits Sourabaya to transact some business with the Tesmans and stays at Schomberg's hotel. He is in no mood for frivolous entertainment and spends his evenings sitting apart on the verandah of the hotel. He has nowhere to go, no one to see. He has lately become aware of this fact: "And though he had made up his mind to retire from the world in hermit fashion, yet he was irrationally moved by this sense of loneliness which had come to him in the hour of renunciation." (66) Heyst is "driven to desperation by the rasped, squeaked, scraped snatches of tunes" (67) which come from hotel's concert-room. He goes to the hall and feels disgusted with what he sees there: "He remained, astonished at himself for remaining, since nothing could have been more repulsive to his tastes, more painful to his senses, and, so to speak, more contrary to his genius, than this rude exhibition of vigour. The Zangiacomo band was not making music; it was simply murdering silence with a vulgar, ferocious energy." (68)

Heyst feels a sudden pity for the helpless orchestra ladies who are being exploited by their band leader. He is particularly impressed by a young girl, one of the band members, who is still on stage: "She had captured Heyst's awakened faculty of observation; . . . He looked at her anxiously, as no man ever looks at another man; and he positively forgot where he was." (71) Impulsively, Heyst goes up to the girl and expresses concern at the fact that Mr. Zangiacomo has pinched her cruelly on the stage. The state of awakened sympathy prompts Heyst to rescue the girl. Adrift in a hostile male environment, the helpless girl immediately accepts his offer: "I haven't come across so many pleasant people as all that, in my life." (75) Heyst is irresistibly attracted by her voice. It seduces him by its amazing quality. It is, he feels, a voice fit to utter the most exquisite things. In coming to the girl's aid, Heyst once again defies his father's teaching. But he justifies his action by saying that he helped out Lena to hear more of her voice.

Heyst's incertitude about reality vanishes when he meets Lena. Looking at her in Schomberg's pavilion, he has the "sensation of a new experience." (71) At their next meeting, Heyst finds her glance to be "real, the most real impression of his detached existence—so far." (93)

Lena makes Heyst aware of her forlorn position. Her background is sordid and she is unattached to any ties. Her father had been a musician and her mother had deserted them when she was a child. She had lived unstable life in the grip of poverty. The poorly educated girl was forced to take an odious employment with Zangiacomo Ladies' Orchestra. And though she was just twenty years old, she had been wooed and pestered by several lewd admirers. Trapped in the depths of inertia and despair, she has nothing in life to look forward to: "And I am here . . . with no one to care." (78) When she meets Heyst, both have been existing in total isolation. Except his tie with Morrison, Heyst has lived a solitary existence. He has been a detached spectator and wanderer. The books, tables, chairs, and pictures from his father's house have been the only objects having reality for him.

After his second inexplicable adventure in the hazardous business of rescuing those in distress, Heyst once again becomes passive. He becomes aware that he has engaged himself by a rash promise; he wonders where his action might end. Lena's query what she is to do once she arrives at Samburan, leaves him disillusioned: "Heyst seemed to see the illusion of human fellowship on earth vanish before the naked truth of her existence, and leave them both face to face in a moral desert as arid as the sands of Sahara, without restful shade, without refreshing water." (80) Though Heyst has resolved to aid Lena, he remains wavering and uncertain. He paces to and fro for a long time at night, trying to find logic for his action.

It is clear that Heyst is now entering into a phase of self-discovery. He suspects that, as a result of his encounter with the girl, his physical appearance has changed during the night. He has become aware of feelings he never had earlier. This emotional experience has confused him and made him feel like a different person. Though Heyst rescues Lena, he does not stand on a firm ground. He still feels unauthentic:

> It was the very essence of his life to be a solitary achievement, accomplished not by hermit-like withdrawal with its silence and immobility, but by a system of restless wandering, by the detachment of an impermanent dweller amongst changing scenes. In this scheme he had perceived the means of passing through life without suffering and almost without a single care in the world—invulnerable because elusive. (90)

By relinquishing herself wholly to Heyst, Lena makes him realize his responsibility for her existence. Later, she tries to make her identity reside in Heyst: "Do you know, it seems to me, somehow, that if you were to stop thinking of me I shouldn't be in the world at all!" (187) Before Heyst renames her Lena, the girl bore two names which suggest her dual character.[29] Her first name was Alma, which in Latin means 'soul,' and the other was Magdalen, meaning a whore or a street girl. But she adds that she is willing to accept any name given by Heyst: "you can call me by whatever name you choose. Yes, you give me a name. Think of one you would like the sound of—something quite new. How I should like to forget everything that has gone before, as one forgets a dream that's done with, fright and all!" (88)

A sinister element is introduced in the novel with the arrival of Jones, Ricardo, and Pedro at Schomberg's hotel. These three men are no ordinary agents of corruption; they are the evil incarnate. They have no ideals, no imperatives. Having a contempt for humanity, they consider themselves outside the realm of human civilization. The languid emaciated Jones leads the group of invaders. Jones is characterized as evil intelligence, Ricardo as instinctive savagery, and Pedro as brute force.

Jones's need to relieve boredom takes him to Samburan. Added to this is Schomberg's attempt to get rid of Ricardo and Jones by using Heyst as a bait. Schomberg tells Ricardo tales of the wealth Heyst acquired by betraying Morrison and portrays Heyst in such a light that Ricardo is irresistibly drawn towards him: "a Heyst fattened by years of private and public rapines, the murderer of Morrison, the swindler of many shareholders, a wonderful mixture of craft and impudence, of deep purposes and simple wiles, of mystery and futility." (156) Induced to go to Samburan, Ricardo decides to keep Lena's presence on the island a secret from Jones who has a hysterical loathing of women.

Heyst's conscious ideal is his father and he spends a lot of money to transport the books and the portrait of his father to his refuge in Samburan. He gives these a pride of place in his house. For Heyst, the objects "familiar to his childhood and his youth and associated with the memory of an old man, were the only realities, something having an absolute existence." (176) His acquaintances are mystified by the fact that he lives alone on the island. To Davidson, he has become "a spirit which had renounced all outside nourishment, and was sustaining itself proudly on its own contempt of the usual coarse ailments which life offers to the common appetites of men." (177)

Heyst is unable to act because he is not sure whether he can trust Lena, or trust his own feelings for her. On the Samburan island, he meditates on the mystery of his actions. He elaborates the philosophic basis for this. Realizing the significance of his involvement with Lena, Heyst says: "There must be a lot of the original Adam in me, after all." (173)

Heyst's choice to run away with Lena engulfs him in the absurdity of worldly pursuits and meaningless actions. He recalls the teachings of his father who had warned him that the world was contemptible, and that Heyst should merely "look on—make no sound." (175) The father was a "destroyer of systems, of hopes, of beliefs" and a "bitter contemner of life." (175) Heyst therefore sees Lena's effect upon him as totally physical, an entrapment which he wishes to resist. His dilemma leads to a sarcastic comment on his relationship with Lena: "And I, the son of my father, have been caught too, like the silliest fish of them all." (174)

The elder Heyst's precepts have a paralyzing effect upon Heyst's capacity for fulfilment, his capacity for spontaneous emotion. Following his father's advice, Heyst allows himself only the emotion of pity towards those in distress. His rescues of Morrison and Lena occur in context of sceptical detachment contained only by a pity that does not engage a deeper commitment to life. He therefore is incapable of grasping the significance of these curiously affirmative acts.

Heyst is incapable of deciding whether he should really have fled with Lena. He is ill-at-ease and suspects that his escapade may prove to be a stupid act of impetuosity. Even Wang, his Chinese servant, senses that Heyst's relationship with the girl contains "unexpected possibilities of good and evil, which had to be watched for with prudence and care." (184) While Heyst meditates over books, Wang looks after the necessities of physical survival. The spell of his father's pessimistic philosophy is cast off at least temporarily when he is in Lena's company, and her love gives him a greater sense of his own reality than ever before. When during their discussion Lena pauses for a moment, Heyst's comment on her silence is significant: "Thought, action—so many snares! If you begin to think you will be unhappy." (194) "Thinking," writes Conrad in the "Author's Note" to the novel, "is the great enemy of perfection. The habit of profound reflection, I am compelled to say, is the most pernicious of all the habits formed by the civilized man." (x-xi) Again, in *A Personal Record,* Conrad observes: "Nothing humanely great—great, I mean, as affecting a whole mass of lives—has come from reflection." (ix) These statements of Conrad reveal that, like Dostoevsky, he condemned the habit of excessive reflection.

Heyst feels restless and dissatisfied with seeming emptiness of his existence. His attitude is discouragement, dismay and indecisiveness, extending to apathy and ennui. Even in Lena's company, he cannot fully overcome his deep-rooted feeling of disappointment: "But even then there still lingered in him a sense of incompleteness not altogether overcome—which, it seemed, nothing ever would overcome—the fatal imperfection of all the gifts of life, which makes of them a delusion and a snare." (212) He wants to forget who he is. He would like to cease to exist, if possible. He tells Lena: "In past years, in moments of doubt that will come to a man determined to remain free from absurdities of existence, I often asked myself, with a momentary dread, in what way would life try to get hold of me?" (202)

Geographically isolated on the island, Heyst and Lena are isolated from each other also. Lena doubts his love and realizes that he can never love her for herself alone: "sometimes it seems to me that you can never love me for myself, only for myself, as people do love each other when it is to be for ever." (221) Sometimes she finds it difficult to understand the meaning of what Heyst says: "I hear what you say; but what does it mean?" (325)

Unsure of her situation, Lena get suspicious of Heyst's relationship with Morrison. When Heyst divulges to her the cause of his solitary confinement, she tells him of Schomberg's version of the story. Heyst is quite disturbed to hear Schomberg's malicious lies about Morrison's death. He has attempted to create a world of absolute moral and ethical values. And he is shocked by the fact that the world, so complex and contradictory, does not conform to these values: "No, this earth must be the appointed hatching planet of calumny enough to furnish the whole universe! I feel a disgust at my own person, as if I had tumbled into some filthy hole." (215)

Heyst's concern for his reputation represents the most critical breach in his isolation. A man of his beliefs and temperament should not be upset by such trifles. Lena's recollection of Schomberg's calumny awakens him to his inability to fully cut himself off from the world: he can destroy neither his origins there nor his past.

Lena seeks knowledge of Heyst for fuller communion of being. Her intense desire is to make herself indispensable to Heyst. During their three months on the island, Heyst and Lena spend many hours together and try to know each other. Lena intends to give him pleasure while delivering herself from the horrors of an assault by Schomberg. Her capacity for love is emphasized by her "irresistible desire to give herself up to him more completely, by some act of absolute sacrifice." (201)

In the midst of his existential malaise, Heyst is torn between his desire to love Lena whole-heartedly and the desire to withdraw into himself. He vacillates in his attitude towards Lena. At one moment, he thinks of Lena with appreciation for her charms. And a moment later, he is reminded of the writings of his father. While reading one of his father's books, Heyst runs into a page of the chapter entitled "Storm and Dust." In it, the elder Heyst has asserted that life offers no real consolation; everything is an illusion, and man is a prisoner of those illusions, of which love is the most oppressive: "Of the stratagems of life the most cruel is the consolation of love—the most subtle, too; for the desire is the bed of dreams." (219) In his writings, the elder Heyst has considered the universal nothingness with great serenity.

It is ironical that Heyst welcomes the arrival of the infernal trio who have come to lay waste his Edenic world at Samburan. When Jones, Ricardo and Pedro reach there, they are nearly dead from thirst and are unable to talk. Heyst helps them out with water which performs a miracle on them. Friendship and loyalty are like cases in man's moral desert but the selfish trio does not understand it. Though Heyst has saved their lives, they plan to rob and murder him. If Lena represents life and involvement, the three cut-throats stand for death and destruction.[30] Interestingly, they have come from the very world from which Heyst has tried to escape. Heyst's facade of aloofness and indifference is insufficient to protect him from them. Once again, he is face to face with the absurd world.

Heyst's alienation is further increased by the absurd and entirely irrational behaviour of the trio. When he apprehends danger from them, Heyst realizes a responsibility to protect Lena. The impending doom, however, is implicit in Lena's sense of aloneness: "The desolate feeling of being alone persisted. She was really alone." (250) She experiences the sensation of having been abandoned to her own devices. Even Heyst feels that she is unprotected and imagines himself in the form of a girl, lying defenceless, alone in the bed. When his revolver is lost, he seems incapable of defying Jones and his two menacing companions. He feels so separated from Lena that he does not share with her the loss of his revolver.

Conrad's juxtaposing of Lena with Ricardo is significant; they represent the forces of good and evil which contend for Heyst. Ricardo, not Jones, is the activist who takes the lead and sets the events in motion. He is concerned with the practical side of every situation: "To him life was not a matter of passive renunciation, but of a particularly active warfare. . . . Though very far from being a pessimist, he was not a man of foolish illusions." (260) He cannot abide inaction, for, unlike Heyst, he is not prone to reflection. When he creeps into Heyst's bungalow and surveys its interior, he is surprised at the number of books Heyst owns and does not understand their presence. He is an unthinking man and an antithesis to all that stands for an existentialist. He embodies the destructiveness of Heyst's philosophy.

For Heyst and Lena, the two detached people, Samburan seems to be a utopia. But this utopian world is shattered when evil interrupts their lives. Ricardo's visit to Lena is the first time she is actively tested. Previous to this, all her declarations of sacrifice and martyrdom have been isolated from any opportunity for action. She rises to the occasion when the opportunity comes. She overpowers Ricardo without any hesitation: "She resisted without a moment of faltering, because she was no longer deprived of moral support; because she was no longer depending herself for herself alone; because of the faith that had been born in her—the faith in the man of her destiny." (292) By taking action, she seeks to establish a bond with Heyst.

Lena wants to save Heyst, his very identity. After Ricardo's attack, she clarifies her own deepening feelings about Heyst: "She was appalled by the situation; but already all her aroused femininity, understanding that whether Heyst loved her or not she loved him." (298) Looking at Ricardo, she feels that he "was an unavoidable presence, which had attended all her life. He was the embodied evil of the world." (298)

Heyst feels the predicament of an existential protagonist. He experiences a sense of uneasiness, and his self-confidence deteriorates considerably. He regrets that he has neither the force nor the conviction to face the evil intruders. He is totally estranged from them. At one point, his discussion with Lena turns into moral philosophy. She asks him whether this danger of evil is a sort of punishment for the way they are living. Assuming a typical Heystian pose, he observes with surprise: "What? Are our visitors then messengers of morality, avengers of righteousness, agents of Providence? That's certainly an original view. How flattered they would be if they could hear you!" (354) Heyst adds that he is not conscious of any sin but Lena replies that the guilt is hers: "Woman is the tempter. . . . I threw myself at you." (354) She understands the danger Ricardo represents for them. In a bid to protect Heyst from undue worry and tension, she keeps Ricardo's visit a secret from him.

Heyst seems a defeated and resigned victim of blind fate. He bemoans his plight and feels, as if he has ceased to exist: "He considered himself a dead man already, yet forced to pretend that he was alive for her sake, for her defence. He regretted that he had no Heaven to which he could recommend this fair, palpitating handful of ashes and dust—warm, living, sentient, his own—and exposed helplessly to insult, outrage, degradation, and infinite misery of the body." (354-55) He is so overwhelmed by man's insignificance in the cosmic scheme that he does not feel like dealing with the evil that threatens him.

The anguished Heyst fails to act when he confronts Jones in the bungalow. As Jones learns about the girl's presence, he seems frozen still. Heyst realizes that "if I want to kill him, this is my time," (387) but does not move. Characterized by a Hamlet-like proclivity for reflection, Heyst cannot bring himself to act violently and suffers from a kind of moral paralysis. It is in conformity to his earlier statement to Lena: "There is a strain in me which lays me under an insensate obligation to avoid even the appearance of murder. I have never pulled a trigger or lifted my hand on a man, even in self-defence." (329) In his confrontation with Jones, Heyst has failed to comprehend the behaviour of the latter.

Heyst's faith in life is shattered when he discovers Lena playing the part of a courtesan to Ricardo. Nothing could have been more disgusting for Heyst; he thinks Lena to be licentious and doubts her fidelity: "Doubt entered into him—a doubt of a new kind, formless, hideous. . . . He stopped suddenly, with a thought that he who experienced such a feeling had no business to live—or perhaps was no longer living." (391-92) He misunderstands Lena and seems to be convinced of his father's teaching that love is both cruel and subtle. Jones also feels repulsed when he sees Ricardo fawning at the feet of Lena. The outraged Jones tells Heyst that he will have to shoot Ricardo and not Heyst.

Ricardo makes Lena conscious that she is living not for herself but for Heyst. Surprisingly, it is Ricardo and not Heyst who promises Lena a meaningful existence—a life of equals, both true and both free. He asks her to live like a rover, a free person: "We'll go on wandering the world over, you and I, both free and both true. You are no cage bird. We'll rove together, for we are of them that have no homes. We are born rovers!" (397) But Lena wants a complete fusion with Heyst which Ricardo fails to understand.

Lena acts with complete self-assurance. As she had asserted earlier, she knows how to stand by a man. Hers is a genuine, spiritual love for Heyst. She thinks herself responsible for Heyst's being in trouble, and decides to expiate her sin by eliminating the danger before him. The noble feeling prompts her to camouflage and shrewdly disarm Ricardo by taking in possession the knife that has the sting of death in it. She uses her physical charm to do this. However, her plan to wrest danger solely by gaining possession of the knife is quite inane.

Though she dies in the process of safeguarding Heyst, Lena becomes a woman capable of ultimate sacrifice. She dies "triumphant," with "divine radiance on her lips." (407) In the "Author's Note" to the novel, Conrad himself writes about Lena's triumph: "And in view of her triumphant end what more could I have done for her rehabilitation and her happiness?" (xvii)

Lena is capable of unselfish giving. Her last words to Heyst are: "I've saved you! Why don't you take me into your arms and carry me out of this lonely place?" (406) Heyst lifts her into his arms and cherishes her love in his heart for ever. However, he remains unable to make a total commitment even at this stage; his profound mistrust of life and women keeps the true cry of love from his lips. He curses himself inwardly for his inability to speak words of love even when she is dying.

As an existential protagonist, Heyst has to choose values and commit himself. He affirms faith in human condition, despite potentiality of evil present in man. He fully appreciates Lena's love for the first time in his last words to Davidson: "Ah, Davidson, woe to the man whose heart has not learned while young to hope, to love—and to put its trust in life!" (410) The story has come full circle, with Heyst, through the tragedy of lost opportunity, realizing the emptiness and error of his negation. He achieves self-recognition and wishes that he had learned to love and trust earlier in life. In Conrad's novels, recognition is synonymous with revelation. A letter that Conrad wrote to Garnett about the latter's criticism of "Karain" is illustrative: "the full comprehension of what you objected to came to me like a flash of light into a dark cavern. It came and went, but it left me informed with such knowledge as comes of a short vision. The best kind of knowledge because the most akin to revelation."[31]

Love is a supremely capable emotion and offers a valued means of exploring life because it can serve both to define the self and to foster solidarity with others. In Lena's death, Heyst grasps for the first time the need of a deep commitment to human love. His final pronouncement on life indicates his realization of the inadequacy of the negative philosophy of his father. Through Lena's presence on the island, he has grappled with life and eventually realized that he must commit himself to life. He comes to conclude that virtue has no meaning apart from action. The dangers of isolation are exposed; the surest antidotes to cynicism and pessimism are the warmth and love of fellow men. Heyst feels that the only proper course for him is to commit himself, along with Lena's corpse and his father's books, to the fire that purifies everything. His decision to immolate himself is a symbolic rejection of his former life.[32] It is an act of existential affirmation of the values one should cherish in life.

NOTES

1. *The Secret Agent* (Garden City, New York: Doubleday, Page, 1925).
2. Joseph I. Fradin, "Conrad's Everyman: *The Secret Agent*," *Texas Studies in Literature and Language*, XL (1969), p. 1023.
3. Avrom Fleishman, "The Design of Conrad's *The Secret Agent*," ELH, XXXII (1965), p. 202.
4. Paul Dolan, "The Plot in *The Secret Agent*," *Conradiana* XVI (1984), p. 232.
5. J. Hillis Miller aptly comments: "It is a positive awareness of nothing.... It is a living death whose horror is its inability to escape from itself." *Poets of Reality: Six Twentieth-Century Writers*, rep. in *The Secret Agent: A Casebook*, ed. Ian Watt (London: Macmillan, 1973), p. 195.
6. *The Rebel*, p. 16.
7. Likewise, R.W. Stallman says: "The nihilism of *The Secret Agent* ends in a covert affirmation of the supremacy of life." "Time and *The Secret Agent*, p. 122.
8. *The Secret Sharer* in *'Twixt Land and Sea* (Garden City, New York: Doubleday, Page, 1925).
9. Albert J. Guerard, *Conrad the Novelist* (Cambridge: Harvard University Press, 1958), p. 24.
10. Jean-Aubry, *Joseph Conrad: Life and Letters*, II, p. 143.
11. *Existentialism and Humanism*, p. 29.
12. "*The Secret Sharer* and the Existential Hero," *Conradiana*, III (1971), p. 23.
13. Steve Ressler too argues that only through action can the captain's uncertainties be overcome: "There was never any doubt as to Leggatt striking out for freedom, and I think the imperative here is self-directed, an exhortation to make the necessary rupture, to authenticate self by severing the incapacitating dependency he has

developed for his twin." "Conrad's *The Secret Sharer:* Affirmation of Action," *Conradiana,* XVI (1984), p. 203.

14. In a similar vein, Joan E. Steiner asserts: "By consciously facing danger and challenging his vulnerability, the captain overcomes his crippling sense of duality and demonstrates his ability to command, thereby belatedly earning the respect of his crew." "Conrad's *The Secret Sharer:* Complexities of the Doubling Relationship," *Conradiana,* XII (1980), p. 182.
15. M.D. Zabel, "Introduction to *Under Western Eyes,*" *Under Western Eyes* by Joseph Conrad (Anchor Books, Doubleday, 1963); rep. Marvin Mudrick, ed., *Conrad: A Collection of Critical Essays* (New Jersey: Prentice-Hall, 1966), p. 133.
16. Christopher Cooper, *Conrad and the Human Dilemma* (London: Chatto and Windus, 1970), p. 81.
17. Discussing the alternatives Razumov has before him, Steve Ressler points out that "despite Razumov's excruciating dilemma where risk is implicit in any choice, the only just act would have been to have banished Haldin from the apartment once he announced his assassin's role. However, Razumov is incapable psychologically and morally of such decisiveness because of his present unformed character." "Conrad's *The Secret Sharer:* Affirmation of Action," p. 196.
18. John Hagan, "Conrad's *Under Wester Eyes:* The Question of Razumov's 'Guilt' and 'Remorse,'" *Studies in the Novel,* I (1969), p. 319.
19. Avrom Fleishman, *Conrad's Politics: Community and Anarchy in the Fiction of Joseph Conrad* (Baltimore: Johns Hopkins University Press, 1967), p. 232.
20. John A. Palmer, *Joseph Conrad's Fiction: A Study in Literary Growth* (New York: Cornell University Press, 1968), p. 130.
21. Albert J. Guerard, *Conrad the Novelist,* p. 231.
22. "Razumov," remarks Tony Tanner, "tries to regulate his life according to his intelligence—he has to, it is all he has got. But he discovers that sanity and inner peace are not the products or reason, cannot be purchased by the deductions of aware intelligence. Therefore—life is absurd in the sense to which we are only now accustoming ourselves." "Nightmare and Complacency: Razumov and the Western Eye," *Critical Quarterly,* IV (1962); rep. C.B. Cox, ed., *Heart of Darkness, Nostromo, and Under Western Eyes: A Casebook* (London: Macmillan, 1981), p. 184.

23. *The Rebel*, p. 30.
24. John A. Gee and Paul J. Sturm, eds., *Letters of Joseph Conrad to Marguerite Poradowska*, p. 36.
25. Frederick R. Karl likens Razumov's situation to that of Sisyphus: "Razumov recognizes himself as a Sisyphus who, morally speaking, can never escape his burden." "The Rise and Fall of *Under Western Eyes*," *Nineteenth Century Fiction*, XIII (1958-59), p. 315.
26. Jean-Aubry, *Joseph Conrad: Life and Letters*, II, p. 342.
27. *Victory* (Garden City, New York: Doubleday, Page, 1925).
28. Approaching *Victory* in the light of Camus's chapter "Rebellion and Art" in *The Rebel*, Gary Geddes holds the view that Heyst imposes his own form on the lives of Morrison and Lena because he cannot tolerate the senselessness evident in their lives. *Conrad's Later Novels* (Montreal: MacGill-Queen's University Press, 1980), pp. 48-52.
29. Cedric Watts gives a new interpretation of the name "Lena." It is, in his opinion, an abbreviation of "Helena"—the name of Helen of Troy. Substantiating this, he writes: "The action of *Victory* is a parodic counterpart to the legend which prompted *The Iliad*. Paris abducted Helen; because of this the Greeks besieged Troy, and eventually the city was destroyed in conflagaration after bloodshed. Heyst abducts Lena; because of this action, Schomberg sends Jones, Pedro and Ricardo to assail Heyst's settlement, and the buildings are finally destroyed in conflagaration after bloodshed." "Reflections on *Victory*," *Conradiana*, XV (1983), p. 75.
30. Cedric Watts shows how Jones serves as a contrast to Lena: "Jones, spectral and skeletal but with a sting, patently represents sterility and death, while womankind, and particularly Lena, represents fecundity and life." *Ibid.*, p. 74.
31. Edward Garnett, ed., *Letters from Joseph Conrad: 1895-1924*, p. 92.
32. Rose Orlich similarly argues that Lena's love is rooted in a sound psychology of authentic love, and that Conrad was able to envision genuine love in a Christian existentialist sense. Concluding her article entitled "The Psychology of Love in Conrad's *Victory*," she remarks that Lena's love "nourishes the latent capacities within him (Heyst) and draws him into a gradually deepening experience of authentic love with its final consummation by fire." *Conradiana*, XIII (1981), p. 71.

Summing up

An attempt has been made in the preceding chapters to examine comprehensively and exhaustively Conrad's major novels in the light of humanistic school of existential philosophy. The study demonstrates that Conrad, though not a formal thinker or philosopher, shares many of the preoccupations of the modern existentialist thinkers. And what is significant is the way in which Conrad's work foreshadows much of the literature produced by the existentialist writers. It has been emphasized that Conrad's own experiences contributed to his preoccupation with the theme of isolation and existence in his novels. The basic philosophic position of Conrad, like that of Camus and Sartre, is that he thinks of man as a being isolated in an alien universe. Conrad depicts the loneliness and isolation of his protagonists and the anguish resulting from this isolation. In each of his novels, the existential perception of the void is at the centre of things.

Conrad's heroes, like those of Camus and Sartre, have no close family ties. James Wait, Kurtz, Jim, Nostromo, Decoud, Verloc, the captain in *The Secret Sharer,* Razumov, Heyst and Lena are all isolated beings without any such ties. Very few of Conrad's protagonists have living fathers and those who are there exert a baleful effect on their sons. Razumov is the illegitimate son of Prince K— who never acknowledges him as his son and in fact destroys Razumov's career by taking him to the police chief. Jim and Leggatt are always worried as to how their conduct would be viewed by their parson fathers. In the case of Charles Gould and Heyst, the fatherly influence reaches out from the grave. It is only his dead father's passion for the mine which leads Charles Gould to decide to reopen it. And Heyst consciously tries to live according to his father's doctrine of non-commitment which leads to his destruction.

In exploring man's feeling of solitariness, Conrad describes problems of communication which men suffer from. Even marriage proves insufficient to save men from isolation. The Verlocs in *The Secret Agent* experience solitariness in their marriage relationship and fail to communicate with each other. Similarly Heyst-Lena and the Schombergs in *Victory* find no comfort in marriage.

The sense of being a stranger in a hostile world where one's conception of oneself seems at odds with the conventional world appears in many of Conrad's works. The disorderly universe in which we live gives us only an experience of futility and worthlessness. In his non-fictional writings, especially in letters to his friends, Conrad gives expression to his views on man, God, and the universe. He describes the universe as a knitting machine that will not embroider, no matter what we do with it. He even suspects that the aim of creation cannot be ethical at all. Conrad portrays man and the universe as odd-shaped pieces in some gigantic, meaningless puzzle. Man in Conrad's fiction is trapped or adrift in a valueless universe. Existence itself is contingent, gratuitous and unjustifiable. Conrad's heroes suffer the absurdity of being in the world. In Sartrean terms, they are condemned to exist.

The Conradian hero feels shattered by the mysterious forces of the universe. Central to his core of consciousness is the realization that the world is indeed absurd in the sense that though man must have a meaning to live, no meaningful potential exists. His nausea is a representation of the absurd—of man pitted against the enormous universe. Like the mythical Sisyphus, he continues his job, fights against all odds. To be aware of the recalcitrance of existence is in some sense to surmount it.

In the absurd and meaningless world in which he lives, Conrad's protagonist is confronted with making a choice. In this respect, Conrad anticipates Sartre who holds that man's fate is not determined by a prior superimposed essence; rather his fate is determined by his free decisions and actions. Almayer, Nina, Willems, Kurtz, Jim, Decoud, Nostromo, Winnie, Razumov, Heyst and the captain in *The Secret Sharer* define themselves in their choice and action.

Man's freedom thus becomes an inseparable burden, a source of perpetual anguish. In Conrad's world, man is faced with the seemingly impossible predicament for rational meaning in an irrational world; he must rise up in protest against the chaotic universe that challenges human significance. Conrad shares the existentialist belief in revolt against the absurdity of existence. Unable to escape the evils of the world, man must find his happiness within the limits of his finite existence. Conrad holds the existentialist conviction that however meaningless and hopeless things are, we must cherish our ideals and with their aid turn defeat into a kind of victory. His protagonists thus embody the affirmative, life-embracing aspect of existentialism rather than its destructive aspect. In this respect, Conrad anticipates the humanistic school of existentialism, termed as "existential humanism" by Sartre.[1]

A close study of Conrad's novels reveals the novelist's preoccupation with the tenets of existential philosophy which subsequently came to dominate the literary scene. *Almayer's Folly* is a record of the dreary existence of a solitary Dutchman named Kaspar Almayer. Imprisoned in the fundamental isolation of his being, he tries desperately to give his life meaning. In the beginning, he is a singularly unheroic protagonist who has allowed Lingard to make important decisions for him. He hopes to give Nina wealth and prestige in Europe. It is ironical that the search for gold with which Almayer hopes to provide Nina with a new life is instrumental in driving his half-caste daughter forever from European civilization. Almayer's life reveals that existence without love and compassion is not worthwhile.

An Outcast of the Islands repeats the themes of betrayal, the dangers of imagining a splendid future, the tensions between black and white, and the perils of isolation. Peter Willems, the protagonist of the novel, is a man in process. He suffers his fall from a position of trust and responsibility. In his life at Sambir, Willems experiences loneliness and isolation. He finds himself separated from his natural surroundings and from his kind in space. Even love proves ineffective in dispelling his solitude. He sees the river as a means of escape from the Malay jungles but it turns out to be the source of death. But the fact that he wants to and does make an attempt to return to the white world raises Willems above the common run of humanity.

The Nigger of the "Narcissus" concerns itself with the problem of existence. It deals with the conduct of the crewmen and their consequent anguish in the face of death. James Wait is a negro and, because of his blackness, remains a lonely and isolated figure in an all-white crew. The peaceful life on board the *Narcissus* is disrupted by Wait's presence. With his knowledge of death, Wait exerts a terrifying moral blackmail on the crew. His presence demoralizes the small world of the ship which threatens to founder both physically and morally. Captain Allistoun and Singleton, however, remain unperturbed. It is only after Wait's body is consigned to the sea that the crew members become sure that they have not been fooled. They become aware of death and face it very bravely. They take full responsibility for their actions and have a sense of commitment. They are authentic individuals who do not turn away from trying situations.

Youth centres around the testing of a young man by an ordeal at sea.

At the age of twenty, Marlow, as second mate of the *Judea*, was filled with the youthful conviction that he could handle any situation. His conviction is put to test aboard this jinxed ship which eventually explodes near Java. Marlow's voyage on the sea is an endless struggle with the elements. The young Marlow does not despair at the hostility of nature and the interminable delays and mishaps. The *Judea*'s repeated attempts to get a new crew and start the journey parallel Sisyphus's repeated attempts to roll the rock up the hill. Marlow, like Sisyphus, remains hopeful despite successive failures. When the *Judea* finally blows up, Marlow rows off from the sinking ship as a commander of one of its lifeboats and has his first glimpse of the East. Marlow's integrity is tested to the limit of his endurance and he survives the ordeal. Like an existential hero, he defines himself in his action. He chooses to part company with the captain and later ignores the homeward-bound ship. He lives the existential man's determination not to reconcile his personal aspirations with the merciless limitations of temporal existence.

Heart of Darkness reveals the profundity of Conrad's comment on the human predicament. Marlow yearns for a meaning in the ineluctable conditions of existence. His trip to the Congo is an ordeal like a weary pilgrimage amongst hints for nightmares. His dark and sombre journey makes Marlow increasingly aware of his state in the world. He is alone in an alien and indifferent universe. His trip to Africa stands for the place where man discovers the truth about himself and, by generic extension, about mankind itself. Civilization provides external checks for persons living in the western world. Without some deep inner check, one would succumb completely to the heart of darkness. The howling natives test Marlow's endurance to its limit. At the Inner Station, Marlow is confronted with his choice of nightmares and chooses Kurtz in preference to the manager. Kurtz has not completely succumbed to the darkness; his dying words are an evidence of moral conviction. Marlow recognizes Kurtz's achievement of insight and ultimate victory. Through an existential encounter with Kurtz, Marlow gains valuable knowledge about himself, the nature of evil and the world. He therefore involves himself with Kurtz's experience by telling a lie to the woman Kurtz cherished. Aware that the innocent idealism of the ignorant should not be destroyed, Marlow lies to the Intended. His lie affirms a moral significance beyond himself, a value which Conrad calls an illusion. The highest hope of mankind lies in the sort of self-purification exemplified by Marlow. He chooses the human over that which would destroy the human.

Lord Jim is concerned with the acute consciousness of lost honour.

Jim forfeits his honour by an act of cowardice and redeems it by subsequent integrity and courage. Characterized by the fine conscience and the exquisite sensibility of a romantic, Jim represents the epitome of the existentialist despair and alienation. His failure to live up to his idealized image of himself makes him miserable. His dereliction of duty on the *Patna* frustrates him. He feels the pricks of conscience throughout his life and tries to undo the *Patna* incident by some heroic gesture. He feels totally alone and is conscious of his loneliness. He suffers intensely, feeling that in some vague way life has let him down. He finds relief from his gnawing sense of guilt in Marlow's presence. Marlow makes an attempt at comprehending the reality of Jim's jump. The perspectives of truth and reality are constantly shifting. In Sartrean terms, it tantamounts to evading the issue. Jim's determination to seek out suitable punishment for his act takes him to Patusan where, after a series of adventures, he establishes himself as an important leader among the men of bugis community. But Gentleman Brown, with his insight into Jim's need to leave white civilization for the shelter of Patusan, touches the soft spot in Jim. Jim's decision to give Brown another chance proves fatal. Even while in a state of confusion about the objective validity of his motives, Jim realizes, almost with an outcry, that individual existence is impossible without individual choice and action. Like a Sartrean hero, he remains faithful to his ideal of conduct, to his view of what life demands of a human being. It is only his confrontation with death that makes him an individual. It is then that he loses fear and dies an authentic individual.

In *Nostromo*, Conrad shifts his emphasis from the spiritual history of a solitary individual to a world in turmoil. Charles Gould consciously chooses to reopen the mine to bring law, order, stability, peace and prosperity to a land of poverty. The mine does bring a certain prosperity to the country but soon it develops into a tyrant. It becomes Gould's evil genius and brings evil on him as well as the rest of the major characters. Decoud is demoralized by the absurdity of an uncaring universe and finds it difficult to live without the human orbit. His existential solitariness makes him realize the futility of his existence. Like an existential hero, Decoud exercises his choice of suicide. He believes that his suicide might have some value or meaning in a meaningless universe. Like that of Almayer, Willems and Kurtz, the character of Nostromo deteriorates through environment. But on his deathbed, Nostromo declares himself responsible for allowing the treasure to ruin his life. Through his confession, Nostromo once again becomes the man of integrity.

The Secret Agent concerns itself with the cruelties and inanities that are enacted in the name of political ideologies and progress in the society. Winnie and Verloc live isolated in their separate worlds and do not let each other into the secret of their personal thoughts. The non-communication between them leads to their fatal illusions: Winnie's that Verloc is like a father to Stevie, and Verloc's that he is loved for his own sake. Verloc fails to share with Winnie the responsibility of the mission thrust upon him by Vladimir. Winnie's indifference makes him feel hopelessly alone in the world. His attempt to damage Greenwich Observatory fails and the premature explosion leads to the blowing up of his brother-in-law, Stevie. The revelation makes Winnie conscious of the great fallacy of her marriage. Anguish and despair accompany the realization. Verloc's act of bad faith, his attempt to force the responsibility of Stevie's death on Winnie, makes Winnie rise in revolt and put an end to Verloc's existence. Like Camus, Conrad holds that rebellion arises from the spectacle of the irrational coupled with an unjust and incomprehensible condition.

The anonymous captain in *The Secret Sharer* is an isolated being, a stranger to the ship as well as to the crew. His decision to harbour the murderous Leggatt tantamounts to abetting a criminal. But he refuses to judge Leggatt according to the letter of law. He feels that Leggatt was morally justified in his action in the face of the danger that threatened the ship during the terrible storm. The ordeal of concealing Leggatt drives the insecure captain close to madness and shipwreck. But from this encounter, he also gains a greater self-assertiveness and self-confidence necessary for a good commander. As Leggatt departs, the captain is able to establish proper rapport with his ship. He manages both to maintain the integrity of his inner life and to command his ship. The departure of Leggatt signifies the integration of what he stands for into the narrator's own character.

Under Western Eyes is concerned with the question of human freedom as it unfolds in Razumov's terrible ordeal, self-recognition and his expiation. It poses the existential queries regarding the ultimate purpose of human life. The sudden appearance of Victor Haldin, an irresponsible and irrational anarchist murderer, forces Razumov to surrender his personal freedom. Betrayal of Haldin dislocates Razumov's life and leads to his exile from the university where he had hoped to become an eminent professor. The feeling of guilt provokes in him the realization that in betraying Haldin, he has in effect betrayed himself and his conscience. Razumov's confession proves Sartre's belief that man is always free to choose his existence anew. His decision to affirm the primacy of love is a radically authentic decision. Ultimately he chooses those humanistic values—symbolized by Nathalie, Sophia and Tekla—which Conrad claimed were at the heart of his artistic vision.

In *Victory,* Conrad demonstrates the danger and futility of Heyst's postured detachment and mistrust in life. There is one difference between Heyst and Conrad's other heroes. While other protagonists unintentionally or inadvertently commit an anti-social or illegal act, Heyst's acts are conventionally moral and social. Imbued with his father's rationalist pessimism and peculiar kind of cynicism, Heyst is reluctant to act. But twice he abandons the nihilistic way of life suggested by his father, first when he comes to the aid of Morrison in distress and, again, when he rescues helpless Lena. In final terms, Conrad asserts that in the face of a godless universe, the gesture of getting involved, of committing oneself, is necessarily and inherently valuable even if it ultimately leads to disaster.

Victory, like *Heart of Darkness*, *Lord Jim, The Secret Sharer* and *Under Western Eyes* depicts the movement of the protagonist towards another human being. The process of moral self-discovery leading to human commitment in these novels is an approach to existential humanism. Conrad's view of commitment, having strong affinity with the existentialist ideology, explains his current appeal to many readers.

Conrad's work prefigures modern existentialist fiction especially of Herman Melville, Graham Greene, William Faulkner, Arthur Koestler, Saul Bellow, Iris Murdoch and V.S. Naipaul. Of these, Naipaul is the one who shows strongest affinities with Conrad. Like Conrad, Naipaul chose to join the English tradition rather than the culture from which he sprang. That is the primary reason of his sharing with Conrad the experience of alienation, a fact which he has readily admitted. He discovers in Conrad as one who has been everywhere before him, writing not like other novelists about "highly organized societies," but of men "as prisoners of their culture." "Conrad's value to me," writes Naipaul, "is that he is someone who 60 to 70 years ago meditated on my world, a world I recognize today. I feel this about no other writer of this century."[2]

Like that of Conrad, Naipaul's major preoccupation in his works—*The Mimic Men, In a Free State,* and *Guerrillas*—is with the theme of alienation. But there is a major difference between the two writers. Conrad's concern is not just to portray states of alienation but also to discover how, with this knowledge, the individual can find a way to go on living. This positive humanism is lacking in Naipaul. For Conrad, there is always the possibility of combating despair, of discovering meaning in the conditions of existence. Conrad's vision includes not only the knowledge of alienation but also the necessity of commitment.

The modern existentialism has touched the domains of our consciousness which for many centuries were considered to be the darkest and the most mysterious. And although existentialism has assumed various shapes according to the deep and crystallized sensitiveness of its exponents, there are no two opinions in regard to the fact that all philosophizing starts from human existence. Indeed, it is to the credit of Conrad who, as early as the first decade of the twentieth century, became conscious of the human condition and explored man's freedom and responsibility in an absurd world. Not only that, he rejected pessimistic nihilism and replaced it with his own affirmation of the humanity of man. In Conrad's view of the world, there is room for all sorts of creeds except despair. When we affirm the continuing modernity of Conrad's art, it must be stressed that his art does not reside in the denial of the positive.

In the Conradian scheme of things, man must accept responsibility for his own deeds and for their consequences. The necessity of struggling is an important aspect of human freedom presented in the Conrad canon. Each of Conrad's novels reinforces the idea that awareness of absurdity need not obviate commitment. Conrad's heroic characters are always those who have seen how ultimately inaccessible to reason is existence; yet they are not paralyzed by the sight. They indeed exemplify what Paul Tillich calls a "courage to be" in the face of despair: "The act of accepting meaninglessness is in itself a meaningful act. It is an act of faith."[3] Conrad holds his faith in man's ability to establish a code of humanistic values in the face of an absurd world. Joseph Conrad is a humanist who gives supreme value to man: man is his *summum bonum*.

NOTES

1. Jean-Paul Sartre, *Existentialism and Humanism,* p. 55.
2. V.S. Naipaul, "The Reality and the Romance," *The Sunday Times Magazine* (27 October 1974), p. 61.
3. Paul Tillich, *The Courage To Be* (New Haven: Yale University Press, 1952), p. 176.

Index